DESTINED FOR GREATNESS
My Storms

Volume Two

DESTINED FOR GREATNESS
My Storms

JACQUELINE DENISE PALMER

XULON PRESS

Xulon Press
2301 Lucien Way #415
Maitland, FL 32751
407.339.4217
www.xulonpress.com

© 2020 by Jacqueline Denise Palmer

All rights reserved solely by the author. The author guarantees all contents are original and do not infringe upon the legal rights of any other person or work. No part of this book may be reproduced in any form without the permission of the author. The views expressed in this book are not necessarily those of the publisher.

Unless otherwise indicated, Scripture quotations taken from the King James Version (KJV)–*public domain*.

Printed in the United States of America.

PAPERBACK ISBN-13: 978-1-63129-383-2

EBOOK ISBN-13: 978-1-63129-384-9

Table of Contents

My Storms 1

The Five Casket Funeral 5

The Eye of the Storm 11

Picking up the Pieces 25

Carla Comes Home 37

A Returned Favor 53

Called to Preach 79

My Three Fathers (The Gifts) 91

Momole 127

Momole's Children 169

Acknowledgements

I dedicate this book to my Mama, Mary Helen (Scott) Ellison. Thank you for introducing me to your God.

I thank you Daniel, my dear husband, for allowing me to tell my story. I look forward to the rest of this journey that we have embarked upon. I know that God has much more in store for our lives, and if we continue to keep Him first, there is no obstacle too big for us to overcome. I love you, my soul mate.

I would like to thank my family and friends for sharing their stories. I know some of the stories were not easy to tell, but by the grace of God, He has helped us to move forward. But I'll say it like Pastor Walter Ballard said in one of his messages, "It Had to Happen." Because of the things we went through, we are stronger, and better because of it. God took the good, bad, and ugly, and made us the men and women that He has called us to be.

I thank Finnie Harris, Mattie Woodard, Bessie Matthews, James Scott, Darnell Scott, Honey Howard, Robert Harris, John Harris Jr., Betty Ashley, James Jones, Annie Jones, Stanley Harris and Patricia Harris for taking the time to share stories about our family's history.

Some the people names were changed in this book to protect their privacy.

Preface

As I glance back over my life, it's hard to comprehend how I was able to survive my life circumstances that I wrote about in Volume One of my book. But then I realized if it had not been for the God I serve, the God who came and got me from the verbal, emotional and physical abuse that I suffered at Curtis (Mama's first husband, my stepfather) getting pregnant at fourteen years of age, selling and using drugs, abortions, nightclubs, failed relationships, depression, hopelessness, suicidal thoughts, homelessness, unforgiving spirit, physical and sexual abuse from my first husband, the grief from losing my Mama to breast cancer, and losing two children, niece, nephew and stepfather in a car wreck, I wouldn't have survived. As I stated in Volume One, "If you don't remember anything else about my life story as you read Volume One and Volume Two, please remember God is a God that forgives, even when I and others thought I had done the unforgivable or unimaginable." "If we confess our sins, he is faithful and just to forgive us our sins, and to cleanse us from all unrighteousness" (1 John 1:9).

I continue telling about the biggest storm of my life here in Volume Two of my book. The biggest storm of my life was working together for my good, even though I couldn't see it at the time. "And we know that all things work together for good to them that love the God, to them who are the called according to his purpose" (Roman 8:28). Only a real God could have brought me through, and I thank God for Mama who introduced me to Him. You will see for yourself how real God truly is as you read about my life storms and the people who surrounded me during those trying times.

"Destined for Greatness." These are the words I heard the Lord speak to me as I lay on my bed of affliction after a car wreck in 1998.

I had just lost my Mama to breast cancer, and my son, daughter, niece and nephew in that same car wreck. My sister was still in the hospital and her survival was uncertain. I was trying to keep from asking the Lord why, but when I did, the Lord replied, "My child, you are destined for greatness. Many can't take what I allowed to happen to you, but I'm going to take you through, and many souls will be saved."

This somewhat brought peace to my soul, because it was then I realized that I was going to be all right. My faith took over and I knew there was a purpose for all my pain. Not only the pain that I felt then, but all I had endured as a child up until this point in my life. We don't realize it as children how much our personalities and behaviors are shaped by the people who surround us daily. It's not always good that shapes us, it's also the bad and the ugly. Sometimes when the bad and ugly shape us for so many years, it becomes generational curses. These curses can have such a hold on you until you don't even understand why you think the way you think and do the things that you do. So, my story veers in the last three chapters from my tragedy to some of the people who shaped my life. For many years, I didn't know who my real father was. At different points in my life I got to know the men who people would tell me was my father. In the end, I felt like I was the luckiest girl alive, because I had the pleasure of knowing three great men who love me.

Momole (my grandmother, aka Viola) was one of the strongest people I ever had the privilege and honor of knowing. Getting to know her story helped me to understand why I thought the way I thought about so many things. In other words, her story helped me to understand myself. She was raised in a household with her father, Mama and two of her father's mistresses, who all slept in the same room. She was married at the age of thirteen years old to a gentleman who was much older and had seven children. After his death, she remarried and had six children. After the second husband's death, she married one more time and had four more children. Momole had seventeen children, so she had to be strong to survive the things she had to endure as a child raising children. Momole loved hard if she loved you. But she also hated hard if she hated you. Momole, like her father before her, ruled her house with a firm hand. As you read her story, you will see me in her.

Chapter One

My Storms

I remember when I was in elementary school, there was a tornado warning one day. As soon as the principal told the teachers to move everyone into the hallway, I got on my bicycle and headed for home instead. By the time I reached my street, the wind was so strong it blew me backwards into a ditch. I crawled out of the ditch and tried to go down the street again. The wind was so strong I had to drop down on my knees and crawl in another direction to get home. I finally made it home. I faced this natural disaster early in life, but it could never compare to the life storms that lay ahead of me.

When Mama died, I thought that was a storm, but little did I know that the wind was just starting to blow. I felt like I was not going to make it. When my children died, I realized I was in the eye of the storm, but the Holy Ghost stood up in me and I knew I was going to come out. I asked God why it seemed like I couldn't take it when my Mama died. God spoke to me and said, "When your Mama died, you were trying to go through the storm standing up. But when your children died, you dropped down and went through the storm on your knees."

I thought I really knew who God was before my life had taken this drastic turn. Yes, I was going to church, saved, sanctified, and filled with the Holy Ghost. I even heard what the preacher was saying and tried (most of the time) to apply these things to my life. I was not always successful. There were times in some of my moments of failure when I asked myself, "Why should I keep trying? I can't get this right." But God, with all His grace and mercy, saw something in me that I couldn't see in myself. Just like the saints of old use to say, "He looked beyond all of my faults and He saw my needs." This was an understatement in my case. I still had no idea how awesome and real God really was. I knew without a doubt that God loved me. I also knew Him as a healer, deliverer, and supplier of my needs. Even though I had experienced God to be these things to me, at certain points in my life, I still had no clue that God was who He said He was. For years, when different trials would come, sometimes I went through in the right way (on my knees), and sometimes not (on my own).

I have learned, in this walk with the Lord, that there will come a time when you will have to know the Lord for yourself. When that time comes, riding on another saint's coattails (depending on others who know God) won't work. In other words, you will have to spend time with God to get the strength you need to pull through whatever trial you're facing. Your Mama, daddy, friends, or pastor can't save you; only God can help you then.

That day finally came for me when the storm began to rage in my life. The wind was so strong that it blew me off a cliff and I began to fall into the abyss. I tried desperately and hopelessly to catch on to something—anything—to break the fall. Have you ever had a dream that you were falling and there was no end to it? Your heart is racing, hurting, and you just can't see your way because it's too dark. That's what it felt like

While in this state of hopelessness, I heard the enemy say, "What are you going to do now?" After hearing the enemy's taunting remarks, I realized that I could no longer ride on Mama's or the saints' coattails. Before the enemy's remarks had a chance to penetrate my heart and mind, I heard my Mama's voice saying, "If you keep your mind stayed on God, He will keep your mind in perfect peace." "Thou wilt keep him in perfect peace, whose mind is stayed on thee: because he trusteth in thee" (Isa. 26:3,).

Without even acknowledging what the devil was saying, I said, "Okay, Lord, I'm going to take You at Your word. If You don't help me, I can't be helped." I got my mind off the bigness of my circumstances and put my mind on the bigness of my God, and perfect peace came. My Mama (Mary) had succumbed to her battle with breast cancer. Four days later, I lost my son (Mauricus, aka Alex), my daughter (Maurisa, aka Simone), my sister Carla's daughter (Lamarien, aka Little Mary), my sister Carla's son (Jeremy), and

Robert E (Mama remarried, second husband) in a car wreck while on my way to Mama's funeral, but I still had a perfect peace. Carla was in a coma and I had a broken femur, arm, wrist, and ribs, and my vertebrae were broken in two places. The doctor told me that if I turned the wrong way, the vertebrae bone could cut my spinal cord and I might never be able to walk again. Still, I had perfect peace.

It was at this point that I stopped falling, grabbed onto the Lord, and held on for dear life. God's word had begun to come alive in my life—all because of the storm. I thank God for the storm! I was finally getting to know who Jesus really was. The reality of who God was didn't sink into my heart, mind, body, and soul until 1998. In other words, I finally learned not to let my circumstances dictate who God was to me. It was in these circumstances that I learned who He was.

Joale Carla, Jeremy & Lamarien 1998

Jacqueline, Simone'; Little Mike, & Alex 1998

Chapter Two

The Five Casket Funeral

If someone had told me I would be able to stand strong through burying five of my family members at one time, I wouldn't have believed them. I think back to the point where I was lying in the emergency room hospital bed and the social worker walked in with a minister following close behind. I am amazed at how clear my mind was when she leaned close to me and said, "There's been a car wreck and there were four fatalities." That was the moment in time that God began to carry me, and this was truly the storm in which I could not walk alone. He was my strength when all my strength seemed to have faded away. It was as if He had sprayed pain repellant around my heart to keep grief from overwhelming me all at once.

The funeral arrangements had been made, and Carla and I were in no shape to be there to say our final goodbyes. The funeral was videotaped as I requested, and it would be a year after the wreck before Carla and I were able to watch it together. Fifteen years later, God nudged my heart to watch the funeral service again, so I could write this chapter of my book. It took me a while to find it after searching through hundreds of VHS tapes, but I found it. The whole time I searched for the tape, I had this overwhelming feeling of dread, because I knew watching the funeral was going to take me to an emotional place I didn't want to visit. This would be the hardest chapter to write about in the book, but I knew if God brought me through in the beginning, He was going to continue to take care of me.

My husband, Daniel asked me not to watch it alone; he wanted to be there with me when I decided to watch the tape. We both sat quietly and watched in disbelief as they wheeled the five coffins in one by one. It was like watching a parade full of flower-covered floats, only there was nothing to cheer about. The funeral home had to double their staff to make the funeral go smoothly. As soon as two of the funeral staff members brought one coffin in, two other staff members were standing by to bring in another. I had never seen anything like that. As I sat there watching, I remember thinking that I was glad I had been in the hospital and was unable to attend. I don't know if I could have handled being there.

The coffins stretched from one side of the church to the other. Mama was in the middle. Carla's two children were on the left side of Mama, and my two were on the right side. Little Mike (aka Michael Jr. my second son) came in with his grandmother, Ruth Sims, and his Aunt Culp. They sat about three seats back from the front. They didn't come in with the family procession; they got a seat while it was available. Little Mike's face and eyes were swollen, blue and black from the wreck. He looked as if he was still in shock as he watched friends and family go up to see the bodies of his loved ones. He sat there looking straight ahead and glancing from side to side occasionally. He wiped away the tears as they crept down his face. I found myself wanting to hold and comfort him. Staring at the TV, I said out loud as if he could hear me, "Everything is going to be okay."

I watched his uncle sit beside him and comfort him throughout the service. The question in my mind, as I watched his uncle and grandmother comfort him, was why my husband wasn't sitting with Little Mike. I looked at my husband and asked him, "Where were you?" He then told me that he was on the other side of the church because the church was so crowded. That hurt me to the core, because he was a good father to our children and should have been sitting with Little Mike.

I watched Jim (my oldest son) being escorted to the front by other family members to view the bodies. The closer he got, the harder it became for him. Before he could view all the bodies, he broke down and was unable to go any further. They assisted him to the front pew, and my heart broke as I watched him lay his head in his lap, sobbing uncontrollably, all while shaking his head in disbelief. I continued to watch as friends and family journeyed from one side of the church to the other to view the bodies. For some, I know it seemed like a mile walk, although it was only a few feet. I could feel the love and support from the people as I watched. The church was full, from front to

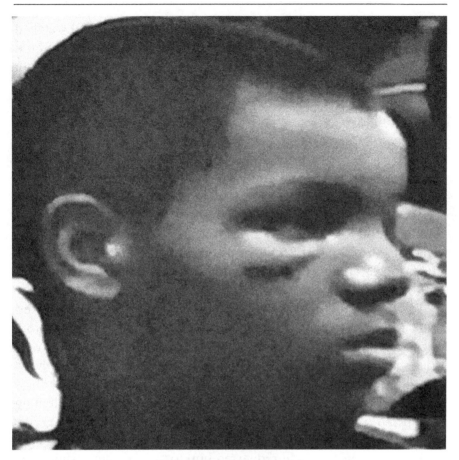

Little Mike at the funeral

back, and the walls were lined with people also. I was told that some were not even able to come in, but they stayed anyway. The pulpit was filled with preachers from every denomination. They had all come together and put their religious differences on the back burner to love and support the family. The funeral home staff finally closed the coffins and the service began.

I'll never forget Mattie's (Mama's sister) words as she stood in front of the coffins and said she could imagine Mama after she had died, yelling, "Lamarien, Jeremy, Alex, Simone, come to Granny!" Doing what they always did when Granny called, they obeyed. Mattie's words comforted my heart for a moment. Mattie had managed to hold herself together even though I knew there was turmoil going on inside of her.

Finnie (Mama's brother) was on program to sing a solo. I watched him as he slowly approached the front of the church, trying to hold his composure. It was no surprise to anyone as he opened his mouth and began singing "Someone Watches Over Me," because this was the song that he sang at all funerals and everyone loved it. I've never known Finnie to ever sing the entire song. My cousin, Pastor James Jones, even teased Finnie about that very thing.

James said, "I want to hear the whole song or is that the whole song? I wonder did he write it on the way to church."

God gave Finnie strength to sing the portion of the song he usually sang, but while he was on his way back to his seat, his legs couldn't hold him up and he began weeping. He was blessed that loved ones rushed to his side and caught and comforted him. The situation was enough to make anyone sick, and it had gotten the best of Finnie.

Pastor Larry Dixon was my pastor at that time, and he talked about the time when God filled my baby, Simone, with the Holy Ghost and she began speaking in tongues. Simone was eight years old at that time. Watching this, a smile came on my face and my heart was filled with joy. Peace filled my soul as I realized that my babies were okay, and God doesn't make any mistakes. I sat there watching the tape with my husband and was pleased with the way the service was going. But nothing touched me as much as seeing Daniel get up to sing after someone had requested him to sing a song. I shook my head in awe and disbelief as he opened his mouth and sang the song, "Be Encouraged."

I looked at him and asked, "How were you able to stand before all those people, with your children behind you in coffins, and tell the people to be encouraged?"

He looked at me and said, "It was God, I was shaking so bad inside."

I knew it had to be God who gave him strength. Mama's pastor from her old church, when she lived in Arkansas, preached the funeral, and he did an awesome job. The service had come to an end and it was time for the viewing of the bodies. There were people I hadn't seen in years who came to pay their last respects. The honorary pallbearers sat on the front row with their heads hung low, wiping away the tears as they tried to fight them back. After everyone had made their rounds, the funeral home staff slowly rolled each coffin from one side of the church to the other, so the immediate family didn't have to get up to view the bodies. It was hard enough when there was one body to view. I watched the family struggle as the funeral staff paraded the coffins one by one in front of them. Time seemed to stand still as I watched the family looking as if they wished it were all over. Tears rolled down the honorary pallbearers' faces as they dropped their heads, trying not to look at the bodies. The parade had finally come to an end as they rolled the coffins out of the church.

I didn't cry at this point, but there was no joy that flooded my soul that time. I had watched the tape several years before this by myself, and at the end of the tape an overwhelming joy flooded my soul and I began walking up and down the hall, praising God. There was a second tape with the burial part of the service on it, which I had never seen. I cried as it all ended. Even though it had been seventeen years since I lost my family, all I wanted to do in that moment was ask God why?

But all that came out of my mouth was, "Thank You, Jesus!" While I praised Him, the weights began to lift, the dark clouds rolled away, and all was well once again.

They had the funeral at Palm Street Church of Christ because it was big enough to accommodate our friends and family. After getting on my feet after the car wreck, I would attend many more funerals in that same church. But not one time did it cross my mind that this was the church where they had my family's homegoing service, at least not until 2016, at my stepsister's funeral. About midway of her homegoing service, the realization came to me as I videotaped her service: Her coffin now stood in the very place those five coffins stood July 14, 1998. Emotions that I could not hold back flooded my heart as my eyes welled up with tears. With my mouth open, I gasped, and it was a few seconds before I realized I was holding my breath. I slowly took a deep breath and was baffled that I hadn't realized this before now. For a moment, I was no longer at my stepsister's funeral. I had slipped back in time, to that dreadful day I was glad to have not been a part of. My heart was now pounding in my ears as my breathing became labored. I fought to corral my emotions and to get my mind on the present situation. It was hard, but I finally made it back and was able to go on with the day. I knew all too well the hurt that everyone was experiencing. So, I began to pray and ask God to give them strength.

Chapter Three

The Eye of the Storm

The eye of the storm is the region of mostly calm weather found at the center of strong tropical cyclones. However, this doesn't mean the storm is over. Sometimes the worst is yet to come. God came in and gave me such peace in my storm, until I felt as if I was in the eye of the tornado. Tornadoes are prevalent in Arkansas. They tell me if you ever get caught in the middle of a tornado, it is calm and peaceful, but on the outside, everything is being torn up. I was in the eye of the storm and I couldn't feel anything but God's joy, peace, and love. The sun was shining, and the atmosphere was calm right in the middle of the biggest storms of my life. God was at work. In a matter of two weeks, I had drawn close to God, until He began to shield my heart from the pain. Things were looking pretty torn up to everyone else, but God had me in His hand.

Daniel came back to the hospital in Albuquerque with me the day after the funeral. He had just finished one song on the album he had been working on in the studio. It was a song we had written together-"Blind Faith." I asked him to play it for me. He put the song on repeat, and I listened to it over and over. I needed something to hold on to. There's this part in the song that says, *"Lord, sometimes I'm walking with tears in my eyes, but Lord I'm depending on you to make everything all right. I go wherever you want me to go, if I'm sure that it's you. Or I'll hold my peace and not say a word; Lord I'll give my life if you want me to."* That part of the song ministered to my soul in my darkest hour. God was all I had to hold on to at that point. I'm so glad God is a loving and forgiving God. God loved me despite my failures and imperfections. He's a God of another chance.

The thing that I had whispered in Mama's ear about being great in the Lord had a great price tag attached to it. There is no triumph without trial, and no greatness without adversity. I didn't know how, but I knew I was going to come out and overcome, and I knew that it would be my pain that would make me reign.

My second day in the hospital, the shock began to wear off and I kept trying to wrap my mind around the children being gone. I had somewhat accepted Mama's death, but not my children's. I didn't know how. My heart began to hurt so bad that I could hardly breathe. So, I looked up and prayed a prayer.

I said, "Lord, I can't tell the people about You like I desire to tell them about You, my heart is too heavy. I need You to lift this load out of my heart."

It didn't take God all night long to take the load out of my heart. God came to see about me, and He took the load. When the nurses came in, they rolled me over and I said, "Lord, I thank You." When the nurses rolled me back over, I told them, "The Lord's been so good to me." The nurse seemed puzzled that I was praising God with all that I had been through. I think they may have thought I was losing my mind because I wasn't reacting like other people would in this situation. Even though I didn't understand why God allowed what He allowed, in time I began to accept His will and trust that He had everything in control.

The nurses asked me if I wanted to see the psychiatrist.

I told them, "Yes, send them on in." The psychiatrist came in and I immediately told them there was nothing they could do to me or for me that the Lord hadn't already done.

"I've got peace of mind; I've got joy in my soul and the burdens have been lifted out of my heart."

The psychiatrist then said, "Mrs. Palmer (me) can we video tape you? We believe you can help someone else."

I wouldn't let them video tape me at that point. I don't know why, I just didn't. I wish I had now. There were moments when I asked God, "Why did You choose me to go through this?" I believe it was because He saw something in me that I couldn't see in myself. If you had told me before this happened that I would go through this situation praising and magnifying God, I wouldn't have believed you. I thought back to Mama as I praised my way through this situation. I didn't realize that I was in school as I watched Mama go through her ordeal of dying. But while I lay there in the hospital bed, I finally understood what her praise was all about. The lesson that I learned, I was now applying to my situation. I learned that God is still God and is worthy of all praises, despite what life circumstances may bring.

Whatever storms come your way; you must still do your reasonable service. You may ask, "What's my reasonable service?" My reasonable service is to continue my praise, thank You, Jesus, Hallelujah Jesus, and serving God with my all, in spite of what life has brought. I do this because God is still God despite the storm life may bring.

I thought, *Mama, I got it, I understand. The joy of the Lord is my strength.*

So, you may ask, how did I make it through the situation? I praised my way through. This was the only way I made it through. The more I praised Him, the more my mind stayed on Him. The more my mind stayed on Him, the more perfect peace I had. Only God could do that. This was the legacy that Mama passed down to me. What a legacy! "I beseech you therefore, brethren, by the mercies of God, that ye present your bodies a living sacrifice, holy, acceptable unto God, which is your reasonable service." (Rom 12:1,), "For this day is holy unto our Lord: neither be ye sorry; for the joy of the LORD is your strength." (Neh 8:10)

Craig (Carla's husband) didn't go to the funeral. He stayed at the hospital with Carla and me. He would go see Carla for a while and then come sit with me for a while. Polly (my best friend) came back to New Mexico with Daniel after the funeral was over. I was so relieved to see them both. When Daniel had to go back home to go back to work, Polly stayed with me. The Bible talks about a friend who sticks closer than a brother "A man that hath friends must shew himself friendly: and there is a friend that sticketh closer than a brother." (Prov 18:24) Polly was this kind of friend. She quit her job that she had been working for thirteen years and came to the hospital with me, left the hospital with me, and stayed with me an entire year until I got on my feet. There was only one other person who would have done this for me and that was Mama. But Mama had already gone on before me. So, God had a ram in the bush. God was looking after me when I couldn't look after myself. Polly (my best friend and husband's aunt) would read the Bible to me and pray with me. This was where I found my most comfort. This was exactly what I needed to endure what I was going through. I had told Polly some years ago, if I ever got sick, read my Bible to me. She honored my request.

The nurses had to log roll me whenever they assisted me to turn. They had to do this because the doctor told me if I was turned the wrong way, the vertebrae bones could cut my spinal cord and I would never be able to walk again. I told the doctors, "You all do all you can do, and God will do the rest." I kept thinking about Carla and wondering how she was doing. I wanted to see her. I was told that her head was so swollen until it was wider than her shoulders. I kept begging the nurses to take me to see Carla. They hesitated to take me because my back was broken in two places, pelvic bone was broken, and I couldn't sit in a wheelchair. They had to take the whole hospital bed if they took me to see her. I prayed to God and told Him that I wanted to see my sister. I felt if I could just lay my hands on her, everything would be all right.

Carla had made a statement before we left Vegas. She said, "Jackie, I have lost all faith in God. If I had a ladder long enough, I would go to heaven, put my hand in His face and ask Him, "Why did you let my Mama suffer as much as she loved You?"

I then told her that the Bible says, "Just like Christ suffered in the flesh, arm yourself likewise." "Forasmuch then as Christ hath suffered for us in the flesh, arm yourselves likewise with the same mind: for he that hath suffered in the flesh hath ceased from sin" (1 Pet 4:1).

Every day is not going to be a bed of roses. Some days you are going to drink tears for water. I've learned it's not what the preacher says anymore, I know now if I keep my hand in God's hand, everything will be all right. I didn't want my sister's soul to be lost. My prayer was, "Lord, bring my sister out in her right mind."

A few days had passed, and I had given up on seeing her. I didn't think it was going to happen because on Monday morning they were supposed to fly me back to Arkansas on a plane, lying down. But God had not forgotten my request. That Sunday night at twelve midnight, two nurses came into my room and they told me they were scheduled to work on the other end of the hall. They had switched places with two other nurses so they could have me for their patient. The nurses went to church earlier that day and told everyone in the church about me. They all prayed for me.

I said, "Look at God." Then I told them I wanted to see Carla. Their reply was, "We'll work it out."

It was twelve midnight when the nurses wheeled me down the hall in my hospital bed, put me on the elevator and took me to see my sister. When I got in the room with her, she was in the room where other patients were visible. They slid my bed beside hers and placed her hand in my hand, and I began to call on the name of the Lord.

I said, "Lord, I don't know why all this happened to us, but I know You haven't brought us this far to leave us." I began to bind and rebuke death. After I got through praying for Carla, I began to say a prayer for the other patients. The nurses were standing by my bed, crying. They wheeled me back to my room, but not before stopping at the nurses' station.

The nurses asked me, "Did you get to see your sister?"

I told them, "The Bible says, 'Everything works together for the good for those who love the Lord and are called according to his purpose.' Of course, I got to see my sister." "And we know that all things work together for good to them that love God, to them who are the called according to his purpose." (Rom 8:28)

The nurses wheeled me to my room, and Polly and I prayed for the nurses and sent them on their way. That next day they flew me back to Arkansas on a plane lying down. Polly was with me and this brought some comfort. But the flight home was almost unbearable. The plane was small, and it looked like a crop-dusting plane. The turbulence was awful, and with every bump there was pain and nausea. They had given me two pain pills when I got ready to leave, but that wasn't helping much. I was glad when we landed and was anxious to get home and see Daniel and Little Mike. I made it home, and Daniel had my hospital bed set up in the living room. We still didn't have that much furniture in our home because we were struggling financially, and furniture was not on the top of the list. The only thing we had in the den was a TV and chair. There was a couch and chair in the living room where my hospital bed was. My husband had placed the hospital bed up front so my friends and family could come in and out to see me.

Polly moved in with me, and her being in my house at this point was God-ordained. Polly didn't know anything about taking care of someone with my injuries. I had to teach her how to bathe me and take care of me. I had been a patient care tech for years. Polly used to say, "I can't do that kind of work; I don't have the stomach for it."

God gave her the stomach to take care of me, and she and Daniel did an awesome job.

My friends and family began to come in and out to see me. I know they expected to see me singing "why me?" and "woe is me." But all I could do was tell them, "The devil meant it for my bad, but God is going to work it for my good. I know that the devil meant to kill me this time. He broke my body, but he messed around and left my mind and my mouth working. If the devil was going to get me, he should have shut me down completely." I began to tell my friends, "This is the day that the Lord has made, I will rejoice and be glad in it. Come on and magnify the Lord with me and let us exalt His name together. I will bless the Lord at all times, His praises shall continually be in my mouth."

The Lord spoke to me and said, "The same joy that I placed in your Mama, I have placed in you."

The Bible says that the joy of the Lord is your strength. I'm here to tell you if you don't have joy, you don't have strength. This scripture had come alive to me; I finally understood my Mama's praise even the more. In biblical teaching, theologians describe my experience as having gone through observation, interpretation and application of the scriptures. So, I say again, if you're wondering how I made it through, I praised my way through.

The power of God filled my house. When my friend Gwen Devine came in to see me and got close enough to my bed, I laid hands on her and she fell to the floor. She rolled on the floor under my bed and God filled her with the Holy Ghost, speaking in tongues. I couldn't help but weep as I watched my friend lie in the floor, loving on God. When the power of God fell in the house most of the time, there wasn't a dry eye in the house. We were all in one place in one accord, giving God the praise. God showed up and showed out each time.

Little Mike was in the den, playing video games when different people would come in and out. He could hear everything that was being said. He would cry a lot while he was playing the game, because he missed his brother and sister. It was like he was an only child now, because Jim (my oldest son) didn't live with us. It would be several months after the wreck before Little Mike finally opened and began to tell me about the things that he saw when we had the wreck. My heart hurt as Little Mike talked about the day that changed our lives forever. He told me he woke up while I was screaming at Robert E, telling him to get back on the road. He saw me for that split second when I braced my hands on the dashboard. The next thing he knew, he woke up in pain outside of the truck.

He went on to say, "There were these people around Simone (my daughter). When they moved, I saw her eyes, they were open, and the veins were red in her eyes. I called her name, but she didn't answer. I saw Jeremy (Carla's son), I called his name, but he did not answer either; he wouldn't even look at me. Jeremy had his hands in the praying position and his lips were moving. He was making this sound like he was speaking in tongues. Alex's (my son) head was turned away from me. I called Alex's name, but he didn't answer. Joale (Carla's daughter) was lying above me next to Jeremy and she was unconscious."

This was a hard thing for me to hear, but I was glad that he was talking to me. Little Mike hadn't talked to anyone about any of these things at that point. I was up and walking at the time he confided in me about the things he saw.

I told him that I was going to send him to talk to a psychiatrist.

Little Mike adamantly told me, "I don't want to see any psychiatrist."

I insisted that he go. I felt as if he needed someone to talk to.

Little Mike said, "I'm going to pray that the Lord touch your mind because I don't want to see a psychiatrist."

After he told me that, I was too through. What could I say to this? He didn't go.

I don't remember Jim coming to visit me when I got home from the hospital, but he did make it to the hospital to see me. He would call after I got home from the hospital, but he was scared to come by the house. Jim had been arrested for selling stolen cars in Texas and was released from jail. He had fines that he was supposed to pay, but he didn't. So, Texas police had a warrant out for his arrest, and he told me that the FBI was hunting for him. He was afraid that I would call them and report him if he came to visit. I don't know if I would have called them or not. I was just worried that they would hurt him if he didn't turn himself in. He eventually went to prison and served his time.

Peter (my first husband) even came by to see me and he brought his girlfriend and his son, who used to come over and stay all night with Alex and Simone. I could see the hurt in his son's eyes, as he came to my bedside to hug me. He was about the same age as Alex and Simone. I was glad to see Peter's son, but Peter himself was up to no good as usual. Peter had contacted Robert E's insurance company and tried to get money from the children's death, and he had even talked to a lawyer. This was a man who was ordered to pay less than $200 a month for two children in child support and was still behind. Peter may have seen the children once a year if that, and it wasn't because I stopped him. This was one sorry excuse for a man.

The people were coming to see me in groups. When they came in, I would tell my story and give God the glory. When one group left, another group would come. I would get tired and feel like I didn't have the strength to tell my story anymore. So, I would ask Polly to call Jesus' name three times. Till this day, I don't know of anyone who could call on Jesus or moan Jesus' name like Polly did. When Polly started calling on the name of Jesus, the anointing was so strong until it would make the hairs on my arms and neck stand up, and a chill would run down my spine. I would ask her to call Jesus name three times because I knew if she called Him enough times, she wouldn't be able to stop. Sure enough, it never failed, Polly would keep telling about God's goodness. This would allow me time to rest and get a second wind. This would go on all day, every day.

I had some difficulty moving my legs, but one day we praised God so, and the power of God was in the house until my legs were going up and down on the bed. I began to have pain later that night, and my pain medication wasn't working. Daniel called the ambulance and they took me to the emergency room. When I got there, the doctor had already heard about me from the nurses who would visit my home.

The doctor walked in the room and said, "Mrs. Palmer, I heard you have been praising God. I'm not going to tell you to stop, but I do want you to take it easy."

I said, "Man, give me my shot so I can get back to my God."

I'll never forget the peace that I felt during those times. Witnessing the power of God move like it did during my storm was an indescribable experience. There are no words; it just puts me in awe! Even as I write about this, there is a peace I feel that I can't explain. The people who witnessed this move of God know what I'm talking about. I wouldn't take anything for my journey now. I've come too far to turn around. I was in the eye of the storm, but the sun was shining. Somebody please, tell the Lord thank you!

Not everyone who came to see me was my friend. Some of my enemies sat at my bedside and started to talk about the things I used to do or things I had done to them when we were children. It was as if they were saying, "Look at you now." They didn't know it, but God was in the plan all along. I would let them talk, but when they got through, I would say, "Yes baby, I did do you wrong, forgive me, but I'm no longer the same, God has made a change in me." I then began to tell them about where God had brought me from.

They started off saying, "Yes Jackie, yes Jackie," but before I would get through telling them about the goodness of Jesus, tears would be flowing down their faces and they would be saying, "Yes Lord, yes Lord." After God had done this a couple of times, I prayed a prayer and said, "Lord, if You have to send every one of my enemies one by one, send them on, Lord. Don't let them be the same, make a change in their lives." I even received a letter in the mail that was several pages. The letter happened to be from one of my classmates. I didn't know this at the time I was reading the letter because she had used her married name. But in the letter, she began to talk about how I treated her when we were children. She said that she struggled with writing the letter. At the end of the letter, she talked about how she had been bleeding for a while and the doctors didn't know why. So, she decided to prepare to die and she asked me if I would raise her children. I still didn't know who had written the letter at this time. There was a phone number at the end of the letter, so I decided to call to see who she was. I called her and she made me know who she was.

I immediately said, "Yes baby, I did do you wrong, but I'm no longer the same." I went on to tell her that she would live and not die, and she would raise her own children. I prayed for her over the phone and she began to speak in tongues and God dried up her issue of blood. Occasionally, when I would be on program at a church to give my testimony, I would look out in the audience and she would be there. Only God can do this, He is who He says He is, and He'll be whatever you need Him to be. God continued to show His mighty hand.

When the home health nurses would come in to see me, they would leave crying and praising God. I remember the day that the air conditioner went out. It was the end of July and the beginning of August and it was so hot. I was laid up in the hospital bed and already miserable because of my injuries. Daniel called the heat and air company to have them send someone out to fix our unit. The gentlemen came in and began to fix the air conditioner.

He glanced back at me while fixing the air conditioner and asked me, "What happened to you?" I began to tell him my story and tears filled his eyes. He stuttered as he said, "I heard about that accident, my church gave money to help." As he said this, he ran out of the door. Daniel and Polly ran behind him to see what was wrong and to pay him. The gentlemen said, "Don't worry about paying me." Daniel was excited and grateful because we still were struggling to pay the bills. Daniel and Polly came back in the house and we praised God for a while.

Nightfall soon came and everyone was gone to bed. I could hear nothing but my thoughts and the Lord when the enemy asked, "What are you going to do now?" I didn't even acknowledge what the devil was saying. Instantly I heard my Mama's voice saying, "If you keep your mind stayed on God, He will keep you in perfect peace." Then I said, "Lord, if You don't help me, I can't be help." I got my mind off the bigness of my circumstances and got my mind on the bigness of my God and perfect peace came.

There is peace, but then there is perfect peace. This perfect peace, you can't get from man and it surpasses all understanding. I felt like I was in a dark room and I couldn't see my way. So, I put my hands in God's hand and He led me out of that dark place where the storm had taken me. Yes, the storm in my life had caused quite a bit of damage, but God had lifted me above the dark clouds, lightning, and rain, and it was peaceful. There were times when it felt like those summer days when I would lie under a tree on a blanket at Momole's (my grandmother) house. I just lay there and stared up at the sky for hours without a care in the world, trying to see shapes in the clouds, just passing the time.

The times that I did struggle were in the middle of the night when everyone had gone to bed. The day's activities always replayed in my mind when all was quiet. There was this one night that I will always hold dear to my heart. I was thinking about the Sunday when Simone' began to cry in church.

I asked her what was wrong, and she hunched her shoulders up and said, "I don't know."

Pastor Dixon was already praying for Little Mike and Alex. So, I told Simone' to go up with her brothers to get prayer. She got up and went and stood by her brothers. By the time she made it to them, she began to cry even more while bowing up and down. Pastor Dixon prayed for her and she turned and walked toward me, still crying. By the time she got halfway back to me, Simone' began to speak in tongues. My baby was seven years old and God had filled her with the Holy Ghost. Church was over for an hour and my baby was still praising God and speaking in tongues. I had time to call Mama on the phone and told her to listen. I held the phone out of the church office door so Mama could hear -- that sweet sound of the rivers of living water flowing from my daughter's belly. "He that believeth on me, as the scripture hath said, out of his belly shall flow rivers of living water." "But this spake he of the Spirit, which they that believe on him should receive: for the Holy Ghost was not yet given; because that Jesus was not yet glorified." (John 7:38-39)

Then Pastor Dixon asked Simone', "Baby, how you feel?"

Simone' replied, while speaking in tongue, "I feel good."

The next thought that ran through my mind was when we had our twenty-one-night revival at our church (Faith Temple). Alex had gone to church with me this night. Church was over and we were on our way back home when Alex surprised me with what he said.

Alex said, "Mama, what must I do to be saved?" Then he said, "I don't ever want to grow up, die and go to hell."

I responded with a question. I asked him, "Baby, do you believe that Jesus Christ is the Son of God?"

Alex said, "Yes, Ma'am."

I said, "Okay, repeat after me," and I led my son through the sinner's prayer. All I had him do was repent, if you're wondering. Alex echoed everything I said.

He said, "I believe that Jesus Christ is the Son of God. Forgive me, Lord, for everything that I done wrong. Come into my heart and change me. I accept You, Jesus, as my Lord and personal Savior."

Then I went on to explain to Alex that if he meant those things he had said from his heart, he was now saved. I then told him, "If God was to crack the sky this night, son, it will be well with your soul."

I laid there in my hospital bed, thanking God for taking my two children who were ready and leaving my two who weren't. My mind also ran back to the time Ruby Terry (a gospel soloist and evangelist) ran a revival at our church a few months before the children died. The last night of that revival, Mrs. Terry said, "I need to pray for the children. Some of them will not be here next year."

I remember thinking, *Lord, please don't let it be mine.*

It was mine. My heart got heavy as this thought passed through my mind. I was struggling, trying to keep from asking God why. But I finally asked God, "Why?"

The Lord spoke to me and said, "My child, you are destined for greatness. Many can't take what I have allowed to happen to you. But I'm going to take you through, and many souls shall be saved."

With humility, and tears rolling down my face, all I could say to His reply was, "Yes, Lord, I'll do what You want to do." In the same breath, I said, "Lord, I want to see Alex." I had seen Simone in a dream at the hospital and she skipped up to me happily and said, "Kiss, kiss, Mama."

Then she happily skipped off. I hadn't seen my son. I thought maybe I could go to sleep and dream about him, but I couldn't go to sleep. I looked down at the end of my bed, fighting to see through the tears, and there my babies stood. Simone walked around on the left side of me and lay in my arms and looked up at me and smiled. Alex came around on the right side and lay across my stomach. Alex began to sing this song that he always sang. He used to sing this song so much until we would say, "Alex, sing your song."

Alex began singing, *"I may be young, may never get old, might not have money, silver or gold, but I got Jesus and if I let Him, He'll take control, I can feel him down in my down in my soul."*

The kids then wiped my face and said, "Mama, stop crying, we're all right."

Then Alex began to sing his song for me one more time. *"I may be young, may never get old, might not have money, silver or gold, but I got Jesus and if I let Him, He'll take control, I can feel him down in my soul."*

Alex and Simone' got up and went back to the end of my bed. When I looked up at them through the mist of my tears, I saw Mama standing between them, smiling at me the way she smiled.

I began to sing all through the house at 2:00 in the morning, *"Can't nobody do me like Jesus."* I made so much commotion until it woke Daniel. Daniel got out bed and came to the front of the house to check on me. I told him what God had done for me and

Daniel called into work and stayed home with me until twelve noon, praising our God.

Polly and Daniel took good care of me. Polly kept my house and me clean while Daniel worked. When Daniel came home from work, he would help Polly with my care. At the end of the week, he would give her a little money. It wasn't much for what she was doing, but she understood our circumstances. Most importantly, Polly and I kept our minds stayed on God all day. When we didn't have visitors, we still praised God. This was what it took for me to go through this storm and keep my sanity.

I told Polly, "I hope you never get sick, but if you do, I'll be there."

I thank God for blessing me with my husband, Daniel. There I was laid up in the bed and couldn't take care of myself. Daniel even had to help me on and off the bed pan at times. I hated this with a passion, and he knew it. But he was so gentle and kind.

Daniel would say, "Baby I know you don't want me to do this, but I got to clean you up, so let's roll over." The whole time he was rolling me over and cleaning me up, Daniel would say, "It's going to be all right baby." I would fight to hold back the tears, and most of the time I wasn't successful.

Daniel is four-and-a-half years younger than I am. He was a young man and could have decided to leave me, but he chose to stay. For two months prior to the dreadful accident, I had left home to take care of my Mama in Las Vegas, except for the one week I came back home. Then when I finally made it home, I was all broken up and still couldn't be a wife to him. But he chose to stay. God gave me a good man, in sickness, and in health, till death do us part. We've been married twenty-six years now, and I look forward too many more.

It was hard lying flat on my back, day in and day out, not being able to do for myself. I had to wear this SCD (sequential compression device) machine on my legs to keep me from getting blood clots. They would squeeze my legs intermittently and they were very hot and uncomfortable. I would wait until I knew no one was paying attention and use my feet to get them off. It would take me a while to get them off, but I would do it. When Polly noticed that I had taken them off, she would put them back on. I would beg her to let me keep them off for an hour. Sometimes she did and sometimes she didn't. The other thing that drove me crazy was the cast that was on my left arm. It had started itching and I would ask somebody to bring me a clothes hanger so I could scratch the itch. The cast was hot, heavy, and I got tired of it. So, I asked Little Mike to bring me a butcher knife and he did. Little Mike didn't know why I was asking for the knife, he just gave it to me and went back in the den. I waited for him to leave the room and began to cut the cast off my arm. Twenty minutes had passed, and Little Mike emerged from the den.

When he caught me cutting the cast off my arm, he ran over to the bed and grabbed my arm, yelling, "Mama, stop, you're going to hurt yourself," while he wrestled the knife away from me.

I yelled at him and said, "You're not supposed to do this to me, I'm your Mama."

All the commotion finally got Polly's attention and she came out of the bedroom to see what was going on.

Little Mike said, "Mama is cutting her cast off her arm!"

I got quite like a mischievous child that had been caught. Polly came to my bedside to investigate. When she looked at my cast, she said, "Give the knife back to her because she almost got the cast off anyway."

Polly helped me get the cast off. When I finally got the cast off my arm, it felt so good. There was this long pin sticking out of my wrist. There was nothing there to keep me from bumping the pin on the bed because I had taken the cast off. When I did bump my wrist, this would send pain shooting up my whole arm. I finally got tired of this and decided to take the pin out one day. I gave the pin a gentle pull and it just slid out. God truly takes care of fools, because this was a foolish thing to do and I thank God that it didn't cause me any further harm.

Chapter Four

Picking up the Pieces

I was now at the point in my life where the wind had stopped blowing so hard, It was time to sift through the rubble that the storms had left behind and pick up the pieces. It wasn't going to be easy, but I had to keep moving forward. One day I got a call from the doctor, telling me they were going to put me in rehab so I could learn how to walk again. I asked the doctor, "Can the physical therapist come to the house and teach me how to walk?"

The doctor replied, "No, I'm putting my foot down, you have to go to rehab to learn how to walk again." Then he went on to say, "Don't look to get out of rehab for a month or more."

Fear took over and I began to cry. I didn't know how they were going to treat me in rehab. Polly and Daniel were taking such good care of me at home; They were waiting on me hand and foot, feeding me turnip greens, sweet potatoes and cornbread. I finally but reluctantly agreed to go. The doctor had an ambulance come to pick me up and take me to Rebsamen Hospital Rehab in Jacksonville, Arkansas. My first day at rehab, it took five people to get me out of the bed and put me in a wheelchair. I was kind of down for a moment, but then I realized that I was in a wheelchair and I could get around for the first time in about two months. I began to go in and out of the patients' rooms, telling them where the Lord had brought me from. I told them that Roman 2:11 says God has no respect of person, what He's done for me He can also do for you. "for there is no respect of persons with God." (Rom 2:11)

The next day those same five people came and got me out of bed, but this time they took me to the rehab room. It was a big open room with a lot of equipment in it. One of the physical therapists put a walker in front of me and I said, "Lord, get in these old legs." There was a person on each side of me. They lifted me up to the walker. My legs were weak, but I was determined not to be in rehab long. I took hold of the walker and began to walk. These were my first steps in nearly sixty days. I walked halfway across the room and I had to sit down and rest. But I told them, "You all might as well give me my walking papers because I'm on my way home."

The next day it didn't take but one person to get me out of bed, and he was a big guy. They took me down to the rehab room. They put a walker in front of me and I said, "Lord, get in these old legs." I grabbed the walker and walked all the way across the room and told them, "You all might as well give me my pink slip because I'm on my way home." When I made it back to the wheelchair, I asked the therapist, "What it's going take for me to get out of here?"

He said, "In order for you to go home, you're going to have to walk 150 feet by yourself, get yourself dressed, get in and out of the bed, and go to the bathroom by yourself."

I had accomplished all except one task. I couldn't get in and out of bed by myself. The next day when they took me down to the rehab room, I got on the walker by myself and walked 150 feet. As I was walking, one of the techs tried to tell on me because I was walking by myself.

The therapist told them to leave me alone. "She's going to do what she wants to do."

When I made it back, I asked them, "Is there anything else?" I could get on the bed, but I couldn't get my left leg in the bed. So, while sitting on the bed, I began to pray. I said, "Lord, I've been lying around too long and it's time for me to be about Your business. Please show me what to do." I looked over to my left, and there lay this device they gave me to help put my socks on. It had a rope on it like a jump rope. I wrapped it around my leg and threw my leg in the bed. I pushed the call light and when they answered, I told them that I had met all their requirements and they were going to have to turn me loose.

They came running in the room and said, "Show us how you got in the bed by yourself."

I showed them and they said that I was cheating because I used the rope to wrap around my foot to put my leg in the bed. I told them,

"You all told me to get in the bed; you didn't tell me how to get in the bed. I have met all your requirements and you all have to turn me loose."

During the day, when I wasn't in the rehab room, I was ministering to the patients. They had given me a room off the dining area and started bringing patients to me so I could read to them and pray for them. When I would go to breakfast, I was the youngest person there. I would do all I could to make the patients' day better.

I would tell them, "I don't want to be here either, but since we are here, let's just make the best out of it." Then I would say, "Time is not as long as it has been, you are one day closer to getting out of here." By the time I got through talking to them, we were all laughing and talking and enjoying our breakfast. We were ready to take on the day.

The nurses finally called the doctor to let him know that I had met all the requirements to be discharged. So, the doctor wrote my discharge orders.

I walked out of the rehab in five days. The nurse told me to go home and take it easy. I told her I was a young woman and I was not about to go home and sit down. Polly took me to the mall the next day. I laugh now when I think about Polly trying to push me up an incline that was in the mall. She had on heels and I could hear her grunting as she tried to get to the top of the incline. Her shoes were sliding, and she kept slipping and sliding backwards down the incline. Polly was about five feet tall and weighed about 125 pounds-I will not tell what I weighed. She was worn out when we got home. I had to use a walker most of the time when I first got out of rehab, but when I had to go places, I would use a wheelchair.

Polly & I at the mall

Now that I was somewhat on my feet, it was time to take care of business at hand. A lawyer from North Little Rock called me while I was in the hospital, and I found out later he was just an ambulance chaser. I only listened to him because he said Katherine (Polly's sister) recommended that he call me. He claimed to be a preacher, and this made me trust him even more. This would prove to be a mistake. I continued to communicate with the lawyer when I got back home. He held onto the case until the statute of limitations had almost run out, then he told me that I didn't have a case. I fired him and he threatened to sue me. Miss Ruth Sims (Little Mike's grandmother) recommended a new lawyer. I was on my feet by this time and I took him the paperwork. I told him what the other lawyer said about me not having a case. The new lawyer told me he would look things over and contact me later. He called me before I could get home.

He said, "Mrs. Palmer, I have checked the paperwork out and you do have a case. I don't know what the other lawyer was talking about."

He took my case and within two months we were sitting before a judge. Meanwhile, I didn't let any grass grow under my wheelchair or feet. Polly took me to different churches to give my testimony. She would push me to the front of the church, and I began telling my story. When I would stand up, my pelvic bone and legs hurt a lot of times and I walked with a limp. But it never failed. As I told my testimony, the anointing of God would fall on me and I couldn't help but come out of my wheelchair proclaiming the goodness of the Lord. I didn't feel any pain as I walked back and forth, telling about what the Lord had done for me. It wasn't until after the anointing would lift off me that I began feeling some pain. God would move every time. I even got an invitation to come back to the rehabilitation center where I had gotten my rehab treatments to give my testimony one Sunday morning. God moved and the patients and family members were blessed.

Carla was still in trouble. She was still fighting for her life. When I left the hospital in Albuquerque, Ewonda Baker, our cousin was also there. She stayed for about three weeks. Craig and Ewonda alternated shifts taking care of Carla. The hospital had discharged Joale and she was doing fine. Joale had a cast on one of her arms and staples in her abdomen and arms. It would take time for her to heal, but she was stable enough to be discharged. Ewonda would bring Joale to visit Carla and me also while I was in the hospital. It soon came time for Ewonda to go back to Arkansas and she brought Joale back with her. The doctors in New Mexico finally thought Carla was stable enough to be transferred to a hospital in Las Vegas. Carla was still very sick and couldn't communicate.

By this time, Bessie (Mama's sister) felt that someone from the family should be out there with Carla. So, she volunteered to go. The rest of the family was happy about this, because we thought with Bessie being at the hospital, we would get all the information we needed about Carla's progress. We knew Craig needed help with Carla and no one else could make the trip at this time. Bessie was not working currently. It seemed like the perfect solution to the problem.

Even though Carla had been in a coma for weeks, we were still praying— "Lord, bring her out in her right mind." Carla was already bitter and blaming God for the suffering that our Mama had to endure. We were worried about how she would react after she found out that she had lost two children, and a niece and nephew. We feared that telling her about the children would hinder her recovery.

When Craig got to their home in Vegas, the lights were off. He had to figure out how to get the lights back on, take care of all the other bills and take care of Carla also. He started working two jobs and would go take care of Carla when he got off. Bessie was staying with Miss Hannah (Mama's friend) Miss Hannah would take Bessie to the hospital some days, and the other days Bessie would take the bus. She stayed with Carla while Craig was at work. This was a big help in one way, and a big mess in another way. A help because she helped take care of Carla. A big mess because she was calling some family members back in Arkansas, telling lies about Craig. She had the whole family back in Arkansas mad at Craig. She was telling everyone that Craig was mistreating Carla, and she even called and said that she caught Craig playing under Carla's clothes. This was not true; he was cleaning her feet. Some of the church members from Craig's church were mad at him also, because Bessie had them and us believing that Craig was on drugs. These lies hurt Craig not only emotionally but financially. Instead of everyone giving him money to help him make it through, they were giving the money to Bessie. Everyone naturally thought that Bessie was doing all the work taking care of Carla and Craig was doing nothing. The church had given Craig money to fly to New Mexico when Carla was in the hospital there, but they would not help him once he got back to Las Vegas with Carla because of the lies.

The church, our family, Bessie's daughter, and Miss. Hannah were all giving Bessie money. Craig had to struggle and survive the best way that he could. Bessie was gambling at the little corner stores in Vegas every chance she got. This was where all the money was going. Robert E was flown back to Las Vegas also and placed in a long-term care facility. He never really got back on his feet. I was told that he was being mean and fighting the nurses and aides at the facility where he lived. His church had taken over some of his financial affairs. Craig and my sister were living in Robert E's brother's (Sam) house. They would pay the rent to Robert E when he was up and around. This was one of the things that the church had taken over, collecting rent for the house that Craig lived in. They didn't even give Craig a chance to get on his feet. Because of the lies they had been told; they had no sympathy for Craig.

At this time, Craig was unable to pay the rent, so he moved in with his family. Even though Craig worked two jobs, he was broke trying to pay the bills and some bills that Carla created that he didn't know about. Carla had gotten several loans from a check cashing place. Craig had to work and pay those off along with everything else. Craig didn't have enough money left after paying the bills to groom properly. He was not able to pay for haircuts or get his beard trimmed. His beard had grown out and he was looking uncared for. This was one of the things that gave Aunt Bessie's lies some momentum. Craig informed me at this time he probably looked like he was on drugs. Craig was not on drugs, he was just a man who loved his wife, and was trying to hold things together the best way he knew how, until his wife woke up and got back on her feet. This was a strong man to endure all the lies and keep going.

Clyde even called Craig from Arkansas and cursed him out because he believed the things that Bessie was telling him. We all believed her. Bessie had money coming in from every direction, she had it 'made in the shade' for little while. Miss Hannah caught on to what she was doing and stopped giving her money. Miss Hannah told her that she could not afford to take care of a grown woman.

When Carla woke up, Craig would go to the hospital every day and give Carla a bath, change her bed, put her on the bed pan, and turn her every two hours. The wounds that had healed on Carla's back would itch and Craig would be up and down all night, scratching and taking care of all of Carla's needs. I understood this because I went through the same thing when I was unable to care for myself. The nurse only had to come in the room to give Carla medication if Craig was there.

It would be months later, after Craig and Carla moved to Arkansas, that the family realized the things Bessie had said about Craig were all lies. I can only imagine what Craig must have felt, moving thousands of miles from his home and family and coming to a place he knew nothing about, with people who had only met him briefly but didn't like him because of lies someone had told them. This coupled with not knowing if his wife would totally recover, and if she did, would she decide to go ahead with the divorce she was planning before the wreck. This took a lot of courage and love, and God was with this man.

After Carla woke up, Bessie didn't hesitate to tell her all the lies she had told everyone else. Even though Carla was not totally in her right mind, she had enough sense to know that Craig was not mistreating her. Things that Bessie was saying did not line up with the things Carla was seeing Craig do. Carla replied to Bessie's comments, "But he seems like a good man." Bessie didn't have anything else to say. The jig was up.

Craig is a good man, and it took Carla losing her memory to realize this. Craig is a meek man, and some people confused his meekness for weakness. Please don't get it twisted, it takes a strong man to endure the things that he endured. Craig didn't tell Carla about the children being gone at first. He was trying to figure how he was going to tell her. Carla had regressed to a childlike state and Craig had to be careful how he handled telling her the news. Carla could not comprehend how bad her condition was. As you may remember, Carla had a very bad head injury and her head was so swollen that it was almost as wide as her shoulders. The swelling had gone down. When her head was swollen, she had this knot in the top of her head and it was bald around this area. When the swelling went down, the knot that was in the top of her head was now on the lower back of her head. That's how swollen her head was.

One day, Carla pushed the call light for the nurse to come in to help her to the bathroom. She didn't realize that she hadn't been walking to the bathroom, they were putting her on the bedpan whenever she needed it. When the nurse came in the room, Carla told the nurse what she wanted.

The nurse asked her, "Can you walk?"

Carla replied, "The board doesn't say I can't walk."

Every day the nurses would put their names and the patient status on the board, but this day they forgot to put on there that Carla couldn't walk. Carla had been reading the board every day. So, the nurse went out of the room to confirm whether Carla could walk. When she walked out of the room, Carla decided to go to the bathroom alone, and after that she planned to make her escape out of the hospital. So, without any hesitation, Carla stepped out of the bed and went straight down to the floor. Her limbs were weak, and she had foot drop (a condition caused by an injury to the peroneal nerve which causes the foot to not to be able to lift.) The nurses ran in and got her back in the bed. I thank God she didn't hit her head.

The fall did something to Carla. Now she realized something was wrong and began to ask questions about what had happened. Craig had to finally give her the bad news about all the children. Craig had carried the burden by himself about the children's deaths for three months. During this, he was wondering and dreading how his wife was going to take the news. Craig told Carla about her children and she said, "Lord, I thank You for leaving me one child because You could have taken them all." Carla went on to say, "Lord, I thank You for sparing my life because if You hadn't, I would have been hell bound."

Two days passed, and the Lord spoke to Carla and said, "You haven't repented."

Carla raised her hands and said, "Lord, I beg Your pardon for all I've done wrong. Forgive me, Lord."

You must understand, when you get wrong the only way to get right is to repent. You can't go around it, under it, or over it; you must go through the door. That door is Jesus Christ. "I am the door: by me if any man enters in, he shall be saved, and shall go in and out, and find pasture." (John 10:9) So, I say stop trying to go around the door and just walk through it. All you have to say is, "God, I'm sorry, forgive me for my sins," and if you mean this from your heart, God forgives all. You haven't done anything so bad that God will not forgive. He knows where you are and can save you. "Behold, the LORD's hand is not shortened, that it cannot save; neither his ear heavy, that it cannot hear." (Isa 59:1, KJV) "But your iniquities have separated between you and your God, and your sins have hid his face from you, that he will not hear." (Isa 59:2) Go ahead and talk to God and get it right.

Ewonda was our cousin, but Joale (Carla's daughter) called her Auntie. She took Joale back to Arkansas with her. Joale was nine years old and her life would never be the same because of the things she had just endured, and because of the things that were about to take place.

JOALE'S PERSPECTIVE:

Here I was nine years old, waking up in the hospital, not understanding how I got there or what had happened. I had stitches on my arms and down the middle of my stomach. I also had a cast on my arm. My hospital bed was up against the wall and there was this little color TV. My family had started coming to see me. I still didn't know what had happened, I just remember waking up in the hospital. I remember Craig, Bessie, Finnie, and Auntie Ewonda and my grandfather Curtis all coming in my room.

Craig pulled up a chair and sat down and he said, "You all were in a car wreck. Lamarien, Jeremy, Alex, and Simone' have all passed away." After Craig said this, I didn't hear anything else that he said. His voice just drifted away. I turned my head toward the wall and tears began to roll down my cheeks. I didn't cry hysterically or panic. I guess I was in shock.

I never even acknowledged what he had said, and I never even mentioned it again. My days just kind of passed while I was in the hospital. I had no appetite and wouldn't eat. Auntie Ewonda took good care of me -- she made me eat and took care of my needs. She would take me to see my Mama and Auntie Jackie (me), but I don't remember much about the visit. I wasn't paying much attention to my surroundings; I was in a daze. All I knew was what I knew, and it wasn't much.

I remember Auntie Ewonda telling me, "We'll be going home soon, and you got to stay with your daddy." I didn't ask any questions, I just said okay. In my mind, I was thinking, *I'm not going to stay with my daddy, I'll just go see him for a little while and then I'll go live with Auntie Ewonda.* All I was thinking about was my Auntie Ewonda because she was all I knew.

When we got to the airport, Auntie Ewonda met up with this high yellow man who didn't say much, He was her husband. We walked through the airport and I walked past this man and lady who were standing in the airport. Auntie Ewonda stopped and started talking to them. I still didn't realize who they were. They caught my attention for the briefest of moments because I thought it was crazy for this man to have on a black pleather (plastic not leather) long sleeve jacket and pleather pants. It was the end of July and it felt like it was 120 degrees. I had on shorts and I was sweating. I just knew that this was not who I was going home with because he didn't have enough sense not to have on a pleather suit in the hottest part of the summer.

Auntie Ewonda handed my daddy and auntie my luggage and said, "I'll call you later. You go with them."

At this point, I was thinking, *I'm going to go with them for a little while but then I'm going to live with my Auntie Ewonda.* As I look back, I felt like a foster child being taken away from everything I knew and being dropped off in a foster home. I couldn't process what was happening, so I just went with the flow. I went with the flow because in the back of my mind, even though I got in this brown van with them and took the trip from Little Rock to Carlisle, I was just going to stay with them for a little while and then I would go stay with my Auntie Ewonda. That was my plan. Because in the back of my mind, I was thinking, *I know that they are not going to leave me here with these people,* but they did.

When we got to Carlisle, we went to my grandmother's apartment (biological father's Mama). She lived in this little apartment. It had one bedroom, bathroom, living room, and a kitchen. There were so many people stuffed into this small apartment, who had come to see me. They started hugging and kissing on me. I had a limp, a sling on my arm, still had staples in my stomach and arm. I remember the first thing that came out of my mouth.

I said, "I just want to lie down and go to sleep." They took me to my grandmother's bed, covered me up and closed the door. I lay there thinking, *I'm just going to sleep for a long time and when I wake up, I'm going to go stay with Auntie Ewonda.* But when I woke up, I was in the same place with the same people.

My daddy said, "Come on, let's get ready to go home."

It was at that moment when reality finally sunk in my heart and mind that I was not going back with Auntie Ewonda. I was nine years old and had lived in Vegas for most of my life. I was now in Arkansas in the country. I didn't know anything about mosquitoes, or this humid heat. I was used to the dry heat of Vegas and being able to play outside. Here I was on my way to the van with my limp and sling, being eaten up by the mosquitoes.

We went to Shaffer Road and there was this little white house sitting in the middle of a field. It was farmland, and there was nothing, but rows and rows of beans planted in the fields and a road. There was no McDonalds; there was nothing but Shaffer Road. We pulled up to this old white house and got my stuff out of the van. When I went into the house, it had a living room, kitchen and two bedrooms. In the middle of the living room was one of those old-time wood burning stoves. This house looked like one of those slave houses on a plantation that I had seen on the TV show, *Roots*. I was standing in the kitchen when my aunt informed me that I would be sleeping in the room with them. The house only had two bedrooms and the people who were going to be staying there were my daddy, auntie, her two children and me. My cousin slept in the room with my daddy and I slept in the room with my auntie and her daughter. When I walked in the bedroom that we were going to be sleeping in, there were clothes everywhere. There were so many clothes and stuff on the floor I couldn't even see the floor. I had to step and wade through piles and piles of clothes and stuff. There was only one bed and it was a bunk bed. Something was wrong with the top bunk, so my auntie, her daughter and I all slept in the bottom bunk.

As I look back at that time in my life, I think about that moment. Everything I had ever known was taken away from me. Here I was with these people I knew nothing about. For as long as I stayed with them, nobody ever asked me how I was doing or if I wanted to talk about all that had happened. They were like, "You want pizza, candy for breakfast, or do you want to do this or that?" They didn't ask, so I never talked about it. This whole situation traumatized me even more.

The happiest time I had during that period was when Daddy would let me go stay with Uncle Clyde. He was my favorite uncle and I knew him. We would do things together; he took me shopping and bought me all new clothes. I got to go stay with my Grandma Meda (Curtis's second wife), and I was happy because I knew her. This was the life I was used to, but Daddy would only let me spend one night. They would let me get this little piece of happiness and then take it away. I would have to go back to the plantation.

I went to stay with Uncle Clyde and his (1st) wife one weekend, and I asked his wife, "Can I stay with you all?"

Clyde's wife replied, "You have to call and ask your daddy."

So, I picked up the phone and called Daddy and asked him, "Can I come live with my Uncle Clyde?"

He replied, "Hell naw, you got to come home tomorrow."

I remember sitting there with my little legs folded under me and I cried. Clyde's wife tried to console me, but I didn't want to hear anything unless she was going to tell me I could stay with them. The next day, with a heavy heart, I packed my things and went back to the plantation house. It wasn't long after that I was able to go stay with my Uncle Clyde. I didn't know how it happened. All I knew was I had gotten my wish. Life for me at this point was great, I was with my favorite uncle and I was going to Lonoke Elementary School. Things were getting back to normal and I was happy once again. **END OF JOALE'S PERSPECTIVE**

Chapter Five

Carla Comes Home

Joale had lost her brother, sister, and two cousins. Her mom was in the hospital and they didn't know whether she was going to make it, or if she did, what condition she would be in. Joale knew very little about her father and his family. I can only imagine the fear and uncertainty that she must have felt. Living with her father would be some of the worst weeks of Joale's life. Her daddy immediately took her to a social services office and tried to get Joale a check. When they asked him where Joale's Mama was, he lied and said that he didn't know. Somebody in Lonoke started a rumor that Carla had died, but she was very much alive. When Carla's mind started coming back to her, she called Arkansas and told Joale's father to take Joale to Clyde and he did. I know that he was shocked to hear from Carla. Clyde took good care of Joale until Carla was able to get to Arkansas.

Carla's mental condition began to improve. Now this had an up and downside to it. We all know what the upside is, of course. The more her mental status improved, the more the reality of the situation began to sink in. The realization of Mama and the children being gone began to overwhelm her and she became depressed and withdrawn. Carla was a woman but had slipped into this childlike state. When she talked, she would talk like a child and whine. It was November 1998 and the wreck had happened in July and she was longing to see her daughter, Joale, and the rest of the family. But she was not well enough to travel, and she still couldn't walk. It would cost her $5,000 to fly home in a plane like I had flown. I don't even remember how I got the money. I think it was from the insurance on Robert E's truck. No one had that kind of money at that time that I knew.

All Carla could think about was getting back to Arkansas so she could take care of Joale. Joale was her new reason to live. The doctors were telling Carla that she could not leave yet because she was not well enough. This, coupled with the fact that some of the nurses and techs were mistreating her, didn't help matters either. When I found out she was in the same hospital Mama was in before she died, all I could do was pray for my sister, because there were a few occasions when Mama was mistreated, and we couldn't leave her by herself.

Carla called me crying. She said, "Jackie, I dropped my call light, so I had to bang on the bed to get the nurse's attention. When she came in, she picked the call light up and threw it at me." Carla began to cry and told me that she told the nurse, "I didn't ask to be here." The next day when the nurse came back, she was nice to Carla. Carla believed someone must have told her why she was in the hospital and this made the nurse more sympathetic to Carla's plight.

On another occasion, two male nurses had to clean Carla up because she had soiled the bed. The whole time they were cleaning her up, they talked about her. Carla reported them but then she was scared that they would come and do something to her. When she expressed this concern to one of the nurses, the nurse reassured her that they had been taken care and wouldn't cause her any harm.

To be a good nurse, you must have compassion and patience. So many nurses went to school just so they could make money. If you are one of these nurses, the patient is the one who suffers. Also, you give the good nurses a bad name. But you must remember the Bible says, what you sow you shall reap. One day you will have to be at someone else's mercy, receiving the same treatment that you put out. "Be not deceived; God is not mocked: for whatsoever a man soweth, that shall he also reap. (Gal 6:7)

Miss Hannah realized the state of mind Carla was in and thought that this might hinder her recovery. Carla had fallen into a deep depression and Miss Hannah believed the best thing for Carla would be to be around her family. The first thing Miss Hannah had to do was convince the doctors to let Carla go, and she did. Secondly, she had to figure out how to get her there. Miss Hannah worked for an airline, and she was trying to figure out how to get Carla on the plane long enough to get her to Arkansas. So, for Carla to be able to endure the flight, the nurses started getting her out of bed and started making her sit up as long as she could stand it. This was hard for Carla to do. There were times when I would call Carla and she would tell me in this whining tone, "Jackie, they won't put me back to bed. I'm tired."

I would then explain to her why it was important for her to sit up. Joale's birthday was that month and Carla wanted to be back in Arkansas for her daughter's birthday. This was her incentive, so this was what I would say to encourage her. Sometimes it worked and other times it didn't. The nursing staff finally got Carla sitting up long enough that they thought she might be able to fly home. The doctor decided to leave the Foley catheter in place, so getting to the bathroom wouldn't be an issue when she was on the plane. Miss Hannah got busy making flight arrangements. This was not going to be easy, but they had to give it a shot. Miss Hannah got a flight for Carla and her husband, Craig. The flight wasn't easy on Carla, but they made it to Arkansas.

Craig had a lot of thinking to do. Carla was planning to divorce him before we had the car wreck. Craig never brought this up to Carla, and she didn't remember. All Carla knew was that Craig was a good man and she loved and appreciated him for taking care of her. God works in mysterious ways. So, the plan was for Craig to fly back to Arkansas with Carla and then fly back to Vegas to tie up loose ends and move their things back to Arkansas later. Craig's father was totally against this, he even told Craig that Joale was not his daughter. True enough, Joale was his stepdaughter, but he was more of a father than her real father had ever been. So, when his father said this, Craig let him know that this was his family and he was going where they were. Craig was also concerned about how our family was going to treat him, after all the lies that had been told. Rumors were all over Lonoke about how bad Craig had treated Carla. I think it took a lot of courage and love for his wife for Craig to overcome this situation and move to Arkansas. When Craig came back to Arkansas and everyone got to know him, they realized that he was nothing like Bessie had said. My brother-in-law was an awesome man and he was God-sent to love and care for my sister. Craig took care of Carla like Daniel had taken care of me. How blessed we are.

We were all waiting at Clyde's house, anticipating Carla's arrival. Clyde went to the airport to pick Craig and Carla up. When they got to Clyde's house (the house we grew up in), Craig lifted Carla out of the car and placed her in the wheelchair. Craig and Clyde had to lift the wheelchair up a couple of stairs because the house did not have a ramp. When they brought Carla in the house, my eyes filled with tears as my mouth fell open in disbelief. Carla had lost so much weight and she looked like Mama's twin. Carla looked so much like Mama it startled me, and it made me flinch. The first words out of my mouth were, "Mama." I couldn't help but stare at her.

I knew she wasn't Mama, but I let my eyes and heart absorb her presence because I knew this would be the closest thing that I would have to seeing Mama again. I held onto her neck and cried while telling her, "You look like Mama." We cried and reminisced. Everyone gathered around Carla and loved on her. She had made it home and it was November 22, 1998, her daughter, Joale's birthday, and my wedding anniversary. Everyone was happy and Carla was content because she had surprised her baby girl, Joale, on her birthday. Or shall I say, we thought everyone was happy. Joale was having mixed emotions about her Mama's arrival. Joale had been through so much and everything was finally feeling normal to her until November 22, 1998. Carla had come home.

JOALE'S PERSPECTIVE

Mama had come home to Lonoke, Arkansas, on my birthday to surprise me. Everyone was happy and overjoyed. You would have thought that I would have been just as happy as everyone else. With all that I had been through, Mama was back. I was supposed to be happy. In Mama's mind, she was thinking, *This is going to be a special moment, I'm going to come back on my daughter's birthday and surprise her and she is going to be so happy.*

I was standing outside the house, and when they took Mama out of the vehicle and wheeled Mama into the house, I wasn't smiling, and I wasn't excited. I feel so guilty about that now, but I was only nine years old and I felt what I felt. I was with my Uncle Clyde and I couldn't have been happier. But my happiness was interrupted by this woman they were rolling in the house who I didn't know. When I saw my Mama, my mind went back to the time when Mama was strong. She was working three jobs, she was independent, and going here and there. Mama and Granny were the two strongest women I knew. But as I watched them bring this weakened, sick person in the house, this was not my Mama.

I said to myself, "My life is just getting back to normal. This is not normal for me." Even before my Mama came home and Auntie Ewonda took me to Las Vegas to see her, I was not happy then either. We would take pictures, and in those pictures, I was smiling, but I was so broken. Mama had a tracheostomy at this time. But in my nine-year-old mind, I was thinking, *By the time Mama comes to Lonoke, she's going to be up and around. Mama's going to be back to her normal self.*

I thought back to Granny, how strong she was fighting her cancer. Even though Granny was sick with cancer, she got up and put her wigs on and went on with her day. I would lie in bed with Granny and we would eat pimento cheese sandwiches and Granny was just fine. So, I was thinking, *Mama is just like Granny. Mama's going to get back up and she's going to walk around and she's going to be fine like Granny and we are going to go to church.*

Even when Granny died, I remember all the kids crying and having a hard time. I didn't cry. I was a kid and I had been sheltered from so much by everybody else. I had two siblings, but I played by myself most of the time and knew how to have my own fun. So, while everyone else was having a fit and crying about Granny dying, I didn't cry. As a kid, I had never dealt with tragedy. I never had tragic moments in my life until this point and time in my life. I knew people died and they didn't come back, but I really didn't understand what death truly was.

Even though Granny was gone, I was okay with that because I had spent my time with Granny. I spent more time with Granny than Lamarien, and she lived there with Granny. I lay in bed with Granny when the other kids just couldn't. In Granny's last days, none of the other kids wanted to walk by that middle bedroom that she was in. This was when Granny's eyes were half open. I wasn't scared; I came right on in the room with Granny. She might have been dying, but this was still Granny. Alex, Jeremy, Lamarien, and Simone' were all scared to go to the bathroom that was down the hall because they had to go past the room that Granny was in. I wasn't afraid when they told me that Granny was dying. I was with her on the days she didn't feel well, and when she was at her best. So, when Granny died, I seemed to have dealt with it or I just didn't understand. But when Mama came back, I just could not find that happiness. She couldn't walk, she was barely talking, and she had to be taken care of. When she did talk, she sounded like a child. There are times even now that she regresses and talks like a child. In my mind, I thought, *Mama, you got to take care of me.* I wanted my Mama to be the same person she was months ago before the wreck. I wanted my Mama back and this was not my Mama. It wasn't until 2014 that I began to accept my mom for who she had become. I didn't want to go in the store with Mama because she was handicapped. I was used to going to the store with the Mama who said, "You better not touch anything."

This new Mama never spanked me; neither did Uncle Clyde, Daddy, or Craig. No one ever got on to me about anything; they gave me everything I wanted, and I was the most disrespectful child. I remember being so mad at my Mama for coming back to me like she was, until I said to myself, *I'm going to use this to my advantage.* When she told me to do things or if I forgot to do something she had told me to do, I knew her memory was bad so I would say, "You remember me telling you that" or "I told you that already." "You got to sign these papers. Remember, Mama, you told me you were going to sign these papers for school." I just used the situation to my advantage. I felt like, "The heck with this." I was not accepting the person she was. You would think I would have been happy about the milestone Mama was making and congratulating her on her progress, but I didn't. I talked to my Mama any kind of way. No one ever asked me what I felt or what I was thinking. I was just lost.

Everything was happening so fast, and none of this was supposed to be happening to me. My life was supposed to be different. This was my life and I could not accept it. There would be times when my Mama would just sneeze, and it would make me sick and mad. She was so childlike, I thought she was faking. I would look at this woman and I knew Mama was somewhere inside of her, but I couldn't find her. Once she started walking, she was falling all the time. I didn't say it out loud, but I felt like, *I can't take care of you. Who is going to take care of me?* Craig was working all the time, so I had to help take care of my Mama. Everyone was still giving me everything I asked for. If I asked for anything, they would break the bank to give it to me. But this was not what I wanted; I wanted my old life back. I wanted someone to tell me, "No, you can't have that." I wanted someone to just discipline or fuss at me. But nobody would do that, I was just running amuck. I had no one to talk to. I wished someone would have talked to me, but they didn't. Even now, I don't even look at the scars on my legs and arms. I don't even acknowledge that they are there. I had just shut that part of my life out.

At thirteen years old, I started smoking weed to escape from everything, if only for a moment. Now I feel like there's no point in feeling anything about what happened. I've wasted eighteen years and there is no point crying about it now or talking about it now, because I should have done it then. I feel that my feelings are not validated. **END OF JOALE'S PERSPECTIVE**

Joale is grown now and has a beautiful baby girl, Lauren. She is finally dealing with what happened all these years later. After Joale got through talking, she felt better to get all of that out for the first time. She had only written her thoughts in her journal at that point. She cried and laughed as I interviewed her. When I got through interviewing Joale, I let her know that God wants to heal her from all her hurts and give her the things He has promised. It would be 2016 when Joale, Little Mike, and Crystal (Stine's daughter) watched the video of the five casket funeral. They were able to say their goodbyes and continue moving forward in their lives

Joale & daughter Lauren

Little Mike & his daughter Symone

 The key is you must want to be healed; stop making excuses. God just wants to know if you want to be made whole. Repent and surrender all the hurt to God. If someone pulled a gun on you and told you to put your hands in the air, and you had no way to defend yourself, you would surrender everything of value and of no value to them, because all you wanted to do was live. There is nothing you have that is worth your life. This is all God wants you to realize, and stop holding hatred, bitterness, and anger in your heart. Because, believe it or not, your life depends on it. Just tell God that you want to live. Stop trying to hold onto things that are keeping you from moving forward in your life, and let God heal you like He desires to heal you. You are the only person standing in the way. "So, if you forgive him. I forgive him. Don't think I'm carrying around a list of personal grudges. The fact is that I'm joining in with your forgiveness, as Christ is with us, guiding us." (2 Cor 2:10, MSG) "After all, we don't want to unwittingly give Satan an opening for yet more mischief—we're not oblivious to his sly ways!" (2 Cor 2:11 MSG)

 Carla stayed with Clyde for a couple of days, but then she decided to stay with me because Clyde couldn't take care of her after Craig went back to Vegas. So, I had a hospital bed set up at my house to make it easier for me to take care of her. Carla was still unable to walk, and I was on a walker and still wasn't getting around very well. But I was willing to try to take care of Carla. With Polly's help, I felt like I might be able to do it. But I hadn't thought about the fact that Polly had started working and would not be there during the daytime with me, and Daniel was also working.

The first day Carla was there, Daniel fixed her breakfast. She had bacon, eggs with cheese, and toast. After she got through eating, she told Daniel, "These are the best cheese eggs I ever had." Of course, she told me the same thing the next day. A couple of days had passed, Craig took care of Carla the couple days he was in Arkansas and he was exhausted, but the time had come for him to return to Vegas. Carla and I were alone now, and I was doing the best I could do, but I had bitten off more than I could chew. I kept thinking about the promise that we had made to one another. We had promised one another that if we got sick, we would take care of each other. We never thought we would be down at the same time. It was hard enough for me to take care of myself, but it was a chore trying to take care of myself and Carla. It was like the blind leading the blind.

I was unable to get Carla out of bed. So, this could have turned into a serious problem quickly. She needed to be out of bed at least part of the day. So, to keep her from getting bed sores, I had to give her a bath, and turn her every two hours. But Carla couldn't stand to lie on one side for very long, so I had to turn her every hour. The scars that had healed on her back were itching all the time. So, I was up and down, scratching her back. This was very hard on my body and it made me hurt. Since I couldn't get her out of bed, I had to put her on and off the bed pan. Like I said earlier, this was difficult for me because I had not fully recovered myself. Taking care of Carla made my body hurt more, but I had to do what I had to do. She didn't have anybody else to do this for her since Craig was gone. I knew I couldn't continue to take care of Carla, and I also knew that this was going to be more of hurt to her in the long run because I couldn't give her the proper care. So, I called the social worker and doctor at Rebsamen Rehab to make plans to get Carla admitted. Carla had the same attitude I had when it came time to go to rehab. Fear of the unknown and she didn't want to go.

Carla's first day in rehab, she got to rest, but the next day they got her out of bed to start her on her road to recovery. Carla hated rehab and was not very cooperative with their instructions. She whined and cried a lot and said she couldn't do what they were asking her to do. More than anything, Carla was depressed. I would stay at the rehab center with her and sat up in a chair all night long, taking care of her. Carla would be awake most of the night and I was up and down all night, scratching her back, turning her and putting her on the bed pan. This was extremely hard on me and my health began to decline.

We had the same doctor and he had come to Carla's room early one morning and caught me sitting in the chair beside her bed. There was nowhere in the room for me to lie down. My legs and feet were swollen and hurting, because I had sat up all night. I would cry when I got home because I was miserable. The doctor looked at me and asked me why I was there.

Then he looked at me and sternly said, "Don't let me catch you here another night, your sister will be all right without you." So, I never stayed another night, and this didn't set too well with Carla.

Carla had foot drop in one of her feet and this caused a problem with her walking. She also had begun to stress eat and this caused her to gain her weight back. So, the doctor ordered her a low-calorie diet. The doctors knew that Carla would get around much better if she lost some weight and this made her very unhappy. So, we started sneaking her food.

Christmas was coming and we had planned to check Carla out of rehab for a few days to spend Christmas with the family. The only problem with this was she told them she was not coming back. We didn't know this until it was too late. They didn't give her a pass for a few days, they discharged her, and we didn't know this. When I tried to get them to pick her up after the few days that she was supposed to be home, the rehab people informed me that she had been discharged. I began to cry, because I knew I was unable to take care of her. I don't know what Carla said to them, but this was a big mess. I immediately called the social worker at the hospital. I wept as I explained the situation. The social worker explained that she would get this worked out and would call me back. Meanwhile, Carla was crying because she didn't want to go back to rehab. She was enjoying everyone waiting on her hand and foot. I, for one, understood this, but it was time for her to get on her feet. I knew this was best for her even though she didn't understand. The social worker got in touch with the right people and Carla was back in rehab that same day. Carla was angry at me and didn't understand why I made her go back.

When I went to visit the next day, Curtis and Carla were sitting at the table in the dining area, visiting. I could tell when I walked in that they had been talking about me. When I sat down and spoke to them, Curtis immediately started asking me why I couldn't take care of Carla. Then he went on to say that she was not able to do the things they were asking her to do in the rehab.

He said, "She's been through a lot."

Then Carla interjected and said, "My kids would still be alive if you had driven." Her words made me feel like she had stabbed me straight through the heart with a dagger. I lost my breath for just a moment.

What she didn't know was that I was already blaming and beating myself up because I felt like there should have been something, I could have done to save my children. I was their Mama. I felt that I should have been able to protect them. Carla was in a coma for a while after the wreck, but I had been aware of everything since the wreck. So, I had been struggling in my mind about the children's deaths. Trying to understand why God allowed this to happen, and why He spared my life. I didn't know why, how, or when, but I knew who Jesus was. I had to stop trying to wrap my mind around the why, how, and when and put all my focus on the who. I had fought with everything in me to get my mind to a place of peace and had succeeded until this moment. Carla's words hurt me in a place deep inside of me that God had begun to heal. Carla didn't realize I had already blamed her, Robert, Clyde, and myself in my mind and heart.

Sometimes the hurt of losing loved ones will make you look for someone to blame, when in truth one day we all will pass this way sooner or later. In other words, life's ups and down are going to happen to us all. You must forgive yourself, everyone else, and hold to God's unchanging hand for the strength you need to move forward in your life. If you don't, you will find yourself stuck in that hopeless rut for years to come. "I took another walk around the neighborhood and realized that on this earth as it is—The race is not always to the swift, Nor the battle to the strong, Nor satisfaction to the wise, Nor riches to the smart, Nor grace to the learned. Sooner or later bad luck hits us all." (Ecc 9:11 MSG) The enemy will have you blaming everyone else. The devil will try to keep your mind in turmoil because he knows there is no peace when your mind is in turmoil. "And the peace of God, which passeth all understanding, shall keep your hearts and minds through Christ Jesus." (Phil 4:7)

The things Carla was saying made me retaliate, and I told her, "I can say the same thing about you. I asked you and Robert E three times to stop and get a motel room, but you all didn't want to stop until we made it to Arkansas. If we had stopped at the hotel, the kids would still be alive." I know this shocked her and she hadn't thought about that. Then I snapped my neck quickly as I turned toward Curtis. I told him, "You and Clyde act like Carla was the only one that was in the car wreck. I was in the wreck too. I lost two children just like she did. I got hurt and had to learn how to walk just like she must. You all got to stop babying her; she can do it if she makes up her mind. I can't take care of her; don't you see that I'm on a walker and barely getting around myself?"

They both sat there and looked really silly. I think what I said about her and Robert E not wanting to stop got her attention.

I had even blamed Clyde because I had asked him more than once to take my children back to Arkansas with him before Mama died. Clyde simply cursed me out and told me he wasn't going to do it. I remember when Clyde would come to visit me when I first got home. I struggled in my mind about that very situation. But I had to forgive, let it go, and move on with my life. Now was not the time to be holding any kind of grudges.

After I said what I had to say to them, I got up and went home. It was two days before I went back to visit. The bottom line was it wasn't anybody's fault. It wasn't my fault, Robert's, Carla's, or Clyde's fault.

God called the children home, and when He calls, no matter where you are and what you are doing, you must go. It was their time to go -- there was nothing no one could do to stop it. We don't know a lot of times by what vehicle we're going to leave this world. It may be cancer or a heart attack, but when it's your time, it's your time. Just get right and live right so you can see God's face in peace when it is your time to leave this world. There is no time to be harboring hate and bitterness in your hearts. Life is too short. Make up your mind to let it go and God will help you do the rest. "And be ye kind one to another, tenderhearted, forgiving one another, even as God for Christ's sake hath forgiven you." (Eph 4:32)

When I went back to rehab, Carla and I apologized to one another. She had a different attitude and had started cooperating with the rehab personnel. The new attitude was fueled by the fact that Carla wanted to take care of Joale, not Joale taking care of her. Carla's focus had shifted from "woe is me" to "I'm going to get better and move on with my life." It wasn't long before she walked out of rehab. She had a noticeable limp because of the foot drop, but thank God she was able to walk again.

Carla decided to go stay with Clyde so she could be with Joale. She was out of rehab by the time Craig got back from Vegas. Before Carla left Vegas, she would call Clyde collect and the phone bill had gotten so high until Clyde was unable to pay it. So, the phone was turned off. It shouldn't have because Clyde had already collected plenty of money from donations due to the tragic accident. After Carla came back to Arkansas, I gave her the insurance policy that Mama had taken out on Lamarien (Carla oldest daughter). It had doubled because Lamarien died in the car wreck. Clyde asked Carla for the money for the phone bill, and Carla instructed Clyde to go get a thousand dollars out of the bank to pay the phone bill. When Clyde came back from the bank, he told Carla nonchalantly, "I got two thousand dollars." He didn't give an explanation why, and Carla's mind wasn't right, and so he took advantage of this.

Clyde made Carla pay half of rent and half on all the bills in the house. The house was paid for and shouldn't have had any rent, but Clyde had taken out a loan from the bank to fix the house up and he still didn't get the things fixed that he should have. The house still needed a roof; the bathroom floor was weak, and soft. Sometimes when Carla and Craig would pay half of the light bill, Clyde would not pay the light bill. The bill would be doubled the next month and he would then ask them to pay half of it. Clyde didn't stop until all Carla's money was gone. After all the money was gone, his attitude changed toward Carla and Craig. One day, one of our cousins came to the house and was about to go to the store. Carla had found a dollar and some change in one of Craig's pants while washing clothes. She handed the money to our cousin and told her to bring her a Coke.

Clyde responded with an attitude, "A Coke, you know you owe me half on the groceries I bought."

Carla stood up for herself at this point and told him, "I found that change in Craig's pocket and I don't have any money." Carla then said, "I want you to know that we won't have this problem anymore, because I'm going to do you one better, I'm moving out of here."

Carla and Craig moved into their own apartment before the month was out. Mama would have been angry about this, because she intended for Carla to have the house. They stayed in the apartment for about a year before moving into Uncle Cortez's (Stines Husband) rent house. Clyde and his wife eventually moved out of the house and moved to Chicago. Clyde convinced Carla and Craig to move back in the house after he had moved to Chicago. They were to pay the loan note that he had gotten to fix the house up, which was a little over $300 a month. Carla and Craig moved in the house, but Clyde did not tell them that the roof was now leaking in the bathroom and in the living room. A new roof was one of the things that Clyde was supposed to get fixed with the money that he had borrowed. Craig and Carla were frustrated because they were struggling financially and could not afford to get these things fixed. They had given up their rent house for a house that was not fit to live in. Craig expressed his concerns about the house to his Mama and she sent them money to get the leaks fixed.

Carla and Craig's situation were bad but would soon get worse. Carla was sitting in the living room watching television when the roof caved in. This was one more thing that they couldn't afford to get fixed. So, they just rigged it up the best they could to keep it from raining in the house. They lived like this for months and were at their wits' end, trying to figure out what to do. The opportunity presented itself that they might possibly be able to buy a new home if they sold the house they were living in as is. So, Carla called Clyde and told him that she wanted to sell the house so they could buy a new one and Clyde agreed. But he didn't tell them the house had a lien against it because of his back taxes. It was not personal property taxes; it was Clyde's taxes that he had failed to pay to the government. Carla and Craig found this out when they went to try to close on the house. Just when it seemed like all hope was lost, a friend who was a realtor stepped in and helped Craig and Carla buy a house. They faced many obstacles while trying to buy their home but overcame them. You cannot close a door that God opens and cannot open a door that God closes. God was in the plan all along.

Clyde eventually lost the house due to back taxes. He got mad at us because he thought that we should have helped him pay the taxes to save the house. I never understood this; we couldn't save him or the house because he was in too deep with the government. The lien on the house was over $15,000. Someone bought the house, fixed it up and rented it out. It hurts my heart when I go to Lonoke and drive by the house. All the times we had in the house were not all bad times. The enemy would like for me only to remember the bad times, but I refuse to. When I pass by the house, I reminisce only about the good times. One of our cousins lives in the house now and I can visit whenever I want to. The first time I visited him, it was a little emotional, but I was glad that he was the one living in the house.

Carla's mind had improved with time, but there were so many things she didn't remember that happened before the wreck. When we would take long trips, Carla would not go to sleep while riding in a car. She would say, "The last time I went to sleep in a car, I woke up three months later, I'm not going to sleep." Usually Carla would ask me questions about things she partially remembered, and I would fill her in on the rest.

For years, I had a lot of animosity against Curtis and Clyde, and it took God for me to forgive and move on with my life. I had been praying for them for years, when one day I saw the move of God and I knew that He was hearing my prayers. We had started getting together on July 14th every year. This was the day we had the wreck. Instead of sitting around being sad about it, Carla and I decided to cook a big dinner and invite everyone over. It worked; we had started getting closer. I knew Mama would have been proud of us. Clyde even apologized to me and I apologized to him. Clyde had given his life to the Lord and was trying to do better in every area of his life. Clyde and his first wife had gotten a divorce and they had two children together. Clyde remarried a wonderful woman who is still standing by his side.

I know Clyde still struggles with the past, but the same God who gave him strength to let it go and forgive yesterday is the same God who will give him strength to let it go and forgive today. Don't let a moment in time control your future. God has greater things in store.

Curtis and I have an awesome relationship currently. Curtis forgave me and I forgave him. I hadn't talked to Curtis for a few weeks, and I was shocked when Curtis called me one day and said, "Girl, you know you still my daughter and I love you." Curtis and Clyde even came to hear me preach one Sunday. This was nothing but the hand of God at work.

Carla and I are very close; we talk to one another at least five times a week. Sometimes five times a day. Craig and Carla are closer than ever and they 're both serving the Lord.

Five years after the wreck, I found a roll of film in my dresser that had not been developed. When I found the roll of film, I said to myself, "I wonder what's on this film; I'm going to take it to Walmart, and have it developed." So, I did. I had it developed in one hour. While I was waiting, I ran into Carla, we said our hellos and went our separate ways in the store. In an hour, I went to the photo department to pick up the pictures. I opened the pictures to check them out. I lost my breath when I realized what the pictures were.

Tears rolled down my face. I couldn't help myself. I immediately thought of Carla. I called her on the phone to see if she was still in the store and she was. I told her to meet me at the McDonalds that was inside Walmart. I told her I had something to show her. I told her to brace herself. She started looking at the pictures and began to cry. We sat there crying and reminiscing for I don't know how long. It was a bittersweet moment.

The roll of film had the pictures we had taken in Vegas with Mama when she was in the hospice facility. I had forgotten all about that day. I thank God for leading me to that roll of film. We were looking at that moment in time that Mama struggled past her pain to leave us pictures to remember her. As we looked at the pictures, we could see the struggle with the pain in my mom's face. Well, she didn't have to struggle anymore. It was over.

Carla and I wiped the tears from ours eyes as we went our separate ways. I made her a copy of the pictures and we both found comfort and joy in them.

Chapter Six

A Returned Favor

A few months after I got out of rehab, I was able to walk without a walker, but I walked with a limp. It was hard sitting at the house day in and day out, doing nothing while everyone else was gone. I didn't know what to do with myself, but I knew I had to do more than what I was doing. My short-term memory was affected after the car wreck and it was hard for me to remember simple things that Daniel had instructed me to do throughout the day. Polly had suggested that I write everything down and keep it next to my chair on the table. Throughout the day, I would look at the tablet to see what I needed to do. This was frustrating to me for a while, but I never stopped praying to God and He restored my mind.

I started going to school after my counselor at Arkansas Rehabilitation Center asked me what I wanted to do before the wreck happened. I told her that I always wanted to be a nurse. She then replied, "Enroll and we will pay for it." True to their word, they did. They even allotted me a certain amount for my books. All I had to do was attend school and meet with my counselor at the rehabilitation center monthly and give her a copy of my grades at the end of the semester. I didn't need many prerequisites because I had already attended Arkansas Baptist College, Philander Smith College, East Arkansas Community College, Shorter College and Pulaski Technical College. I had attended these colleges taking classes so I could become a nurse. But I always had to quit after a semester or two, because something would go wrong with one of my children, mostly Jim (my oldest son). He would get in trouble. Peter (my ex-husband) had beaten me so much at times until I stayed sick or I couldn't find a babysitter. I never gave up. I kept going back.

This determination I had to keep going to school, despite my circumstance finally paid off. When I applied for nursing school and transferred all my credit hours from every school, I didn't need many prerequisites. God was in the plan all along. I got accepted in the LPN program at Pulaski Technical College. I completed LPN school in 2002 and had already enrolled in ASU Jonesboro associate degree nursing program before I finished LPN school. I started at ASU in 2002, about two months out of LPN school. I completed that program in December of 2003. I was already working as an LPN at White County Hospital in Searcy while attending RN school. I graduated in the top five.

In 2005, I got a job at the University of Arkansas Medical Sciences (UAMS) hospital and enrolled in their Bachelor of Nursing program and graduated. In 2001, thanks to Arkansas Rehabilitation Center, I got to go to school to fulfill a long-awaited dream and I will always be indebted to them.

It amazes me how I tried time and time again to go to school and failed. But God has His timing for all things. It didn't feel good when I was trying to better myself and seemingly getting nowhere. God's timing is everything, and if you can walk in God's will and move with His timing, that is the key for success.

Since I had gotten on my feet, Polly (my best friend who took care of me after the wreck) had to make up her mind what she was going to do. She was trying to decide whether she was going to find a place to live in Jacksonville or move back to Moro. Polly only had to fret about that for a little while, because the decision was made for her. One day while we were sitting around talking, she got this phone call. I didn't know who it was, but she had this strange look on her face. She didn't say much while she was on the phone. But this made me curious. When Polly got off the phone, I asked her what was wrong.

She made the statement, "Mama could have asked me if I was coming back before she did that."

I said, "Did what?"

She replied, "Mama burned down my house for the insurance money."

I was shocked, but I couldn't help but laugh. I laughed so hard until she started laughing.

While laughing, she said, "Girl, I bet those snakes and rats were running everywhere."

The house Polly lived in was in the country and it was by this open field and the snakes and rats were bad. We finally stopped laughing and I asked her what she was going to do.

She said, "Well, I know I can't go back to Moro."

Polly got a job at Kmart nearby, and later started working at Regal Ware, a company manufacturing pots and pans. This was where Daniel worked. Polly had left her husband, Blackie, a few years before coming to stay with me, due to his habitual cheating. There's this saying that you can't teach an old dog a new trick. In Blackie's case, this was so true.

It was ordained for Polly to be in my house at the time she was there. Polly had a lot of wisdom. After the wreck, Daniel and I had some trouble communicating. I would talk to Polly at times and tell her about the things I was struggling with. Daniel was talking to her also and I didn't know this at first. She used wisdom not to cause confusion in my home. She helped Daniel and me find our way back to one another. We got closer and stronger.

One day Daniel came in from work and there seemed to be something wrong with him, but he wouldn't tell me what was going on. Every time he would go in and out of the bedroom or bathroom, he would slam the door. He didn't slam the door real hard, but just enough that I could tell something was wrong. Polly and I were sitting in the living room, talking.

I said to her, "I wonder what's wrong with him."

Polly said, "I know what the problem is."

I said, "What is it?"

Polly replied, "The Lord said it's time for you to be a wife to your husband."

I just sat there as my mind ran back to the last time my husband and I had been intimate. It was when I had come home to get the children to take them to Vegas to see Mama. I was currently walking with a walker. I don't understand why this had not crossed my mind, but it hadn't. My husband had been very patient with me and I thank him for it, but it was time for me to be a wife to him. Daniel had not discussed this with Polly, God revealed it to her. I made up my mind right then that I was not going to make Daniel wait another night. It had been about three months too long. So, I talked with Daniel that night and told him that I wanted to come together with him. I didn't tell him about the conversation that Polly and I had.

Daniel had this shocked look on his face and said, "Are you sure? I don't want to hurt you."

I said, "Baby, I'm sure."

Daniel helped me get cleaned up and he was ever so gentle. God came in and He blessed our night. I can't express enough how much Daniel means to me.

This is an example of the wisdom Polly had. The next day when Daniel came home, he wasn't slamming doors, he was singing. Polly and I looked at one another and just laughed.

Polly had been my best friend since I was fifteen years old. She was the one who helped me find my way to the Lord the first time I got saved. Polly taught me how to pray, fast, and give God my all. She used to tell me, "You don't have to be just a saint; there are always higher heights and deeper depths in God. It's not boring to be saved. If you put your all into it, God will use you if you put yourself in a place to be used." Polly even taught me that God will keep you if you want to be kept. I didn't have a husband when I first got saved, but she instilled in me to stay celibate until God sent me my husband. So, I fasted, prayed, and went after God with my whole heart and it worked.

Polly was married to Blackie at the time when I had given my life to the Lord. My desire was to please the Lord, and I would follow Polly's every instruction. Polly was a powerful woman of God and I admired the God who was in her. But I made one mistake: I had put Polly on a pedestal and forgot that she was flesh and blood just like everyone else.

It was 1999 going into the year 2000, I believe, when Polly was making plans for her future. Polly now being single had to live the life of celibacy until God sent her lifelong mate. There were a few men pursuing her at this time, and occasionally she would go on a date with one of them. There was this gentleman in Los Angeles, California she liked, but at the time she said she was not willing to move to California. They stayed friends. Curtis (my first stepfather) also threw his hat in the ring. Polly asked me what I thought about her dating or marrying Curtis. I told her I didn't think he was the one.

"Curtis didn't treat Mama right and he's not going to treat you right without God in his life." I felt as if Curtis didn't deserve Polly.

There was this preacher from Little Rock who was a friend of the husband of one of our friends. He talked good at first about Jesus, but then tried to get Polly to go to bed with him. Polly held her ground and didn't sleep with any of them. But then there was Emanuel, who was the cousin to the husband of her sister Katherine. Emanuel lived in Texas and truly loved Polly for who she was. Emanuel helped Polly out financially with whatever she needed, and he expected nothing in return. He even helped Polly's two children, whenever they needed any kind of assistance. Emanuel was my favorite out of all of Polly's suitors. I believed he was the one God had sent. He had asked her to marry him and she refused, but that didn't stop Emanuel from pursuing Polly. He came to visit her a couple of times while she was taking care of me. He stayed friends with her throughout the years, hoping she would someday change her mind.

Polly had to now live the life she had so adamantly preached about for years, and I know it wasn't easy for her being alone. Even though Blackie was no good, she was not alone most of the time when she had him. I don't blame her for leaving, though. I think she stayed longer than she should have. It was a different story now and the men seemed to be coming out of the woodwork, trying to talk to her. This was a distraction to keep her from seeing who God truly meant for her to be with. That's how the devil works. I asked her why she didn't want to marry Emanuel, and she told me that his credit wasn't good. I thought that this was a mighty poor excuse, but these words would come back to haunt her soon.

I will never forget the day that a wolf in sheep's clothing showed up at my house to see Polly. Leo was one of her classmates and had come to town for his sister's funeral. They met one another at the funeral and made plans to see one another before he left town. Leo was a little taller than Polly, with a small-framed body that he seemed to have consciously taken care of throughout the years. Leo didn't look too bad in the face, either. He lived in California, had his own home, and had a nice job that he had been on for years. To top this off, Leo was talking Jesus. Leo was everything that Polly thought she wanted in a man. He stayed in town for about a week and he wined and dined her. He even asked her to marry him and in just one week, Polly had fallen hard in love with Leo. The couple of times that I met him, he seemed nice enough, but that's how the devil works. After Leo left town, Polly told me that Leo asked her to marry and she had told him yes. So, naturally I trusted her judgment and was happy for her.

At first, he was supposed to come back to Arkansas, and they would get married and go back to California. Polly called a few of her friends to tell them that she was getting married and asked if they would be her bridesmaids. Then Polly and I went wedding dress shopping and we found the perfect dress on sale. Meanwhile, Polly kept working, trying to save money for her move.

Polly and I were sitting around laughing and talking about nothing in general when she said, "I don't know what kind of job I'm going to get when I get there because I don't have a high school diploma."

I didn't know that Polly hadn't graduated from high school. This was my first-time hearing this. I then told her, "Why don't you go to night school at Shorter College to get your GED."

Polly's reply was, "I don't have time, and I'll be leaving soon." The next thing she asked me took me by surprise. She asked, "Will you take the test for me?"

I said, "Girl, I don't look anything like you, I can't do that."

Polly said, "Yes, you can, they don't even look at your driver's license that hard."

She had done so much for me, I felt like I had to at least try. It was 1999 and I hadn't been to school in a while. So, I told her, "If I'm going to do this, I've got to go to a few of the adult education classes at Shorter College to refresh myself."

So, that's what I did. I went to classes for about a week and decided to go take the test. I had lost a lot of weight and had hair weave and it was cut like Polly's. At first glance, I favored Polly. I thought I would be fine if they didn't look at the height or weight, and they didn't. I took the test, but they told me I didn't pass. A few months later, I received Polly's GED in the mail. I didn't understand how it happened. Turns out, I had passed, but they had made a mistake. Polly had already moved to California by this time, so I mailed it to her. Yes, this was wrong on so many levels, so don't try it. I would have looked crazy if we had been caught. But I was already caught by the one it matters the most. Yes, God.

Polly was on the phone talking to Leo a few days after I had taken the GED test for her. When she got off the phone, she was quiet. I don't know what he said, but she was quiet for a couple of days. She finally broke her silence and said, "I'm going to get my husband." She then said, "I'm moving to Fresno and I will get married there."

She didn't tell me at that time, but Leo had changed his mind about getting married. She felt if she was there in person, he would change his mind. So, she packed her things and moved to Fresno, California within a week. I talked to her after she arrived and asked her where she was staying. She told me with Leo, and they would be getting married in a day or two. Well, when I talked to her again that week, she said that she and Leo had gotten married and were enjoying themselves. I teased her about it, and we laughed. I was happy for my friend and praying that everything would work out for them.

Polly had started working at Kmart, which wasn't too far from where they lived. After a few weeks had gone by, I talked to Polly and I knew something was wrong, but she wouldn't tell me. A few days later, I got a call from Emanuel (Polly's friend from Texas) and he asked me if I had talked to Polly. I told him not today. Emanuel let me know that something was troubling Polly and she needed someone to talk to.

Emanuel said, "I told Polly she should call and talk to you because I knew you would understand." So, when I got off the phone with Emanuel, I called Polly to see what was wrong.

Polly hesitated, and choked over her words as she slowly told me, "Jackie, I didn't get married." My mouth fell open in disbelief. She went on to tell me, "He changed his mind and I didn't know what to do."

I got angry, because I knew Leo had never had any intentions of marrying Polly. He had gotten what he wanted and was through with her. Leo was truly a devil in disguise. I told Polly to come home and that she could move back in with Daniel and me.

I asked her, "Where are you?"

Polly had moved in with an elderly friend of Leo's for the time being. To make her feel better, I told her about times that I failed God and how He loved me and forgave me. I could tell that this made her feel better.

Once you have fallen, all you can do is get up, ask the Lord to forgive you, forgive yourself, and move on. This is what my friend, Polly, did. God forgave her. She forgave herself and she moved on. God will give you the strength you need to keep from falling if you spend time in His presence daily. "And he is the propitiation for our sins: and not for ours only, but also for the sins of the whole world." (1 John 2:2, KJV) "Now unto him that is able to keep you from falling, and to present you faultless before the presence of his glory with exceeding joy." (Jude 1:24)

I thought about all the people who had asked me if Polly got married and I had told them yes, not knowing that she hadn't. But little did we know, most of the people back in Arkansas knew anyway because Leo had told his cousin and family that he wasn't married. This was the day I realized Polly was just as human as I was. It's easy for you to tell someone how to handle a situation when you are not the one going through it yourself. But when you are facing the same trial someone else is facing, will you be able to stand? Polly was a strong woman of God and the devil had tricked and deceived her.

The Bible says when you are weak, this is when you are strong. "Therefore I take pleasure in infirmities, in reproaches, in necessities, in persecutions, in distresses for Christ's sake: for when I am weak, then am I strong."(2 Cor 12:10) When you are at your weakest, you depend on God for your strength because you realize that you can't do anything without Him. But when you think you are strong; this is when you think you can do it by your own power. However, you are weak and vulnerable and don't even realize it, because you aren't watching and praying like you should. The scripture that Polly always quoted to me was, "Can a man take fire in his bosom, and his clothes not be burned?" (Prov 6:27) In other words, she was telling me not to put myself in any compromising situation with a man because I might not be strong enough to fight off the temptations.

Even though she failed God, all she had to do was repent, get back up, and keep moving forward. Polly came back to live with me, but she was embarrassed about what other people would think of her. I never treated my best friend any differently than I always did. We prayed, fasted, and read our Bibles together, just like old times. Emanuel loved Polly and still wanted to marry her, but she wouldn't. Polly stayed with me for a few months.

If I'm not mistaken, it was the year 2000 when I received a settlement from the insurance company from Robert E's truck. I helped Polly move back to Fresno, California. This time she would get her own place. Daniel gave me permission to help her drive to Fresno. Within a few days, we packed all her things in her car and headed to

Fresno. We prayed and sang most of the way there and God spoke and set His approval on the decision she had made to move back to Fresno. I drove most of the way because I couldn't stand to sit in the passenger's seat and ride long distances. Another reason I drove was we were going through Santa Rosa, New Mexico, where we had that fatal wreck.

When we arrived in Fresno, it was dark, so we decided to get a hotel room and start fresh the next morning. When we rose the next day, we began praying for guidance. Then we searched the newspaper for affordable apartments not too far from where we were. Leo had no idea that Polly was coming back to town. We got a map and got directions to the apartment complex. The first apartment we looked at, she decided to take it. The rent was reasonable, and the area was quiet and nice. We asked the apartment manager where we could get some furniture. She gave us the address and name of a furniture store. We went to the furniture store and bought a living room set, bedroom set, and the furniture place delivered it before noon. Then we went to Walmart and got all the things Polly needed for the kitchen and bathroom. It was a one-bedroom apartment and it was now her home. Everything went so smoothly; we knew God had to be in the plan. We sat around that night, amazed at how God had moved. The next day Polly started thinking about getting a job. She went back and worked at Kmart for a little while. Fresno was a big place, but it had a small-town feel, sort of like Jacksonville. I stayed a few days, but then I caught a plane back home.

Leo was shocked when he found out Polly was back in town. She didn't let him know right off that she was back. Polly found out Leo was dating this African lady at his church and was doing so the whole time she was there. Polly didn't get caught up with Leo when she went back to Fresno. She talked to him on and off, but she didn't let him make her lose her place with God again.

The first Sunday Polly was off, she went looking for a church to go to. She had stopped in the store for just a few minutes when she heard this little sweet voice telling her how pretty she was. When she turned to see who it was, it was an elderly lady who had such a sweet spirit. Her name was Mrs. Flossie, and she asked Polly where she was going to church. Polly informed her that she was looking for a church to go to.

Mrs. Flossie said, "I know a church you can go to that's not too far from here." She went on to tell Polly that her children attended there. Mrs. Flossie then told her that the church she attended didn't have service until evening time, because they were sharing the building with another church. She gave Polly the name of the church, Evangelist Temple COGIC, and showed her how to get there. Mrs. Flossie then invited Polly to dinner with her family. This was not a chance meeting; God was in the plan.

Polly went to dinner with Mrs. Flossie and her family, and she immediately bonded with all of them. Mrs. Flossie and her family soon became a big part of our lives. When Polly finally went to the church, it turned out that it was located right down the street from her home. The church was located on this dusty rock road. It was like she had gone to church back home. When she met Pastor Thomas and his wife, they just loved on Polly and took her in.

When I would talk with Polly, she talked so highly of everyone until I couldn't wait to meet them. Polly soon switched jobs and began working for Sam's Barbeque. It was a family-owned restaurant run by Sam (the father), Martha (the Mama), Dee (his daughter), their son, and other cousins and friends. They treated Polly like she

Mrs. Flossie

was family. Not only was Polly talking to me about them, she was also telling them about me and all that I had gone through.

I finally got to visit Fresno, and everyone was just as loving as Polly had described. I didn't have to pay for any meals while I was there. Sam and his family fed me every day. I would drop Polly off at work and use her car while she was at work. Before I left the restaurant, I would sit around and talk with the family. My first day meeting them, I remember giving my testimony, telling them where God had brought me from. Sam Sr. stood over me, listening to my story, when tears began to flow down his face.

When I had finished telling my story, Sam looked at me and said, "You are one strong woman. I don't think I could have taken that." As we talked, Sam asked Polly and me to pray for him, because he felt like there was a dark cloud over him, following him everywhere. We prayed and I got up and left.

I also gave my testimony to Mrs. Flossie and her family, and after I gave my testimony Mrs. Flossie made a statement that this story needed to be heard. What she did next shocked me. She got on the phone and let different people know I was in town and these people invited me to their churches so I could give my testimony. There would be no church service going on, but Mrs. Flossie would start a church service. She would invite me to their house and then would call different people and they would all come. They would set a chair in the middle of the floor and I would sit there and minister to the people. They were hungry for God and God used me to feed them. Mrs. Flossie amazed me, and she would say time and time again, "Your story needs to be heard." This was truly a real woman of God and God continued to use her in various ways.

I didn't have my own car while I was there. Mrs. Flossie gave me the keys to her car, and I kept it at Polly's house the whole time I was there. I would go pick her up and take her places like it was my car. Who does this? Family will not even do this. Mrs. Flossie was one of those friends who stuck closer than a brother.

Mrs. Flossie, her family, and friends from different parts of the country and world would call one another at 6:30 in the morning and pray. They would all be on a conference call and a different one would lead prayer every morning. Man, what a prayer. They called this the prayer line. That was in 2000, and at the time of this writing, the prayer line is still going on. Tell the Lord, "Thank You." That's what God loves: persistence and consistency.

I had spoken at three different churches in that one week while I was there, thanks to Mrs. Flossie. That doesn't include the house meetings we would have. I would go to prayer with Mrs. Flossie during the day at church. These people loved God and the only other people I knew who loved God like they did was in Moro, Arkansas. I'm not saying that you don't love God, these are just the people I knew. God used Mrs. Flossy to open doors for me.

It came time for me to go home and Polly had to take me to San Jose, California, to catch my flight home. Leo had called and wanted me to come to his church and give my testimony, but I told him I wouldn't be able to because I would be gone by that time. Polly took me to San Jose and soon went back to Fresno. My flight was delayed because something was wrong with the plane. I sat there in the airport and I began to pray: "Lord, if I'm supposed to stay here and give my testimony at Leo's church, let me know."

After about an hour, they began to load the plane. I was uneasy and couldn't get comfortable. After everyone got on the plane, they still didn't take off, there was still something wrong with the plane, so I continued to pray. I said, "Lord, if there is something that is wrong with this plane, please don't let it take off. I'll obey You and go back to Fresno and give my testimony."

I was exhausted and my voice was gone, but it was not time for me to leave California. By the time I got through praying that prayer, the pilot came over the intercom and said that the flight had been cancelled because something was wrong with the plane. I got off the plane and decided to take another flight another day. I finally got in touch with Polly and they came back to get me.

That Sunday, I went to Leo's church to give my testimony. I wasn't the main speaker. Their main speaker was a preacher from out of town. I'll never forget it-when this gentleman got up to preach, all he talked about was that women were not supposed to try to preach. He went on to say that God didn't call any women to preach. I started praying, I said, "Lord, You told me to come back and now You're going to have to touch these people's minds."

When he got through preaching, the pastor of the church called my name to come up and give my testimony. I was nervous because I had to get up behind what this man had said. I'm not a silent standstill person when the power of God hits me, I've got to move, and my voice goes up about three octaves higher than normal. So, it sounds like I'm preaching when all I'm trying to do is reach. When the pastor handed me the microphone, the anointing of God fell on me and I began to tell my story. The church was full, and the people all jumped to their feet. I glanced at the pulpit, and the speaker and the pastor had this crazy look on their faces. God had just proven him wrong. God sent me back and I obeyed. I don't understand why people feel this way. If God can use a chicken, and a donkey, why can't He use me? After I finished with all God had for me to do, I caught a flight out of San Jose that next day.

I kept in touch with Polly after I got back and called Mrs. Flossie from time to time. A few months after I left, I got a call from Polly and she was crying hysterically. I couldn't understand what she was trying to tell me. She had to repeat herself a couple of times and my heart was pounding from fear. When I finally understood what she was trying to tell me, my mouth dropped open in disbelief. Tears began streaming down my face.

Polly said, "Sam (the owner of Sam's Barbeque) hung himself and he's dead."

My mind raced back to the last time I talked with him. After I had given Sam my testimony, he had told me that he felt like a dark cloud was over him and was following him everywhere. I realized now that this was a spirit of depression and suicide. My heart was heavy, because I kept thinking that there should have been something that I should have been able to do or say to stop this. I asked God why He didn't let me see this before it happened. I didn't know what to say to Polly. I just cried with her and prayed for the family. This was a great loss for not only his family but for the city of Fresno. Sam was loved and admired by so many people and would be missed dearly. Sam had struggled for many years mentally and his family stood by him and got him all the help that they knew how. The family struggled through that time in their lives and they kept the restaurant open for several years after Sam's death. The restaurant is now closed, but Sam will always be remembered and loved.

Polly had begun to talk with this gentleman, Archie, who had joined their church. She was crazy about him and so were a few other women in the church. Archie would take her out to dinner and come visit her. She would call me and talk about how good looking and nice he was. Well, I thought the most important thing was that he was in church. As time passed, Archie left the church and went to another church that was in Fresno. Polly continued to see him and said that he had asked her to marry him and she said yes. It wasn't long before Polly left the church and went to the church he was going to. I was very unhappy about this, because I had visited the church she was attending, and I knew her pastor was a good shepherd. Polly had gotten caught up in Archie and lost sight of what was real. Polly did not have a sexual relationship with Archie or stop serving God, but Archie was another distraction. Polly told me her pastor talked with her and told her she had to be careful because Archie was a womanizer. Polly didn't believe him, and she went ahead and joined the other church. I came to Fresno for another visit and got to meet Archie. He was a nice enough guy, but I had my doubts about him. I visited the church they were attending, but all I could think about was that I wanted to go to church at Evangelist Temple.

After time had passed, I asked Polly what they were waiting on to get married. Polly said that Archie had asked to see her credit report. Polly had a few credit issues on her report, and because of this Archie said he wouldn't marry her until she got those things corrected. The same reason she had given me for not marrying Emanuel was now the same reason Archie was giving for not marrying her. Polly's words were now coming back to haunt her. I truly believe it was just an excuse, and Archie had no intention of marrying Polly. He was just another distraction to keep her from going after God like she needed to.

Polly continued to work at Sam's Barbeque, and about 2002 she started getting sick. Her appetite decreased and she started having a lot of pain in her abdomen. Polly never went to get herself checked out because she said she didn't have any insurance. Dee and the other waitress at the restaurant would make her sit down and they would take up the slack when she couldn't work, and they still paid her. They loved Polly like she was family. Dee tried to persuade Polly to go see a doctor, but it was to no avail. Polly didn't tell anyone at the time, but she had been feeling two knots in her side for two years. I found out later that she had seen blood in her stool while she was in Arkansas taking care of me in 1998. She only told one person about the knot she had been feeling in her side, and that was Emanuel. He tried to convince her to go see a doctor, but she didn't.

In December 2003, I had just finished the registered nursing program at Arkansas State University in Jonesboro. I had only been out of school a week when I got a call from Polly. She was in the hospital and she said, "Jackie, I need you to come take care of me. I'm in the hospital." Polly sounded weak and she was.

Katherine (Polly's sister) had already flown to Fresno. Katherine got on the phone and filled me in on the details. The first thing out of her mouth was, "Don't tell anybody." Polly was a private person, and I couldn't help but think that trying to keep everything private had gotten her into this situation. Katherine went on to tell me Polly was in her bathroom doing her hair when she started hurting and having trouble breathing. Her stomach had been bloated for months and she ignored it because she didn't have insurance. She was in a state now that she could no longer ignore it. Polly called Leo to come take her to the hospital. The next words out of Katherine's mouth made me stop in my tracks. She said, "Jackie, it's bad and they don't know exactly what is going on."

About a month before this happened, Katherine said she was awakened out of her sleep by a voice that said, "Go to California and get your sister. She's dying." Katherine called Polly then but did not tell her about the voice she had heard. She pleaded with Polly to come home, but she refused. Though this was not the first time Katherine had asked her to come home, but this time it was urgent. I talked with Daniel and he agreed to let me go.

We didn't have the money to get a plane ticket, so Katherine rallied the family together and they bought me a plane ticket. I went to take care of my friend. I had to go; she had called and said she needed me. I had made Polly a promise: If she ever got sick and needed me, no matter where she was, I would come and take care of her. Five years had passed since Polly had moved in and taken care of me. Even though I had made this promise to Polly, it was one I hoped I would never have to keep, because I had hope she would live a long and healthy life. This was a favor returned with a heavy heart. Oh, how I wished that I could have returned any favor but this one. I wished this only because my best friend was suffering and there was nothing, I could do to stop it.

When I got to the hospital, I slowly walked into her room. I could not see Polly when I first entered the room. Her bed was on the other side of the room in the corner. When I turned the corner and my eyes met her eyes, I gasped for my breath -- Polly did not look like herself. She was so swollen. Tears flowed down my face as I walked over to the bed and said, "I'm here."

Polly was on a pain pump at that time, and Katherine told me that the doctor had given her three months to live. Polly's oldest son had come to Fresno to see about his mom also. Katherine would have to leave Fresno soon and I was to stay behind and take care of Polly.

The doctor did a colonoscopy on Polly and discovered that she had tumors in her colon, and they were cancerous. Polly was in Stage IV colon cancer which had metastasized to her liver and other parts of her body. The doctors removed the tumors and thought they got it all, but they weren't sure. Polly had to have a colostomy bag at that point. Leo came to the hospital to see Polly and so did Archie. I remembered Archie not understanding the seriousness of the situation.

Archie stood at the head of Polly's bed and said, "We going to be all right, I'll take care of her." This made Polly smile.

I looked at him and thought, *maybe he's not half bad.* He even handed me $100 so I could have some money while I was there. But I knew time would tell. Katherine didn't have much confidence in Archie and neither did I. I told Katherine that I was going to tell him what was really going on so we could see if he was going to stay or run.

Archie came to the hospital to visit Polly. When he got up and walked out of Polly's room, I followed him into the hallway. I walked fast to catch up with him. I said, "Archie, do you realize how bad the situation is?" He listened attentively as I filled him in on Polly's condition; he was in shock because he didn't realize what bad shape Polly was in. I told him he had to make up his mind if he really wanted Polly, because she was going to need someone who would stand by her for the long haul. In other words, her sickness was not going away overnight. Archie said he understood, and he turned and walked slowly down the hallway.

Polly's arms were swollen, and she was weak, so whenever she talked on the phone someone would have to hold the phone to her ear. I called Katherine to tell her that I told Archie all that was going on. Katherine responded, "We will see if he is real or not."

The next day, Archie called the hospital and asked to speak to Polly. So, I held the phone to Polly's ear. She said, "Hello, I'm fine." She never said too much after this. The countenance of her face changed as she listened attentively to what Archie had to say. In a few minutes, she said, "Okay, bye." I took the phone from her ear and hung it up.

Archie had called to say that he got a job out of town and he was moving. I could see the hurt on Polly's face, but she didn't cry at that time, but she might have cried later. I told Polly it was going to be all right. Archie's true colors had shown up. I called Katherine that same day and told her that he ran like we thought he would. Katherine said, "Good, now Polly can focus on God and getting well." Polly never saw or heard from Archie again. He lied-he never left Fresno. I was visiting Fresno in 2014 and found out Archie was still in Fresno and had married one of the other sisters in the church.

After we got rid of Archie, I contacted Pastor Thomas to let him know what was going on. Polly had not talked to him since she left the church. Pastor Thomas talked with me for a little while and said he would come and see Polly. Then he said something I will never forget.

He said, "I don't know why, but California is a graveyard for many preachers. California is full of backsliding preachers."

Pastor Thomas was an awesome, God-fearing man, and he didn't hesitate to come and see about Polly. I didn't tell Polly what I did, but I knew that she needed to get things straight with Pastor Thomas before we left Fresno. When Polly looked up and saw Pastor Thomas, the tears began to roll, and she told him how sorry she was. He told her that it was okay, and he loved her. It was hard for me to hold back my tears at that time. He prayed for Polly and soon left. She was so glad to see him, and I could tell that this took some of the load off her mind.

It was almost Christmas, and Katherine and I started trying to figure out how we could get Polly back to Arkansas. The doctors were saying that she was too critical to move, and they were still running a lot of tests on her. They took her to interventional radiology so they could move the drains in her abdomen because there was no drainage in them. When she got back from the procedure, Polly lifted her leg to get in the bed and this brown cottage cheese looking drainage began to ooze out of her lower abdomen. When the nurse raised her gown to see what the problem was, Polly's abdominal incision had dehisced (come open) and it was oozing this drainage. The oozing soon stopped, and it started pouring out. The drainage filled up two big towels. The nurses asked Polly was she hurting, and Polly said no. The nurse was really frowning as she tried to catch the drainage. Polly couldn't see what we saw.

She looked at how the nurse was frowning and said, "It must be pretty bad because of the expression on your face."

The nurse didn't realize how she was looking, and when Polly said that she straightened her face up. While one nurse was cleaning her up, the other one went to notify the doctor. Polly's chances of coming home were not looking good.

Christmas came and Polly's oldest son and I were missing our families. Mrs. Flossie and her family realized this, and they invited us to their house for Christmas. We all gathered at Regina's (Miss Flossie's daughter) house and they loved on us like we were part of the family. They even bought gifts for us. I will never forget them for this. It was so amazing and emotionally overwhelming, experiencing all this love from these people who barely knew us. This was a God thing and I couldn't help but give Him the glory.

January 2004 had made its arrival and Polly seemed to be doing better. The doctors didn't expect her to live as long as she had. We knew God had the final say in all things and we were putting our trust in God at this point. Polly and I would pray and sing, and I would read to her. Polly's oldest son finally went back home to his family and I was there by myself. Katherine stayed on the doctors about letting Polly come to Arkansas. My husband had driven my Durango truck to Fresno so I could get around to places that I needed to, and he just wanted to see me. We didn't know how long I was going to have to stay.in Fresno and I wanted my car so I could drive Polly back home when it was time.

A few days after Daniel arrived, he caught a plane back to Arkansas. The doctors in Fresno consulted with the doctors in Arkansas and got them to agree to take Polly as a patient. They didn't feel like she was stable enough to be transferred, but Katherine had stayed on them. When they got the doctors in Arkansas to accept Polly as a patient, they changed their minds and started working toward her discharge. Polly had been walking the halls two and three times a day while she was in the hospital, trying to get strong enough for the trip home. She was finally discharged from the hospital.

I had graduated from nursing school, and the knowledge learned made the situation more surreal to me. I took Polly back to her apartment, and the plan was to take a couple of days and put her things into storage and drive home, since I had my truck there. I had been taking Polly's vital signs twice a day and all was well. But when I took her temp that night, she had started running a fever. The doctor had warned us that if Polly started running a fever, we had to bring her back to the hospital. I knew if I took Polly back to the hospital, we would not be going home for a while. So, I got on the phone and called Katherine as soon as I saw Polly's temperature going up. I informed her that if we didn't get Polly home tomorrow, I was going to have to take her back to the hospital.

Katherine said, "Let me call you back." I don't know who she called, but by the time she called me back, she had booked Polly a flight from San Jose to Arkansas at 5:00 in the morning. This meant I had to leave Fresno about 1:00 in the morning, because San Jose was about two-and-a-half hours from Fresno. I gave Polly something for her fever, praying that it would work, and began packing her clothes. The plan was for me to get her on the plane to Arkansas and come back to the house and pack up her things.

Polly made it to Arkansas safely. She was supposed to go to the hospital as soon as she got to Arkansas, but she went to her sister Katherine's house in Brinkley instead. Polly got a chance to visit with lots of her family and friends. Everyone was so glad to see her. The visit was short-lived because the same brown cottage cheese drainage began to flow out of her lower abdomen again. Katherine took Polly to the hospital, and when she got there the doctor told her that they were expecting her yesterday. When they examined her stomach and saw all the drainage, they asked her if she was hurting. She replied, "No." They admitted her to the hospital and immediately began to perform tests to see what stage her cancer was and if they would be able to help her.

Meanwhile, I was still in Fresno, trying to figure out what to do with Polly's things. I was ready to come home since she had made it to Arkansas safely. I began packing all of her things that I could get in my Dodge Durango. I quickly pulled her clothes out of her closet, but tears filled my eyes and overwhelming sadness filled my heart as I pulled her wedding dress out of the closet. This was the wedding dress Polly had bought in Arkansas to marry Leo. I sat there on the bed with the wedding dress in my hand as I shook my head in confusion and sadness. Polly would never get a chance to become the bride she had so desired to be. I sat there for a while, lost in my thoughts, trying to get clarity from God, but it never came. I had come to the conclusion that I had to accept what God allowed. Most of the men Polly had allowed in her life were what I called Time Wasters.

A Time Waster is a person who comes in your life and makes you feel like he or she is that special person for you, but they have no intention of doing the right thing. All they want is what they can get from you at that time. Time Wasters are those people who will stay with you for ten, fifteen years, and then walk out on you and marry someone else. When there is a Time Waster in your life, they're in the way of the person who God truly has for you. Time Wasters are blessing blockers and users. Yes, they are smooth with their conversations and will make you weak in the knees and feel good, but in the end, Time Wasters make you cry more than they make you laugh. Please don't get stuck with a Time Waster; life is too short, and God has greater for you. God knows who is deserving of your time and is not going to waste it. Life is too short to be wasting time. "Whatever turns up, grab it and do it. And heartily! This is your last and only chance at it, For there's neither work to do nor thoughts to think In the company of the dead, were you're most certainly headed" (Ecc 9:10 MSG) In other words, stop wasting time and do what you are going to do, because you can't do it when you are dead.

When I got through packing Polly's things in my truck, I couldn't see out of the back or side window. I took her TV to Mrs. Flossie's house, sold some things and gave away most of it. I told Katherine I didn't put anything in storage, and I was coming home. I cleaned the apartment the best I could and informed the apartment manager about what was going on. Mrs. Flossie had a brother in Oklahoma, so she decided to ride with me, and I would drop her off at his house. This was great because Oklahoma was only a few hours from Arkansas, and I wouldn't have to make the trip alone. I will never forget that trip. I was struggling in my mind and heart because we had to drive through Santa Rosa, and Albuquerque, New Mexico was the place where we had the wreck. Before we got there, I was tired, and we decided to stop and get a hotel room and start fresh the next day.

When we got back on the road the next day, we started singing and praying and the power of God filled the car. I was crying until I could hardly see the road. The Lord began to speak and let us know that He was with us. Mrs. Flossie and I were praising God with everything we had. When we came to ourselves, we were on the other side of Albuquerque. I couldn't believe it. God is an awesome God. I said it time and time again, "If I'm not sure about anything else in this old world, I know that God loves me." We made it to Oklahoma in good time that day. Mrs. Flossie's brother was just as nice as her other family. He fed us and put us up in a hotel. He was a pastor of a church; I got a chance to give him my testimony before I left for home and He wept as I told my story. Mrs. Flossie told me when he went to church that Sunday, he preached with a new zeal and told the people what God expected of them.

I finally made it home, and was so glad to see Daniel, and he was glad to see me. He held on to me as if he thought that I would disappear any moment, and I held on to him. I went to see Polly at the hospital the next day. When I got there, a lot of her friends and family had begun to come in to see her. Polly and I talked. I just assumed she would be coming home with me when she got out of the hospital, but Katherine made her come home with her. I understood Polly was her sister and she wanted to take care of her, so I didn't say anything.

Polly had been in the hospital for about a week when the doctor came in and told her, "I need for you to call your family in because I need to talk to them." Polly acknowledged what the doctor had said and kept on talking about the goodness of the Lord.

A couple of days passed by and the doctor came in again and said, "I need you to call in the rest of your family because I need to talk to them." This time the doctor seemed kind of moved, because he didn't think we were taking him seriously.

Polly looked at him and told him, "I will," but then she turned to us and began to talk about the goodness of the Lord. What the doctor didn't understand was that most of Polly's family were preachers and missionaries. It wasn't that we didn't understand what the doctors were saying, it's just we were praying and believing God for a different outcome. She wasn't gone yet, and as long as she had breath in her body, we knew God was able. So, we continued to praise Him despite what it looked like. When the doctor came in the next day, some of the family was there, but not all. The doctor told the family that Polly only had three months to live. We didn't say a word.

Polly looked at him and said, "Okay, thank you sir," and she turned to us and began talking about the goodness of the Lord. At that point, I know the doctor thought we were crazy because we didn't react like he thought we should have when we heard the bad news.

When those three months had passed, Polly was still here. She had to go in and out of the hospital for blood products and chemo. They decided to try a different chemo, since Polly made it past the three months. I remember walking in the hallway with Polly one day when the doctor passed by her in the hallway. He stopped and just looked at her and shook his head because he was amazed that she was still here and walking the halls. Polly went to stay with Katherine after she got out of the hospital and Katherine would take her back and forth to her doctor's appointments.

Polly put on weight and was looking good. I'll never forget the first time she came to church. Boy, did we have a time in the Lord. Polly was little in stature, but she was tall in the Lord. She reminded me of Samson. She had lost her anointing fooling around with the devil, but God had taken her back to her former glory. Chill bumps were all over my arms and chills ran up and down my spine as she opened her mouth to tell where God had brought her from.

With her preaching voice, Polly bellowed out, "Y'all, the doctor said that I only had three months to live. I heard what the doctor said, but I also heard what God said. God said, 'live and not die.'" Just about everyone in the church stood and began to praise God. God had given Polly back her anointing. It doesn't matter what you did yesterday but get it right today. Polly had her place with God back and that was all that mattered.

Most people don't understand that God forgives if you repent from your heart. I didn't tell Polly's story for gossip. I told her story to let everyone know that God forgives. God forgave me and my friend and gave us back our anointing. If you don't remember anything else, I said in this book, remember God forgives. Get up and move on.

The chemo they tried was not working, so they decided to try a stronger one. It turned Polly's feet and hands black and she broke out all over. Polly couldn't take it. The chemo was too strong, so she told the doctor to stop. It was December 2004 when Polly's pain became unbearable. Katherine told me about the nights she would hold Polly in her arms as she cried and said, "It hurts so bad, I've never felt pain like this."

Blackie (Polly's ex-husband) had come by Katherine's house one day to talk with Polly. Blackie apologized for all he had done to her and begged her to take him back. Polly told him that she forgave him a long time ago, but she would not take him back. Blackie left that day realizing that Polly was the best thing that had ever happened to him and he would have to live with his regrets.

Polly was admitted to the hospital in January 2005 for the last time. Her pain had become too much for her to bear. Emanuel (the friend who had asked her to marry him for several years) had come to the hospital and asked Polly to marry him one more time. Polly looked at him and said, "Do you realize the shape that I'm in?" Emanuel didn't care. He loved Polly with all his heart. He always had. Polly could see this now, but it was too late. Polly told him yes and accepted his ring.

So many women have missed the one God has for them, looking for tall, dark, and handsome. Most of the time when you get him, he will not love you or treat you right. Ask God to send you what you need. God knows who is going to love you for better or worse, through the thick and the thin. So, what if he's not tall, dark, and handsome? God will not give you anyone that you can't stand to look at or love. He takes all that into consideration, trust him.

Emanuel, Katherine, and I took turns staying at the hospital with Polly. There were some nights that Katherine and I would stay there together. Polly had gotten to the point where we couldn't understand what she was saying most of the time. One night she began trying to tell Katherine and me something. We got close to her bed so we could hear what she was saying. Polly told us she wanted to get up. Katherine and I knew we couldn't get her out of bed, so we placed our hands in her back and sat her up in the bed.

Polly then said, "I said if you walk like I walk, talk like I talk, if I'm getting good results you should get the same results. Do you understand what I'm saying now?"

Katherine and I looked at her and said, "Oh yes, we understand what you're saying." Polly was preaching her last message, and what a powerful message it was.

The last night of Polly's life, I was there with her. She was restless during the night and so I called the nurse a couple of times to give her some pain medication. It seemed to calm her for a while. I dozed off to sleep for a while. I would wake up when the nurses would come in and out to check on her, but I didn't get up. Everything seemed to be going fine. About five o'clock the next morning, I sat up to see how

Polly was doing. She couldn't talk, but I could see she was in a lot of pain. Her breathing was labored, and her body was wrenching from the pain. I pushed the call light for the nurse to bring her something for pain. I told Polly to hold on, the nurses were bringing something. As I examined Polly, I noticed that her IV line had been broken or cut. The lock was connected to her port, but the IV line had been severed. I got angry and went to the nursing station and told them her IV line had been cut. Polly's IV line had been cut for a while, because her bed and clothes were wet. She had gotten the dose just before I went to sleep, because she calmed down. But the last two times the nurse came in the room to check on her and give her meds, I don't know if she got them. How the IV line got cut, I don't know. The nurses gave her pain medication and called the doctor to report what had taken place. I don't know what the doctor ordered, but when they gave it to her, Polly shook her head yes.

Polly had finally gotten some relief from the pain. At this point, her breathing began to slow down. I knew she was leaving. Just as she took her last breath, her Mama and sister walked through the door and I told them she was gone. It was a bittersweet moment. I hated to see her go, but I didn't want her to suffer anymore. There was no more pain. She was resting. Polly's family buried her with the ring Emanuel had given her.

Emanuel struggled with Polly's dying because he was the only one Polly had told about the growths she had felt in her side. Because of an altercation they had, he had stopped talking to her for a period. During the time they weren't communicating, Polly's health declined, and Emanuel felt as though he had turned his back on Polly when she needed him most. But Emanuel must understand Polly would not want him to feel this way. God chose to call her, and we cannot stop God when He calls. She was grown and made her choices in life. She loved Emanuel but she didn't realize how much until the end. She didn't blame Emanuel for anything, she was just glad that he loved her as much as he did. Polly cherished that thought until she took her final rest. She realized that Emanuel was her God-sent husband. She had wasted so much time listening and looking at time wasters. The right one was there all the time.

Blackie didn't attend Polly's funeral and it would be a year after Polly's death before I saw him again. I had gone to a doctor's appointment and as I pulled up in front of the building to park, I saw this dark-skinned man who looked like Blackie, but I wasn't sure. I walked toward the building and the closer I got, I realized it was him. I called his name to get his attention and he turned to look at me. At first, he tried to pretend he didn't see me and turned and walked away. So, I walked toward him and asked him how he was doing. Blackie was angry and immediately began to talk about his children.

Blackie said, "They could have let me come to the funeral. I wanted to be there."

I told Blackie, "If you wanted to come to the funeral, no one could have stopped you if you really wanted to be there." The real problem was that Blackie wanted to sit on the front row with his sons at the funeral, and they told him he couldn't do that. Blackie could have come to the funeral, but he would have to sit with everyone else, not the family. I understood that, even if he didn't.

Blackie had his head tipped toward his shoulder, which seemed to be frozen in a raised position. I changed the subject by asking him, "What happened to your shoulder?" He told me that some guys threw him out of a moving vehicle one night and broke his shoulder. He said, "I never went to the doctor to see about it and my shoulder is stuck like this." I felt sorry for him, because life had already taken its toll on him and I could see it in his face. But I knew this was just the beginning of his sorrows.

Chapter Seven

Called to Preach

After Polly died, I had to pick up the pieces of my life and move forward. I started working at the University Arkansas Medical Science and decided to further my education. I got my bachelor's degree in nursing my first year there and then I enrolled in the Bachelor to Advanced Practice Nursing (APN) program. I was finally accomplishing some things in my life that I had desired all my life, but God interrupted those plans because He had another mission for me. I had to drop out after a year to raise my grandson, Tom. Jim was Tom's father, and he was in and out of jail, strung out on drugs. Tom's Mama, Honey, was in and out of the State Hospital. Floe (Honey's mom) said Honey was at a party and someone put drugs in her drink. Honey's mind had not been right since.

I had no intention of raising my grandson. I had just gotten used to being at my house by myself. Daniel was a truck driver and was gone most of the time. It was hard at first, but I soon got used to it. I had bought a two-seat, hardtop gray Miata convertible. I only worked weekends, so I would go and do whatever I wanted during the week. Daniel didn't mind, he just wanted me to call and let him know where I was going and when I arrived, so he would know I was safe. Things were going well until I found out about the situation Tom was in. I didn't get to see him often because Tom's family moved a lot. It would sometimes be a year before I could find them after they had moved. This time was no different. I got a call from a friend who told me where they were living, so I went by the house to see Tom and to ask if he could come stay a couple of days with me. Usually when I picked up Tom, I would bring his oldest sister, who was not my grandchild, with me, but this time, I didn't. I always had to buy all new clothes when I picked him up and I had to take him straight to the bathtub. Tom was so filthy the bath water would almost be muddy looking. I had picked him up a couple of consecutive weekends and would take him back on Sunday.

This Sunday, when I went to drop Tom off., he didn't just get out of the car and say, "Bye, Grandma," as usual. When I pulled up to the house, Tom dropped his head and said, "Grandma we don't have no lights, gas, or water on. Can I stay with you?"

I looked at him in disbelief and said, "What?" and then asked him, "How long have they been off." He told me three months. By this time, his sisters had made it out to my car, and we had to stop the conversation. I told him I would see what I could do, but he had to stay there a little longer. He got out of the car and I left with a heavy heart as the tears flowed down my face. I called Daniel and told him what had happened. I went to see a lawyer that same day so I could see what my choices were. The lawyer wanted $1,500 up front, then informed me that I could call social services to report this. I talked to Daniel more about the situation. I decided that I would leave the situation alone because I didn't know if I was ready to take on raising another child. This would be a life-changing decision. I now had freedom to go and come as I pleased, and I was not ready to give it up. I reasoned within myself, *Everyone falls on hard times at one point or the other. Maybe they will get the utilities on soon and everything will be all right.*

I went to pick up Tom the next weekend and I decided to talk to Floe about the utilities. Floe was not at home, she was at a neighbor's house cooking her family something to eat. So, one of the children walked down the street to show me where she was. I asked Floe to let Tom and his two sisters come stay with me until they got the utilities on. I informed her that I would get them back and forth to school.

Floe replied, "No, they need to know what hard times are."

I was shocked, and said, "Hard times? It is our responsibility as adults to supply a child's basic needs, lights, gas, water, food, and clothing. A child should not have to experience hard times like that." I could see maybe one utility off, but not all three. Then I went on to ask her how much it cost to get the utilities back on. When she told me that the water bill was over $300, I knew there was nothing I could do to save them. The thought that crossed my mind was that someone must be doing drugs for the water bill to be so high, because water was the lowest bill we had. My next thought was that I must get Tom out of that situation. I couldn't do anything about the other two, but I had to get my grandson out. I didn't understand how they allowed things to get so bad. There were at least five grownups living in the house, along with six to seven children. One or two of the adult girls would get their own places for short periods of time, but someone always got evicted and they would all move in with whoever had the house at the time.

I remember Honey calling me one time and saying, "Mrs. Palmer, I'm so tired of my situation. Every time I move, they all follow me and move in with me. I can't have anything of my own. I'm thinking about moving out of the state just to get away from them." I let Honey know that I would be praying for her and her family. Honey never moved, and shortly after our conversation she ended up in the State Hospital.

I left their house angry about the situation. I went home praying about what to do. I was sweeping the kitchen floor when the Lord spoke to me and said, "Get him and teach him My ways. I've called him to preach." I cried and began to praise God. I called Daniel on the phone and told him what God had told me to do.

He didn't hesitate. He said, "Okay, baby, I'm with you."

I got on the phone and called DHS and reported the situation. They informed me that Floe was already under investigation. They also informed me that if Tom got in the system, it would be hard for me to get him. So, I made up my mind when I picked up Tom that this time, I was not going to take him back. When I picked up Tom, I was careful not to let Floe know that there was anything wrong.

When Monday came, I didn't return him. Then his grandmother realized I wasn't bringing him back. Floe called me and I let her know what my plans were and that I had reported her to DHS. Floe called DHS and informed them that I would not bring her grandson back. DHS informed her that I was his grandmother too and I had just as much right to him as she did.

I had hired a lawyer and paid him to help me get custody. Tom was eight years old at this time and he informed me that he had been put out of school for an entire year for terroristic threatening. I couldn't believe it! Tom had missed so many days of school until he couldn't be promoted to the next grade. The days he missed were before they had put him out of school. I had to have a letter from his mom to get access to Tom's school records and to be able to try to get him in school, Honey was still his legal guardian and she was in the State Hospital. I had to visit her there to get the paper signed.

I typed a simple note that stated that she gave me permission to take care of Tom by taking him to the doctor, to the school, etc. I called the State Hospital and asked what I needed to do to visit. They told me what to do. I called Honey to let her know that we were coming to visit. Honey gave a list of things that she wanted to eat, and she also wanted me to bring a perm for her hair and I did. When we got there, I didn't bring the letter up at first. I let her and Tom visit a while.

The first thing Honey said to Tom was, "I heard you got in a fight." Tom shook his head yes. Honey asked him, "Did you win?"

Tom replied, "Yes."

Honey said, "That's all that matters then." Then she asked him something that I found very strange. Honey asked Tom, "You still having those staring spells?" Tom's reaction to the question was not answered with words, he just hunched his back over and began squinting his eyes and staring across the room.

I then replied, "Boy, ain't nothing wrong with you. Straighten up and act right." Tom immediately straightened up and never did that again.

Floe and Honey were having Tom pretend to have seizures so they could get a check for him. The gig was up. I was a nurse and I knew about seizures and Tom never had a seizure. He visited with his Mama for a while, and then I showed her the letter and told her what I was trying to do. She signed the letter and I was able to go to bat for my grandson. I wanted him to have a chance at life. I knew if I left him in that bad situation, his chances would be slim. Floe was furious with Honey after she found out that she had signed the paper giving me permission to take care of Tom. I had to go before the school board and talked them into letting him get back in school so that I could transfer him to school in Jacksonville. After I explained his living conditions, they understood Tom's anger and attitude. He had no way to take a bath, see to do homework, and his mom was in the State Hospital. His basic needs were being denied and he was angry and lashing out. He was failing most, if not all his classes.

Tom was released to me and the suspension was lifted so I could get him back in school. When we went to court for the custody hearing, some of the staff from the State Hospital brought Honey to the court. I remember looking at Honey and feeling sorry for her as she sat at the table alone. Honey's hair was all over her head and she looked like life had gotten the best of her. Tom had to wait on the outside of the courtroom with Daniel. My lawyer and I sat at the table across from Honey. The school secretary, school assistant principal, and a friend of mine had come to court with me to testify on my behalf. When the principal took the stand, she talked about all the days Tom had missed from school, and the disciplinary problems that she had with Tom on different occasions. There were pages and pages of reports about their hygiene and how she had to pick up the kids and their grandmother to take them to meetings they were not able to get to. While taking them to the meetings in her car, she had to roll down the windows because Floe and all the children smelled so bad. I know this to be true, because when Daniel or I picked up Tom, we had to roll down the window because of the smell.

My lawyer called each one of my witnesses. The judge never really looked up; he just kept writing on the paper in front of him. After my lawyer got through questioning a witness who had come on my behalf, the judge asked Honey if she had any questions for this witness.

Honey replied, "Yes." The school assistant principal was on the witness stand. Honey slowly got up from her seat and walked toward the witness stand. When she got close enough, she said, "Why didn't anybody tell me Tom didn't go to school?"

The principal replied, "You all were contacted."

Honey went on to say, "Didn't nobody call me and tell me." I knew her mind was bad and so did everyone else, because she was the one who kept him at home. She slowly went back to her seat after the judge asked her if she had any more questions. As she went back to her seat, she kept saying, "Didn't anybody tell me he missed them many days." Honey began to cry at this point. My heart hurt for her because she was so lost. But I knew for now this was the best thing for Tom.

The whole time we were in court, Floe kept looking at me with this mean look on her face. I did my best not to make eye contact with her. As soon as all the witnesses had testified, the judge did not hesitate to give me custody of Tom. He knew this would be the best thing for Tom at this time. He didn't even give Floe or Honey visitation rights, but I had decided I would take him to visit sometimes. Floe, Honey, and her other two children were downstairs when we were getting ready to leave the courthouse. They all hugged him and cried and said their goodbyes. Floe continued looking at me like she wanted to beat me down.

It took a few days for the situation to sink in Tom's head that he was not going to live with them anymore. When it did, he began to cry and say, "I want to go home." I explained to him, "This is your home, but I will take you to see them soon." Tom was all right in a few days. But as time passed, Tom longed to see Honey and his siblings.

It was Christmas 2006, and Tom was a little more settled in, so I decided to take him to visit his mom and sisters. Precious (my stepdaughter) went with me because I was afraid to go alone. When I arrived, everyone was glad to see Tom and he was glad to see them also. Honey had gotten out of the State Hospital, but she was not at the house at the time we arrived. Someone made a phone call to let her know Tom was at the house. Floe just sat at the table and didn't say a word, she just stared at me. I don't even remember her even acknowledging Tom. Tom tried to talk with her, but she hardly responded to him. Honey finally made her entrance and when she did, you could tell she was a little tipsy. Honey had a cup that contained alcohol she was sipping on. Honey hugged, kissed, and talked with Tom for a while. Then Tom went to the back of the house to play with his siblings. I took some pictures of him, his mom, and siblings. Floe continued to stare and not say a word, and this made me very uncomfortable. I didn't want to rush out, but I felt that my life might be in danger. So, I let Tom visit for an hour, then I told him, "Let's get ready to go." Tom asked if he could spend the night. I looked at him and gently told him maybe another day.

I remember thinking, *When I get out of here, Lord, I will not put myself back in this situation.* I figured I would give them more time to cool down. A year after that, I decided to check to see if they still lived in the same house. They had moved and I didn't know where they had moved to.

When Tom started school, he could barely read or do math. I knew I had my work cut out for me. I would sit at the table in the evening time and drill him with his times tables and spelling words.

One day when Daniel walked in the house, Tom told him while crying, "Paw Paw, Grandma hard on me."

Daniel replied, "No she's not, son, she loves you."

I told Tom he was being lazy, and he was a smart kid. I went on to tell him that I was going to help him learn everything he needed to learn so he could have a chance in this world. Then I said, "I want you to grow up and be a productive citizen." This was the explanation I gave Tom every time he felt like he couldn't do it.

The last time I told Tom I wanted him to grow up and be a productive citizen, Tom wiped tears from his eyes, looked up at me and said, "I don't want to be a productive citizen." It took everything in me not to just fall over and laugh. I never used the words *productive citizen* again.

There were many days I asked myself, "Lord, what I have gotten myself into?" Tom had a habit of lying and stealing. These were two of the hardest things to get him to stop doing.

I would tell him, "You do not have to steal. If Daniel and I are able, we will probably buy it for you if it is within reason."

My digital camera disappeared for several months. We later found it in his room under the bed. So, from time to time while he was at school, I would do room searches, and sure enough, I would find things he had taken. Some of the things he had taken were hard to understand why he had taken them. Nevertheless, my grandson got better in school. I had to stay on him constantly about his schoolwork, but he finally realized he could do it. In the beginning I had to go to the school a lot, but eventually that became less and less.

Tom turned out to be a blessing to me. I had gotten sick and Daniel was on the road. There were a lot of things I was not able to do. Tom stepped in and he was the man of the house when Daniel was not there. I had taught Tom how to cook and wash his own clothes. So, when I didn't cook, he knew how to fix himself something to eat. He mowed the yard and planted my flower garden in the summertime. I believe Tom is going to make some lucky young lady a good husband someday.

Tom lived with Daniel and me for about seven-and-a-half years. We lost track of his family because they moved from place to place. I worked with a young lady who was married to Floe's brother, she didn't even know where they stayed. Tom had got a lot better and it seemed like he was trying to do better in school. He was in the tenth grade, struggling to keep his grades together, but he was managing. One day all of this changed. He started skipping school, doing a lot of cursing, and being disrespectful. We finally found out what the problem was. He had found Floe and Honey through his cousin on Facebook. They had been talking to him for about a month, filling his head with a lot of lies. Tom, Daniel, and I had this big altercation and he told us he didn't want to live with us anymore.

I told Tom, "If I knew where your people were, you could go stay with them, but you can't stay in the streets."

Tom then responded, "I know where they are, and I got the number."

I then told him, "Please give me the number and let's call them." When I finally got Floe on the phone, I told her who I was and immediately told her that Tom wanted to come and stay with them. I had her on speakerphone, so Tom could hear our conversation.

Floe responded, "Tom needs to stay there, Tom need to stay there."

I replied, "He said he's not going to follow our rules and that he wants to stay with you all."

Tom was shocked to hear her say that he couldn't come live with them. Floe said, "Let me speak to Tom." Floe told Tom, "You need to stay there and behave yourself. You can come spend the night, but you need to stay there." When Tom got off the phone, he was in shock. He couldn't believe that Floe just didn't say, "Come on and stay with us."

Tom said, "If they don't want me, I don't want to go with them."

What made me so mad about this situation was that they wanted him to stay in my house and cause all this trouble after they had filled his head with lies. Floe did not want the responsibility.

The following weekend, we went to Rick's (my brother) house in Georgia. I did not intend to take Tom with me. I was going to let him go stay with his mom, but he didn't want to go because he was hurt about them not wanting him to stay with them. So, I decided to leave him with my sister-in-law, but then Daniel came to me and let me know that Tom was sorry for what he had done.

I told my husband, "No he's not. He's just saying that so he can go on this trip with us."

We went ahead and took Tom because he apologized for the way he had been acting. My oldest two granddaughters made the trip with us also. Daniel was a truck driver. He and Tom met us in a small town about three hours from where Rick lived, and they got in the car with us. We stopped and got something to eat. When we did, Tom sat with his sisters, Cara and Kenyatta and ate. Tom told them that he lied about being sorry. "I just said that so I could come on this trip." I was so angry, and I let Tom know that his sister had told me what he said. The entire time we were in Georgia, Tom talked about Daniel and me like dogs to anyone who would listen.

Cara, Kenyatta, and my sister Carla told Tom, "Boy, you are a fool. I wish I had half the things you got. You got it made in the shade and don't even know it."

Tom didn't listen to them -- all he could think about was going to live with his mom. I truly understood that, I just wished he had gone about it in a different way. When we got back home, Tom was not telling us all these crazy things he was talking about to his sisters and they were telling me everything he was saying. Tom knew this and this was just what he wanted. I told Cara I didn't want to hear anymore.

I had a dream a few weeks before all this happened. The Lord spoke to me in the dream and told me I was going to have to let him go. I didn't know what He was talking about until Tom, Daniel, and I had that altercation. The Lord spoke to me during the altercation and said, "Let him go." So, when I went to bed, I cried because I didn't want to let him go and I knew the time had come.

Daniel talked to Tom the next day and told him, "Son, you need to leave here in the right way so you will be able to come back home if you need to. If you leave in the wrong way, you can't come back. You think you're ready for what life has to offer, son, but you are not ready."

Tom's attitude didn't change. When I woke up the next morning, I prayed for direction. Cara came in the room to tell me more things that Tom had said. I called Tom to my room so we could talk. I asked him if he was sure he wanted to go live with his mom. His reply was yes. I talked with Tom about a few other things and let him know that we would always love him.

He admitted to doing all the things Cara had told me he was doing: skipping school to have sex with his girlfriend, and smoking weed.

I had one final question for Tom, and I asked him, "What have Paw Paw and I done to you that's so terrible that you are treating us like you are?"

The next words out of his mouth confirmed that Floe and Honey had poisoned his mind. Tom said, "You took me from my Mama."

I had never told Tom the whole story of how I got him. Tom sat there while I told him the whole story. When I got through, I asked him, "Are you ready to go?" Tom said yes. I told Tom to go pack all his things, I was taking him to his Mama.

Tom didn't understand that I had done all I did for him so he could have a better life. It was the beginning of spring break. I got up and got dressed and helped him pack. I had just bought Tom $500 worth of church clothes, with shoes and socks to match the suits, and tags were still on the clothes.

Tom looked up at me and said, "Can I take these suits and shoes?"

I told him, "They are yours. I can't do anything with them." I told him to hurry. It was eight o'clock in the morning and I wanted to drop him off and get it over with. I called my sister and told her to ride with me over to their house. I was afraid to go alone because I didn't know what I was getting into. I called Floe and let her know that I was on my way to drop Tom off. She didn't know that I was bringing him for good. When Tom got through packing, he had two contractors' trash bags full of clothes. Precious came to the house just as we were getting ready to leave. She began to cry and tried to talk Tom into staying with us. She let Tom know that he had it good and he was making a big mistake. Tom refused to listen to her. We loaded everything up in the car and headed to southwest Little Rock. While we were on our way, Carla asked Tom if he was sure this was what he wanted to do. Tom replied, "Yes."

When we arrived, I called the phone number that I had and told his cousin to come help him get his things out of the car. I told Tom, "If at the end of the week Floe says you can't stay, call me, because you can't live in the streets."

Tom got out and got all his things and I pulled off before Floe had a chance to come outside. Tom called me at the end of the week and said that Floe said he could stay. That was fine with me, but we couldn't get him in school in Little Rock because I had custody of him, and I lived in Jacksonville. The secretary at the school board told me that they could not let him in because of the way the court paperwork was worded. The paperwork didn't allow Floe or Honey to have any rights. We had to go back to court to have this changed for him to go to school in Little Rock. I didn't know what to do at first. My heart was heavy, and I began to cry. I felt that my grandson was making a big mistake, but he was old enough now to make this choice. So, I hired the same lawyer that helped me get custody.

When I told him what was going on, the lawyer said, "Mrs. Palmer, are you sure?" I told him this was what Tom wanted. He then replied, "Tom's fifteen, he doesn't know what he wants."

I said, "I know this, but I'm going to have to let him have what he thinks he wants."

So, for a month-and-a-half, my sister and I picked Tom up every day in Little Rock to bring him back to Jacksonville to school until the custody case was settled. It cost me $100 a week in gas to do this. This was money I didn't have because I had retired from my job on January 31, two months prior to this, because of health issues. Some days when I picked him up, Tom didn't have his face washed, hair combed, or belt on. He had already started taking on that 'I don't care' attitude. He knew I always made him wear a belt because I couldn't stand to see his pants sagging, so he would leave his belt off on purpose, to try to get a rise out of me. I didn't say a word. The Lord told me to just pray all the way to school and all the way back from school, and that was what I did.

In May 2014, Floe was granted custody of Tom and she was able to get him back in school. Floe and her family had not changed. They were living in a two or three-bedroom apartment with six grown people and about six children. Floe even told me that the lights still got cut off sometimes. I asked her how the lights got cut off in a place where they just paid rent. She replied, the apartment owner didn't pay the bill. All I could do for Tom and them was pray. I called Tom once a week to let him know that I loved him and that he could be and do anything that he set his mind to. I let him know he was somebody. I did what God had instructed me to do, I taught him God's word and I lived a clean life in his presence. It was hard to let go but I had to. God had told me to get Tom, and now God was telling me it was time to let him go.

I figured Tom wouldn't really realize I was only trying to give him a better life until he was grown and had children of his own. But only a few months after he was gone, Daniel and I got a text from Tom, telling us that he was sorry for all he had said and done. He went on to say, "Everything you all said was true." At the time Tom sent this message, some of the utilities were off at their house. I let him know that I loved him, and I would be praying for him. Tom would come over for the holidays with his other siblings and sometimes he would stay all night.

I believe God has great plans for my grandson, and I pray that he realizes the greatness that he has in him also.

Chapter Eight

My Three Fathers (The Gifts)

Curtis

Some people go a lifetime without ever knowing who their fathers were. Their fathers were absent from their lives for one reason or another. Some fathers choose to be absent because they didn't believe that the child was theirs, some were absent because they didn't know the child existed, and some were absent because the Mama didn't want them in the child's life, others died, and so on and so forth. But I was blessed in this lifetime to have three fathers to love me and accept me as their daughter. But it had not always been like that.

God answered the prayers of a little girl who longed to see her real father. For many years that little girl would sit on top of her dresser, staring into the mirror, looking at herself staring back as the tears rolled down her face, wishing and hoping to know her real father. This would happen mostly after she had been disciplined by her stepfather, Curtis or Mama, Mary. As she stared at herself, she would whimper, "One day my real daddy is going to come get me." This little girl felt like an outsider and the black sheep of her family of six. She felt no love from her stepfather and sometimes none from her Mama or siblings. The little girl wanted to be loved and the little girl was me. I spent hours sitting on top of that dresser with my legs crossed, staring into the mirror, crying and saying, "One day my real daddy is going to come and get me." He never came and the years continued passing by. But God had not forgotten my deepest desires. He was yet in the plan. God remembered the prayer and longing I had just to know who my real father was.

Years later, God stepped in with His grace and mercy and mended Curtis's and my relationship. A few years after Mama had died, Curtis had a heart attack and he and I began to let go some of our past hurts. Reality had begun to sink into our hearts and minds that life was too short to hold grudges. I found it took less energy to love him than to hate him. Before then, I thought I had forgiven him, but would stay away from him most of the time, because I never knew what he might say or do to hurt me. This part of his personality had become a part of me over the years and I hurt a lot of people's feelings the same way.

When Curtis would say different things to get under my skin or hurt me, it would make my mind go back to past hurts and disappointments. My first reaction to this situation would be to lash out at him. So, instead of lashing out, I chose to stay away from him and not deal with the gap in our relationship. God could not mend or heal what I chose not to deal with. It's true, God had worked a work in Curtis's and my relationship, but He was not finished. God could not finish the work He had started if I continued to run when trouble arose instead of facing it.

After Curtis had his heart attack, I made up my mind to love Curtis past anything he might say or do. When he got out of the hospital, I would go by his house to check on him. Whenever I got ready to leave, I would look back at him and say, "Daddy, I love you." His response to me the first day was, "Girl gone on out here with that mushy stuff." I didn't respond to the harsh words that he was hiding behind. I knew he felt vulnerable and at everyone's mercy, because he was not able to completely take care of himself at this time. So, I simply said, "I don't care what you do or say, I'll be back tomorrow." I closed the door with a smile on my face, because I knew that I handled the situation like God wanted me to handle it. I didn't know what effect it was going to have on him, but I knew God was working on me and him. I finally understood the only way I was going to heal was to let God deal with the thing that was in me and not worry so much about the thing that was in him.

So the next day, I got up and prayed and went back to help Curtis with whatever he needed me to help him with. I looked up at him as I opened the door to leave and said, "I love you, Daddy," He replied, "Girl, I done told you to get on away from here with that mushy stuff." I then replied, "I don't care what you say, I ain't going nowhere and I will see you tomorrow."

This time when I said this, he smiled and said, "What you say girl, you don't care what I say?" I replied, "That's right, I don't care what you say, I'll see you tomorrow." I knew then for sure God was doing a work. I came back the next day as I had promised with a smile on my face and joy in my heart. After completing all tasks, I opened the door to leave and turned and told him, "Daddy, I love you." Without any hesitation, he replied, "I love you too, girl." With a full heart, I smiled and told him, "I'll see you tomorrow." As I walked to the car with tears in my eyes, praising God for what He had done, I realized this was the first time that Curtis had told me that he loved me.

Love conquers all and I can't help but think of this scripture, "The LORD hath appeared of old unto me, saying, Yea, I have loved thee with an everlasting love: therefore, with lovingkindness have I drawn thee." (Jer 31:3) God loved me despite all the things I had said and done. It was this unconditional love that drew me into God's loving arms. God continued to close the gap that separated Curtis and me over the years, and he would tell me he loved me on few other occasions, but on Christmas of 2015, Curtis did something that I will cherish until the day I die. I knew how much God had worked on my heart, but I didn't realize how great of a work He had done in Curtis's heart until 2015. He called my sister Carla and told her that he had bought his girls a gift for Christmas. He went on to say that he knew he hadn't ever bought us anything before and just wanted to do something for us before he died. When Carla called me to tell me what he had said, it overwhelmed my heart and I began to cry, because I knew God had worked a work. My husband was a truck driver and I was on the road with him at the time Carla called. She sent me a picture of the gift, and it was a silver necklace with a heart on it, with the inscription that read 'daughter.' It was the perfect gift from a loving father, and I cried even more. When I got home and picked up my gift, I went to visit Curtis. We talked and I told him how much I appreciated the gift.

I thought that day couldn't get any better, but what happened next was priceless. When I stood up to leave, I decided to hug him and tell him that I loved him. I had never hugged Curtis before, and I was fifty-two years old at the time of this writing. Without any hesitation, he opened his arms, hugged me back and told me that he loved me too. Only God can heal like that. I hugged Curtis, and my mind fell back to the time my Mama was praying on her deathbed. She said, "Lord, You said You were going to save him." Mama had prayed for years for our relationship to be healed also. God may not come when you want Him, but He is always on time. I managed to hold back the tears, but they filled my heart and eyes as I got in my car. Still in awe, as I sat in my car, all I could say was, "God, You are God."

As the years passed, I had to continue to fight to have a relationship with Curtis. In Volume One of my book, I wrote about all the things we went through and how God gave me the mind and strength to forgive him. But Curtis could not forgive himself. This really showed up the last year of his life.

I remember a dream that I had as a little girl, that I had to take care of Curtis when he got old. I was so excited about the dream, until I told him about it. Curtis then whipped me for telling him the dream. For years I didn't understand this. After Curtis had his legs amputated, my sister moved him in with her to take care of him. Sometimes I would have to help her out. Curtis hated it with a passion when I had to help clean him up. It didn't matter how gentle or compassionate I was, he didn't like it. I had no doubt that Curtis would think about the things he put me through and the dream that I had when I was a child. He wanted me to visit, but he didn't want me to have to help. There were many days Carla called me, crying because Curtis had cursed her out. He would even talk bad about me and my oldest son. He got mad at Carla because she told him, "Daddy, you are taking about Jackie, and the only thing she has done wrong to you is not being your biological daughter." He talked about my oldest son the same way. Carla also told him, "You better watch how you talk about that boy. He will be the one that will have to take care of you." This made him even angrier. My oldest son lived with Carla, and sure enough he had to help take care of Curtis.

Curtis did not accept the Lord Jesus as his personal Savior when he had the heart attacks, and in the back of my mind, I wondered what it was going to take for him to surrender. In 2017, Curtis had a stroke and another heart attack. He recovered but did not turn to God. It was January 7, 2019, when Curtis finally accepted Jesus Christ has his personal Savior.

It was the end of 2018 when I saw Curtis break down and cry. Both his legs had been amputated and he looked up at me with tears rolling down his face and said, "I believe God is mad at me. I know I've done some things." I realized in that moment; Curtis was trying to apologize for all he had done to me.

With tears rolling down my face, I said, "Daddy, it's okay, God is not mad at you, He just wants you to come to Him and repent."

He then said, "I have, but He's not hearing me."

I then told him, "Daddy, He hears you."

Curtis said, "Why won't He let me die, then?"

I sweetly told him, "It's not your time yet. He's still working some things in and out of you. Just keep talking to Him."

We prayed together and he settled down. It took Curtis losing both of his legs, having bedsore's that were all the way to his bone, and having uncontrollable pain for Curtis to cry out to God for mercy and forgiveness. It doesn't matter how you start the race, but what counts is how you finish the race.

I was a child and it took a while before I got the courage to ask my Mama who my real father was. The conversation happened sooner rather than later because my hands were being forced by some of the grown-ups in Lonoke. Growing up in the small town of Lonoke, I learned at an early age that some grown-ups could be cruel at times. I remember Big John always asking me who was my daddy whenever I passed by his house. I didn't have an answer, because I didn't know, but he would tell me, "Roy Cole is your daddy." There would

Roy

even be times that I was at relatives' houses and they would ask the same question. My grandmother also told me that Roy Cole was my father. Some of the grown-ups were just being messy, trying to stir up confusion in our home. They were hoping I went back to tell Mama. Most of the time I would curse Big John out and call him one-eyed. He would never be alone when he asked me about my father, he and his friends would be under his shed, drinking and laughing.

This hurt me, because I couldn't understand why Roy didn't come see me or say something to me if he was my father. We lived in the same town and I saw him on many different occasions. But what I didn't know was that he had tried on several occasions to get permission to see me. Years later, I found out that he approached Curtis and asked him if he could come to see me. Curtis quickly cursed him out and said, "No, she's not your daughter anyway." Roy had no other choice but to leave the situation alone. He did what he had to do to keep confusion down.

I would see Roy out on different occasions and wanted to approach him and say something to him, but I was scared. I didn't say anything to Mama for a long time. But one day after I had gotten a whipping, I asked her who my father was. She was a little shocked as she sat down on the side of the bed to tell me who my father was. She said, "Robert Hodges is your father." I was about seven years old at the time and I looked up at her and said everyone else was telling me Roy Cole was my father. She looked at me and said, "Girl, I know who your father is, and I don't care what they say." I then asked her where Robert Hodges lived and she responded, "I don't know, but I met him in Pine Bluff."

The situation didn't soothe anything in me, but I accepted the answer she gave me. I thought at least I could tell someone who my father was if they asked me again. So, when I was playing at relative's house and they asked me who my father was, I would say Mama told me Robert Hodges and they would say, "Girl, Roy Cole is your father." Even though Mama had told me this, there was a part of me that wished she had said Roy Cole was my father, because at least he was in the same town and I could see him. For a while I was content with just a name but longed to meet the man Mama said was my real father.

I had accepted the answer my Mama had given me about who my father was, until I overheard a conversation, she was having with someone. I was about twelve years old. My Mama had gone to a program at St John Baptist church. While she was at church, she saw Roy's daughter, who was about two years old at the time. Roy's daughter looked so much like me, she said to herself, "Lord, did I make a mistake?" I listened as Mama talked on the phone. I don't remember saying anything to Mama at that time, but the things that I heard her say, I held them close to my heart.

Not long after that incident, something happened to change my life forever. Curtis and Mama had left the house together and left us at the house by ourselves. I don't know why, but every time they left, we would go through their things in their room. I was searching through their closet when I ran across my birth certificate and I sat down on the side of the bed and began to read it. When I got to the part about my father, it read *Roy Cole*. This, coupled with what I had heard her talking about, made me angry, because I thought she had lied to me all this time about who my father was. On the other hand, I was glad to see this, because I finally had something in writing that was concrete to me as to who my father was.

As soon as I could talk to Mama without Curtis being around, I did. The first thing out of my mouth was, "I thought you said that Robert Hodges was my father." At the time I said this, I was handing her my birth certificate. She unfolded the birth certificate and said, "Momole made me put Roy's name on your birth certificate." It really didn't matter what she said to me at this point. I had it in writing, and I had made up my mind that I was going to approach Roy and tell him he was my father. All I wanted was to know my real father and I wanted a father who was going to love me and treat me better than I was being treated at that time.

I couldn't wait to see Roy again, and that day finally came. I took a deep breath and approached him. I looked up at him and told him, "I heard that you were my daddy." He then looked at me with a small smile on his face and said, "Who did your Mama tell you your daddy was?" I said without any hesitation, "Your name is on my birth certificate." I don't remember what all we talked about, but my heart was happy that he didn't reject me. Roy went home and talked to his wife, Edith and asked if it was all right for him to buy me some school clothes. Edith agreed and that week they bought me several new outfits. When I showed Mama the clothes, she didn't say anything against Roy, she was just happy for me.

Edith has always accepted me and been there for me since that day. She never made me feel like she didn't love me. Roy and his family became a big part of my life for years to come. Whenever I saw them, or sometimes when he was alone, they would always stop and talk to me. They would be in their vehicle and I would stand there sometimes an hour or more and talk. This killed a lot of the small-town gossip about who my father was. Whenever someone asked me who my father was, I would proudly tell them Roy Cole.

I was fourteen years old when I got pregnant with my oldest son. Roy was disappointed, but never treated me any different. I didn't have a close relationship with him, as I tried to find my way in this world during my teenage years. Whenever we did talk, he always talked to me about making the right decisions for my life. He understood, because I had made a mistake and gotten pregnant at such a young age, it was not the end of the world or my life. During my teen years, I didn't spend much time at Roy's house. I didn't spend time with them as a family, but this was not Roy's fault, he did what he had to do to keep the peace.

I only brought one boyfriend to his house to meet him, and it was Benson (the preacher's son). I thought Roy would be happy about that, but he told me later not to bring anyone else to his house. I respected his wishes and held no ill feeling against him. I always wondered why he didn't want me to bring any of my friends to his house, but I never asked. There were times I would disappear, doing my own thing. After Roy hadn't heard from me in a while, he would always track me down no matter what town I was in. I believed Roy could tell when things were going wrong in my life. He did this when I was a teenager and after I married my first husband, Peter. He was right every time he showed up.

They came to visit me in Brinkley when I was married to Peter. It was his gut feeling that let him know that something was wrong. When they got there, I was combing Simone's hair. Everything looked like all was well, but it was far from it. It would be years later when I told him how bad things were.

Roy's and my relationship blossomed after I got saved and had gotten married to Daniel (my husband now). I felt more like part of the family at this time. I visited their home more and Roy visited me and Daniel in our home often. By the time I turned my life around, he was a deacon in the church. Roy was not just a deacon in name only. He would visit the sick and shut-in daily, whether they were in the hospital or at home. He would go to the store for the people he visited, to get whatever they needed. He didn't just drop in and say hello. He would stay a while to keep them company and minister to them about the Lord. A lot of people looked forward to his weekly visit. Roy was well known and loved by so many. Our relationship got even better, because we truly had something in common now. Even though we had gotten closer, I know the thought was fresh in the back of his mind whether he was my father. But Roy understood that this was a question he had to ask Mama.

In 1998, Mama had come from Las Vegas to Arkansas to make her funeral arrangements, because the doctor had given her six months to live. Roy was visiting his brother's wife who lived next door to Mama's house in Lonoke. He realized Mama was in town visiting, so he decided to go ask her if he was my father. Roy knocked on the door and entered when Mama told him to come in. When he stepped through the door, Mama was surprised to see him. Mama's hand was in a sling, all her hair was gone, and she was in a lot of pain. When Roy saw her, he realized how sick she was and changed his mind about asking her what he had intended on asking. Roy spoke and they made small talk for a while. He soon left with his question unanswered. The tragedy of me losing my children in the car wreck in 1998 drew me closer to Roy and his entire family. They stepped in and did all that they could do for me without any hesitation. They were there in word and deed.

I was hurt after seeing no one acknowledged Roy on the obituary or at the funeral service as my father or my children's grandfather. I felt as if he deserved to be acknowledged. He had been in my life since I was twelve, and my family knew this. I was not trying to think the worst of anyone, so I thought maybe the situation was too much and they just didn't think about it. I knew this bothered him, because it bothered me after I saw it. Roy managed to keep his heart in the right place in spite of the situation. His desire to know if I was his daughter grew, but it didn't hinder his love for me even though the hurt was deep. I thank God for the God in him that gave him the strength to move past the hurt.

They were there for me even after everyone else had gone on with their lives. They would always come by the house and visit after they got through shopping and taking care of business. Polly was still there taking care of me and we would sit there an hour or two, talking about the goodness of Jesus. These times were some of my best times that I spent with them. If he started the conversation off first, I couldn't get a word in edgewise. If I started it off, he couldn't get a word in edgewise. He'd preach a while, then I would preach a while. Either one or both of us would end up crying before the conversation was over. Edith would sit back and just let us go at it, and she would throw an Amen in here and there. When they got up to leave, he would hand me a check that he had gotten from his church, St John Baptist Church. Even after I had gotten on my feet, up to a year after the wreck, the people of St John Baptist Church continued to give me financial love tokens. Usually after a time period people go on with their lives and forget about you and your troubles. They never did, and I will always be grateful to them for that.

My Three Fathers (the Gifts)

I would always tell my husband, if I died before he did, to just put Curtis (my stepfather) down on the obituary as my father, because I didn't want to hurt anybody. Then I would tell him Mama should have straightened this out before she died. One day while talking to Roy, I made this same statement. I didn't know at the time, but this hurt him. About a month or two after I had made the statement, I got a call from Roy and he let me know that the statement hurt him deeply. My heart ached to hear this, because the last thing I wanted to do was hurt him. I listened as he expressed what was on his heart. He caught me off guard when he said that he wanted to get a DNA test. I agreed that this would be a good idea. Then he went on to say that he had me in his will. I asked him to take me out of his will. I did this because I wanted to let him know that I loved him whether he had me in his will or not. My love for Roy was not based on anything material that he could give me. He was a big part of my life, and I didn't want anything to hinder our relationship. I didn't care what the DNA test said; it was too late in the game for him and his family not to be a part of my life. I didn't want our relationship to change no matter what the DNA test said.

I hadn't seen them for about a month after this, and this concerned me. I was sitting around the house watching television when I heard a knock at the door, and it was Roy and Edith. I was so glad to see them, my eyes welled up with tears as I hugged them. When I hugged them this time, I held on to each of them for a while. We sat and talked just like we usually did, and he never brought up a DNA test to me again. However, he did mention his will again some years later, and I told him what I told him the first time, "Take me out of the will." All I wanted was a relationship with him and the rest of the family, the rest didn't matter. I did tell him about Robert Hodges that day, but it didn't get in the way of his love for me. As time passed, Roy and I became even closer. I would learn later that Edith reminded Roy that I had no choice as to who my father was.

After I recovered from the accident, I would go and minister at different churches. Roy would come to hear me minister when he could. I will always be grateful to God for the years he allowed us to love and know one another. In 2009, God called Roy home, and I was at his bedside with the rest of the family. It happened so quickly, it seemed as if he was here one day and gone the next.

I was doing a lot of fasting and praying at that time. I was praying for God to heal him, and I believed He could if He just would. I remember one night, we were at the hospital and Roy was in ICU, fighting for his life, and had not responded to any of us that day. He had taken a turn for the worse. I decided to go to Old Landmark House of Prayer Church around the corner for their service. When I got there, they were praying, and I got on my knees and cried out to God for Roy's healing with everything in me. I felt the power of God so strongly. So, as soon as church was over, I headed straight to the hospital to lay hands on him and prayed for him. I believed God for the supernatural. When I walked into his room, Edith was on the couch at his bedside. I spoke to her and immediately began to walk around his bed and call down the power of God. She was praying with me and God showed up. I was calling on God with all my might when Roy's whole body began to shake. He started shaking his head as if to say, "No, stop praying." It seemed as if I had interrupted his journey to the other side and God was pulling him back this way. The nurse ran in the room and I stopped praying. When I stopped praying, he stopped shaking. It was then I understood that he had gotten a glimpse of the other side, and as much as he loved his family, he didn't want to come back. I think Edith and I came to the same conclusion. Roy was a proud man and would not have wanted to be down sick in the bed. He let go of this world the next day and I had to accept what God allowed.

Edith and I have grown even closer over the years. She's there for me during my good and bad times. We go out to lunch at Roy's favorite eating place whenever we get a chance. Whenever we get together, there are times we pray, cry, and laugh together. She's now one of my natural and spiritual leaning posts, my Mama and friend. God always has a ram in the bush.

I was about eighteen years old and had started hanging out in Pine Bluff, partying with Bessie (my Mama's sister) and her daughter, Betty. Each time I went to Pine Bluff, the memory of what my Mama had told me about Robert Hodges (aka Loba) would ease from the back of my mind to the front. The place to start asking questions was my Bessie. She was the only one of my relatives who would tell me as a little girl that Robert Hodges was my father. She and Loba used to be running buddies and he hung out at her house during the time she was married to George (her first husband) and then Grady (her

Robert

second husband). I began asking her if she knew where Loba was, or if she knew any of his relatives. Bessie didn't know exactly where he was, but she had heard that he moved to California. But she did tell me stories about how wild he was and how he loved to fight. This was all I knew about Loba for years.

Since Bessie was unable to tell me how I could get in touch with Loba at that time, I pushed the desire to meet him to the back of my mind and heart for the time being. I hung out in Pine Bluff for so long until I decided to move there. I stayed between Betty's house and my boyfriend's house. Aunt Bert (Bessie first husband sister) was sick and dying of cancer. She wasn't my aunt, but I called her Aunt Bert just like everyone else. She had gotten to the point where she wasn't able to take care of herself. She needed someone to help take care of her activities of daily living. Since I wasn't working at the time, I stepped in to take care of her. It wasn't a problem taking care of her, since I had worked in nursing homes before. So, I did my best to make sure she was comfortable.

I loved our time together and have never forgotten some of the things we talked about. She was sitting up and was in a lot of pain. After I assisted her back to bed, she talked to me. She said, "If you ever feel a pain in your female parts, don't ignore it, go get yourself checked." She had been having pain for years but had ignored it, and now she was dying of cancer. Even to this day, every time I have any female pain, I think of what she said. Aunt Bert soon changed the subject to something a little more pleasant.

"You know I used to be crazy about your Uncle Louis," (Mama's brother) she said. When we got through talking about that, she said, "I got a taste for some frog legs and rice. Do you know how to cook that?" I told her yes and she told me where everything was. After I got through cooking, she nibbled but didn't eat very much.

Aunt Bert only lived a few more days after that. I didn't go to the funeral, I stayed at the house to receive the food that people were bringing over for the family. I was sitting at the table when the family begun coming back to the house. After we got through eating, we sat around the table and talked.

There was this lady at the table I didn't know. She looked at me and said, "I don't know you. Who are your people?"

I replied, "Bessie is my aunt."

Then she asked me who my father was. The thought crossed my mind that she might know Loba or at least know some of his people. So, I quickly blurted out, "Robert Hodges."

Before I could get another word out, she said, "I know your people."

My heart skipped a beat as I listened to all she had to say. Then I interjected, "I never met him, and I want to."

She gave me the phone number of one of Loba's cousin, Lillie Bell Barnes. I couldn't believe it. I kept staring at the number, and I was anxious to make that call, but knew I had to wait until I was alone. Betty (Bessie's daughter) walked into the room and I quickly told her the good news. She was happy for me. As soon as I had the chance, I made the call. I could tell from the voice that the person was elderly. I explained who I was and how I got her number, and I could hear the excitement in her voice. She told me where she lived, and I was as excited about meeting her as she was about meeting me. She gave me instructions on how to get to her house and then I realized she was in walking distance from where I lived. This was perfect, because I didn't have a car.

When I got to the house, I knocked and heard this little voice with a southern twang, that said, "Come on in." When I stepped through the door, Cousin Lillie Bell was sitting in her easy chair, and she said, "Wooooo, you got legs just like Froney's." I didn't know who Froney was at that time, but later I found out she was Loba's Mama. She then said, "You look like Loba."

I asked her, "Why they called him Loba?"

She then replied, "We called him Lofa before they started calling him Loba. He loved bread and would sometimes walk around with a loaf of bread under his arms. Other people thought we were saying Loba and so as time passed, Lofa became Loba."

I began telling her my story and how I wanted to meet him. She didn't know his number, but she told me she could get it from her son. She then told me to come back the next day and she would have the number. When I left her house, I was pleased with the way the visit had gone and I thought about how warm and inviting she was. This made my heart happy. So, the next day I arrived at her home as she had instructed and true to her word, she had the number. When she gave me the number, I got butterflies in my stomach. I asked her if I could call him from her phone and she said yes. I took a deep breath and dialed the number. I didn't know if he was going to accept me or reject me. All I wanted to do was meet him. I didn't want anything from him. I just wanted to see what he looked like. Someone answered the phone and I said, "May I speak to Robert?"

The voice on the other end said, "This is he."

I went on to explain who I was. The next words out of his mouth cut me to the core.

He said, "What do you want?"

This made me mad and without any hesitation, I said, "Nigga, I don't want anything from you, I'm grown. I just wanted to meet you before one of us die." I then told him bye and hung up the phone. With a heavy heart, I went back into the living room and told Cousin Lillie Bell what transpired. She was just as disappointed as I was, but the situation didn't stop her from accepting me and loving me. She then informed me that her daughter, Ernestine and son in-law, Jerry only lived a couple of blocks from her. They would be coming by after they got off from work to meet me. I sat there and talked with her until they came over. They finally made it and we sat there and talked like we had known each other for years. There was a bond made that would be unbreakable as the years passed.

I got to meet all of Cousin Lillie Bell's children before that year was out. It was Cousin Lillie Bell's son who told Uncle Jessie (Loba's brother) about me. Years later, Uncle Jessie convinced Loba to meet me. I was hurt about not being able to meet Loba after finding him, but the love that his family showed me made me get over it. Ernestine and Jerry invited me to their home, and I began hanging out with them quite a bit. I even stayed all night with them two and three times a week. They had one child and I would sometimes even babysit for them. When I first started hanging out with them, I didn't let them know that I smoked weed. I had to keep up this good girl imagine for a little while until I found out what they were all about. They didn't look like the type of people who smoked weed. They looked like the type of people who drank a little when they were socializing.

I had known them for less than a month when Ernestine and I were sitting in the den talking. She asked me if I smoked weed and my eyes lit up and my heart was overjoyed when I blurted out, "Yes." By this time, Jerry was coming into the den with a container that contained their stash of weed. Jerry rolled the joint, fired it up, passed it to Ernestine, and she passed it to me. After hitting it a couple of times, I realized this was some good stuff. It hit me like a ton of bricks. I think it hit them quick too, because we all started laughing for nothing. We sat around and laughed and talked for what seemed like hours.

After our high started coming down some, Ernestine looked at me and said, "I'm hungry." Then she turned and said, "Jerry, go fix us something eat."

We all laughed and agreed that we were hungry. But no one wanted to get up and go cook.

Ernestine then asked, "What's in there to eat?" After discussing what was in there to eat, no one would motion to go cook it. Ernestine said, "I'll cook the eggs." I said, "I'll cook the bacon and sausage." Jerry would cook the toast and fix something to drink. Then we all got up to go cook whatever we agreed to.

This was what we did many times after we came home from a club or house party. During these times, their daughter would be at her grandmother's house. Some of the best times we had were when they would invite their friends over, and we would get high and play this game with the alphabet. We waited for everyone to get high and then they would start the game. The first person maybe says, "I'm going to the grocery store and going to buy some apples." The next person would say, "I going to the grocery store and going to buy some apples and bananas." The next person would have to say what everyone said before him and come up with something that began with the next letter in the alphabet. If you messed up, you were out of the game. This was hilarious and hard to do when you were high.

Other times we just played card games, Tonk or Biz Wiz. It was just good clean fun with no confusion. I remember this one night, Jerry had gone out with some of his friends, and my boyfriend Dan was hanging out at the Juke Joint on West Baraque. Ernestine and I were hanging out at their house, getting high and just relaxing. Ernestine had gone to the kitchen for something and when she started coming back down the hall, there was a baby snake at the end of the hallway. Ernestine didn't scream and her voice didn't sound like anything was wrong when she called my name to come there. So, I came out of the den, all high and jolly without a care in the world. When I turned the corner to go down the hall, she never said a word, she just stared down at the floor with fear in her eyes and she finally said, "A snake."

I didn't see the snake, I just started hopping and running, trying to get away. When I finally reached the end of the hallway where she was, the snake had part of its body off the floor, ready to strike. We ran into the kitchen and stood up on the kitchen table chairs. We were at a panic and high, trying to figure out what to do. I finally came up with the idea to call the Juke Joint to ask Dan to come help us. When we called the Juke Joint, the music was so loud, he could hardly hear me. Ernestine and I were laughing because I was trying to sound serious and scared when I told Dan about the snake, so he would believe me. I kept saying, "It's a snake, a snake is in the house, come help us." He finally understood what we were saying and hung up the phone to come see about us.

Meanwhile, Ernestine and I stood on the chairs, scared and laughing. We stopped laughing and started screaming when the snake came down the hall to the kitchen. I grabbed an iron skillet from off the counter and dropped it on the snake. The handle broke off the skillet when it hit the snake, killing it. When Dan arrived, we were still standing on the chairs, looking at the dead snake. He laughed and took the snake out of the house. We laughed and talked about that snake for the years to come.

I might not have known Loba, but the love his family had shown me was enough for me at that time. It was about five years after that initial phone call with Loba before I heard from him again. I had moved to Little Rock and was working at Taco Bell. I worked evening shift, and when I got to work my boss told me that my father had called looking for me. Then he went on to say that he would be calling back around five o'clock. The first person who came to my mind after my boss told me this was Curtis. I thought at that moment, *why would Curtis be calling me.*? At that point, Curtis and I didn't get along. I put the conversation in the back of my mind and went to work. Five o'clock soon came and he called. I rushed to the phone when I heard it ring. I answered the phone, expecting to hear Curtis's voice, but to my surprise it wasn't. When I realized that it wasn't Curtis, I said, "Who is this?"

The person on the other end said, "It's your daddy from Detroit, Robert."

I was stunned and angry once I realized who I was talking to. The hurt and rejection that I felt when I had talked to him five years prior rushed in and flooded my heart, mind, and emotions. I quickly responded to him the same way he responded to me five years prior: "What do you want?" He was trying hard to be nice, but no matter what questions he asked, I was cold and abrupt with my answers. I soon grew tired of the conversation and told him that I had to go back to work. When I got off the phone, it took me a while to get the conversation off my mind. I felt good about what I had done, even though it was wrong. I didn't think about that at the time, all I could think about was that this ought to make him understand how I felt five years ago.

I was twenty-three at that time, and I would be about twenty-nine years old before I contacted him again. The next time, it was different. I forgave him and he forgave me. We talked on and off for about a year before I met him. His brother, Jessie and his family were coming to Arkansas for a family reunion that year, and Loba told him to stop by my house in Lonoke to meet me. He did, and I went to the family reunion to meet more of the family. This was during the time I had gotten out of church, but it wasn't long after Uncle Jessie's visit that I found my way back to the Lord.

I would talk to Loba on the phone for hours, and I began to learn more about his past and how he met Mama. Mama used to go to Pine Bluff and babysit for Bessie, and that was how she met Loba. I asked Bessie, did Loba ever come see me when I was a baby? Bessie told me he came to see me once when I was first born, and he even asked Momole (my grandmother) if he could marry Mama. Momole didn't like Loba from the start, and she told him no. Bessie told me Mama cried that day. Mattie (Mama's sister) and Mama got so drunk until they were falling in the ditch. Loba left Lonoke that day to never return, and shortly after he moved to California.

Loba was out partying with some of his friends and they had told him earlier that day that they were going to California. Loba saw this as an opportunity to better his life, and he wasn't going to let it pass. He informed his friends that he was going with them. So, he packed the few clothes he had in a bag and followed his friends all that day and night. He told me that they had planned on leaving him behind, so he didn't let them out of his sight. When he first moved to California, he lived with his cousin, Charles. Life was not easy for him. His life in California brought many dark days that he had to endure. No matter where Loba went, he didn't have to look for trouble, it seemed to find him. Some guys beat him and left him for dead in an alley one night, and there was even a point where he was homeless while he was in California. God was in the plan all along. During the time he was homeless, he found a Bible in a dumpster and he dried it out and began to read it every day.

Loba was raised by his grandmother and she was a praying woman. Loba's father, Mama, and the other siblings did live in Pine Bluff for a time, but they moved. When they moved, they were supposed to come back and get him and his brothers. When they returned, they took everyone but Loba and one of his cousins. They left Loba behind to be raised by his grandmother. Loba struggled with this for years and didn't understand why they didn't take him with them. But God was in the plan. It was during those hard times in California he remembered the things his praying grandmother had instilled in him, and these things began to press their way to the forefront of his mind and heart. His mind revisited the time that his grandmother and some of the ladies from the neighborhood would be in prayer at his grandmother's house. The power of God would linger in the house. He didn't understand it then as a child but began to understand by and by who God was and the call that was on his life. There were times that Loba would accidently come in the house while his grandmother and friends were praying, and she made him stay and pray with them. God was giving him the equipment he would need to face hard times in his life, but it would be years before he surrendered to God's call.

After he struggled in California for a while, his brother Jessie convinced him to come to Detroit. Before leaving California, he fathered another child, and her name was Diane. Loba later married his childhood sweetheart from Pine Bluff and they had five children together. This was his first wife and he was married to her when I talked with him the first time on the phone. I'm glad I didn't know him then. He and I wouldn't have gotten along because I was just as bad as he was.

God had His timing and the time had come. Loba had given his life to the Lord and so had I. We had the best thing in common and that was Jesus. This was when Loba's and my relationship went to another level. Loba and I talked for what seemed like hours about the Lord on the phone. I was in awe about the way he talked about God. He had been saved for a while, and usually when people are saved for a while, they lose some of their zeal for God. Not Loba. He talked about God as if he had just met Him and had fallen in love. I would listen attentively to the things he would say. When he talked about God, the anointing would be so strong, until the tears streamed down my cheeks. This would remind me of the times I had spent with Polly when I first got saved. He also had a great sense of humor. He wasn't so heavenly minded he was no earthly good. Sometimes I would talk to him on my way to church and he would say, "If you see any devils in Arkansas with Detroit on them, he's the one that got away. Could you please get him for me?"

I would tell him, "I got him."

There was this one time he told me, "Church was so good until I felt like Scooby Doo, and I felt like I could go eight different ways at one time."

I laughed, and I have been using this statement ever since I heard it. Another statement he would say was, "All God's shalls are loaded and God don't shoot any blanks." Then he would go on to say, "Every knee shall bow, and every tongue shall confess, that Jesus Christ is Lord."

Loba was a member of International Gospel Center in Ecorse, Michigan, where Apostle Charles O Miles was the pastor. I sat on the edge of my seat as he told me about their travels to the Holy Land and other foreign countries. Loba was a part of Apostle Miles' security team. There were times when Apostle Miles would preach in these foreign lands and the security had to be extra tight. Apostle Miles was preaching to thousands of people who had traveled near and far to hear a word from the Lord. Sitting on the edge of my seat, I listened as Loba told me about Apostle Miles walking through the crowd of people while he preached. As he walked through the crowd someone yelled out, "I'll kill you!"

At this point, Loba turned his back to Apostle Miles' back, and every time Apostle Miles took a step, Loba took a step backwards with him, while watching the crowd. Back to back they slowly moved through the crowd. One of the other security guards had positioned himself in a karate stance, ready to fight. Loba kept backing up with Apostle Miles as he walked through the crowd, when out of nowhere this man launched his body toward them, yelling, "I'll kill you!"

Loba caught the man midair, laying his hand on his head, and yelled out in Jesus' name. The man's legs went straight out as his body got stiff and he fell to the ground. Loba never missed a beat. He kept following Apostle Miles as he preached the word of God. Apostle Miles and Loba were awesome men of God, and oh how I desired to see and experience some of the things he would talk about. The desire to meet Loba became even more overwhelming.

It was 1993 and I had gotten remarried. Daniel and I were struggling financially, but I had expressed the desire to meet my father. He was equally impressed with my father's relationship with God. He had talked with him on several occasions, seeking spiritual advice. After talking with Daniel, he agreed and began to help me get the finances together to make the journey. I was thirty years old and was finally going to get the chance to meet my last father. I called Uncle Jessie (Loba's brother) to let him know that I was coming and wanted to surprise Loba. Uncle Jessie and I had been conversing on the phone before I started talking to Loba. He was the one who talked with Loba constantly about him getting in touch with me. He agreed it was time for me to meet Loba, and he invited me to stay with him and his wife, Jackie, at their house while I was there. But he didn't think it was a good idea to surprise Loba.

I didn't know it at the time, but Loba was going through some financial difficulties. He was a welder and business were not good. He had just gotten a job at Chrysler and had only worked two weeks. His lights were off at his house and he had just gotten them on the day before I arrived. Loba shared his situation with me later that week. I didn't get to see him that first day I came, but Uncle Jessie and his wife Aunt Jackie loved on me and made me feel at home. It was like

I had known them all my life. Uncle Jessie was like the family historian; he had researched the family tree and knew who everyone was. I was fascinated as he talked about his father, Mama, and other relatives. I found out that Loba had another daughter in Los Angeles, California. I finally got to meet her years later. He talked about his sisters and where each one of them lived. I only got to meet one of his sisters on that visit, and that was his baby sister, Dot. I got to meet all his brothers but one.

I was enjoying my time with Uncle Jessie, but in the back of my mind, I couldn't help but wonder about Loba. I was curious as to what he looked like. Would he like me? How was I going to react when I saw him? Loba had to work and it would be the next evening before I got a chance to meet him. I thought the time would never come, but it finally did. When Loba pulled up outside, I became even more anxious, and I didn't know what to do with myself. So, I stood up, waiting for him to appear in the living room. I could hear him greet Uncle Jessie as he walked in the house, and I found myself holding my breath, looking at the doorway. When he finally made it to the living room, I exhaled, and it seemed as though time stood still for a few seconds as we stood there, staring at one another.

He smiled and broke the silence and said, "Girl, it's good to finally meet you." We sat in the living room and laughed and talked as if we had known each other for years. When he got ready to leave, he asked me if I wanted to come and stay with him for the rest of the week, and of course I said yes. He had remarried at this time, and his wife Lizzie was wonderful and nice to me, but I would find out that it was all a front some years later.

It was an awesome week. Each day I got to meet someone new. I met Loba's baby brother, Joe, and his family that same day and his brother, Beebe the next day. They were just as funny as Loba was, especially when they got together and talked about the times when they were growing up. I laughed so hard until I almost peed myself as they talked about old times.

Loba told the story about the time they were with their father and they were on the back of the wagon. Every few minutes, their father's hat would fly off his head, and when it did their father would say, "Al Joe, go get my hat." Well after Joe jumped off the wagon about four or five times and then had to run and catch back up with the wagon, he had gotten tired. Al Joe said in frustration, while bending to get the hat, "Eeeeevery time Al Joe go get hat."

They all threw their heads back at the same time and laughed about the days gone by. I listened and laughed as they told story after story. They even laughed and joked about the time Beebe (Loba's brother) got his fingers cut off. Beebe and Jessie were small children when Jessie accidentally chopped off Beebe's fingers. Beebe was holding a rubber strap while his brother, Jessie, tried to cut it with the ax. Jessie missed the strap and cut some of his brother's fingers off. It wasn't funny at the time it happened, but they all managed to laugh about it at this time. Beebe's fingers being gone worked in his favor a many days after this, because when it came time for them to get a whipping about something, Beebe would say that his hand hurt. This excuse worked sometimes, but not all the time.

Years ago, black people didn't go to town every day. They might have gone to town once a month. When they did go to town, it was an all-day event, traveling by horse and wagon. Because of this, if they had the money, they would buy food in bulk. Menya (aka Froney their Mama) would buy 100 pounds of sugar when she would make her trips to the store, and she expected it to last a while. It would have if it hadn't been for the children's sweet tooth. The children could hardly wait until their parents left the house after grocery shopping. As soon as the opportunity would arise, Jessie headed straight for the sugar and would make a glass of sugar water. The other children were right behind him. Jessie would tell them that they needed to share because Menya was sure to notice some of the sugar missing with seven children making sugar water. But they wouldn't listen to him, and Beebe then took it to another level. He filled a fruit jar with sugar and then put just a little water in it, and of course it made him sick. This was the day that they got caught and had to pay for their actions.

Even after they got whippings for some of the things they had gotten into, they continued to get in and out of more mischief. They were all outside playing when Jessie got a dead snake out of a hole and started whooping Loba with it. Loba was about four years old and this scared Loba so bad, he ran so fast until his feet were hitting him on his behind. Loba was trying to run in the house, but he picked up so much speed he passed the back door and had to make another circle around the house. Yelling and screaming for help, Loba fell through the door sideways to safety.

They lived in the country and there wasn't too much to do. So, with each new day came new adventures. When their Mama and father went to town, they would figure out something to do for entertainment, and it never had anything to do with what was right. Loba said Jessie was the mastermind behind most of their diabolical plans. They just followed him in whatever he told them to do. They would sometimes get their father's .22 pistols and his shotgun and shoot birds and other things while their parents were away from the house. Loba was about three years old when Beebe got his father's pistol one time and shot it through the floor and through the ash pan in front of the wood stove. This scared James (their brother). Their father and Mama were not too far from home, killing hogs, when James came to tell them what Beebe was doing. It had only been a year since Jessie cut Beebe's fingers off, and every time Beebe was about to get a whooping, he would say that his hand was hurting. Beebe tried to hide behind his hand hurting, but it didn't work. Their Mama whooped hand and all that day.

There was never a dull moment in the Hodges household. Years ago, it wasn't uncommon for a black family to have numerous children. The parents worked hard to ensure that there was food on the table. Food wasn't as plenteous as it is now, and when food was set before the children, they didn't complain about what it was. They were just glad to be eating and wasted nothing. Menya had just finished cooking breakfast and the smell of salt pork, Burr Rabbit Molasses, biscuits and buttermilk filled the air as the children sat around the table, eating and talking. Beebe had a dog named Nellie Brown that sat under the table, hoping for a morsel of food to be given or dropped. I don't know about anywhere else in Arkansas, but in Portland, everyone knew you didn't get but one piece of meat at mealtime and sometimes not that. While enjoying the meal and trying to savor the moment, Beebe's salt pork slipped from his hand and hit the floor. Unfortunately, he was not quick enough to pick it up before Nellie Brown sunk his teeth into it. Without hesitation and only a thought for his lost salt pork, Beebe grabbed Nellie Brown around the neck and began choking him. While choking the family's dog, he cried and yelled repeatedly, "He got my meeeeeeat!" Menya told Beebe to let go of the dog but he couldn't hear her, he wanted his meat. Menya quickly picked up a stick of stove wood and began hitting Beebe across his back. He paid this no attention and continued choking the dog and yelling, "He got my meeeeeat!" He finally let go of the dog and his salt meat was gone.

Jessie talked about how greedy all of them were. Their Mama would be in the kitchen cooking, and when she got through cooking, she would say, "Arrah, y'all come and eat." This day she only got "Arrah" out of her mouth and Jessie ran in the kitchen. To his surprise, she was still cooking. When Menya said "Arrah," she was about to say something else this time. Jessie was right on her heels before she could finish her thoughts. She was kneading biscuit dough at the time and had flour all over her hands. Just as Jessie ran in the kitchen, she popped him on his forehead with her flour covered hands. Jessie's pride and feelings were hurt, and he felt like crying, but he sucked it up so the other children wouldn't know that Menya had hit him. When Jessie went back to the room with the other children, they asked him, "Did she hit you?" Jessie replied, "No." They all laughed at him. They knew he was lying because flour was all over his head.

I listened attentively as Loba told me the story about the time Menya whooped Papa (aka Ervin Menya's husband) while trying to whip Beebe. Beebe had experienced his Mama's wrath on numerous occasions, and he refused to take a whooping standing still. He knew all too well that it was hard to hit a moving target. After Menya hit Beebe a couple of times, she was already exhausted from chasing him. So, she petitioned Ervin to hold Beebe while she disciplined him for his wrongdoings. She yelled, "Hold him, Ervin!" Beebe was already hopping around, trying to soothe the pain from a couple of lashes that he had already received. Ervin grabbed him from behind, trying with all his might to hold him still. His Mama drew back the strap with all her might and grunted as she swung the strap to hit Beebe. All he could think about was the pain, and he knew his timing had to be perfect because he couldn't break free from his papa's grip. Just as the strap was about to contact Beebe's legs, he raised them high off the floor. The strap missed Beebe's legs and hit Papa's legs. Papa hollered out from the pain of the strap and he said, "If you hit me again, I'm going to let him go." Menya drew back with all her might and grunted as she swung the strap. Beebe lifted his legs just in time for the strap to hit Papa again. Papa yelled out from the pain while loosening his grip on Beebe. He then said, "Gone, Willie (Beebe's real name), she's mad at me about something and whooping my tail instead of yours."

I listened to story after story, holding them in my heart and memory. Then Loba began telling me about some of the hard times that they endured growing up. Just like other families experienced hard times, his family was not exempt. There were days the cupboards were bare, and their stomachs were empty. During some of these times, they would throw crumbs or whatever they could find in the front yard to attract the blackbirds. As soon as the birds would all gather in the front yard and were busy eating, someone would shoot the shotgun that was loaded with buckshot. There were so many birds, whoever was doing the shooting didn't have to take careful aim. They just pointed the gun toward the birds. After cleaning and cooking the birds, they all sat down to enjoy the feast. Sooner or later, someone would bite down on a piece or two of the buckshot that was still in the birds. Biting down on the buckshot that had brought the feast to their table didn't discourage them. They just spit it out one side of their mouths while putting more of the bird in the other side. Everyone was just happy that they didn't have to go to bed hungry.

I enjoyed the stories so much and could hardly wait to meet the rest of the family. I was hoping they would be as fun to meet as Loba and his brothers were. After everyone left, Loba began telling of the times he and my Aunt Bessie were partners in crime. He said they had gone out one night and one of his friends at the club was going out of town and wanted to borrow his pistol. He reluctantly loaned it to him that night. Well, he found out that was a big mistake later that night. Loba got into a fight with two guys and they got the best of him. After everything was over, Loba sat outside of the club's steps and cried like a baby. When Bessie asked him what was wrong, he said, "I'm crying because I'm mad at myself for loaning someone my pistol." I thank God for that.

Before the end of the week, I got to meet Loba's other children who lived in Detroit. When they walked in the door, I could immediately see they were their father's children. All of them looked like Loba. His son, Robert Jr., looked just like him, and they all had that Hodges long bottom lip. We all laughed and talked for a while. Robert Jr. seemed to relax right off and engaged in whatever conversation that was going on. Tracey and Tranice (Robert's daughters) didn't talk much but seemed to relax as the time passed. Tranice did less talking than anybody, but she and Robert Jr. were the ones I eventually bonded with. Tranice and I stayed in touch with one another over

My Three Fathers (the Gifts)

the years for a while. Robert Jr. and I keep in touch with one another on Facebook and the phone from time to time.

All and all, my visit was a success, but the best was yet to come. The night finally came for us to go to Loba's church, International Gospel Center in Ecorse, Michigan. Loba had told me so many good things about the church, I could hardly wait to get there. I was just as excited about going to Loba's church as I was about meeting him. When we got to church, he began introducing me to the different people he had talked about for so long. The two people that I was most excited to meet were his Pastor and First Lady, and of course Mother Deming and Mother Poole. I wanted to meet the people who had helped Loba become the spiritual giant that he was. Just like Polly had taught me and was my spiritual mentor, they mentored him. They mentored him at a time when his health was bad, his marriage was broken, and a child had died, at his darkest hour with his back up against the wall with nowhere to turn. They showed him the path to Jesus, the way, the truth, and the light. He found his healing and peace. They taught him how to fast, pray, and be consistent in season and out of season. With this consistency came growth and maturity in God. The church and the people he talked so adamantly about were everything I dreamed they would be and more. Being in their presence made me realize there were no limits in the place you could go in God. Well, the end of the week came, and I had to go home. But I was making plans to return that next year during a mega conference they had yearly at his church, and this time my husband would be going with me.

Loba and I continued to converse over the phone after I got home, and I talked with him about my father, Roy. He told me Roy sounded like a good man and to make sure I didn't do anything to hurt him. He knew Roy had been a father to me when I needed a father the most, and he was not trying to interfere with that. I was thirty years old and what I needed most at this time was not a natural father, but a spiritual one. Loba stepped in and instructed me to new heights in my walk with God. Polly had taken me a long way in my spiritual walk with God, but God placed Loba in my life to instruct me on how to get to that next level in Him. This, to me, was worth more than any weight in gold.

Daniel and I planned our vacation every year during the time that Loba's church (International Gospel Center) had their yearly conference. During those conferences, we would always experience a mighty move of God. The way God moved will always be etched in my memory. We saw many people healed, demons cast out of individuals, and they were set free. We left each conference with a greater awareness of the power of God.

I was rejuvenated, hungry for the power of God, and more determined to hold on to God as we journeyed back to Arkansas. We felt spiritually free regardless of the trials and tribulations that we were going through, but when we returned to our church in Lonoke, we always had to fight to keep that spiritual freedom. It is one thing to get free, but totally another to stay free. We would do our best to obey those who had rule over us. But it was a struggle when we were told things like we were praying too loud while we were in prayer. I know God is not deaf, but He doesn't mind if you are loud if the prayer is coming from your heart. Trials and tribulations were coming left and right in my life, and the church was the one place I thought I could really be myself and be honest with God about the way I felt. I would go to church hoping I didn't leave the same way I came in.

It took a while to get that breakthrough because I was worried about whether I was too loud. I tried to do it their way for a while, but it made me feel bound and trapped. I testified one day and I told the church, "Maybe everything has gone well for you this week, maybe all your children are saved, maybe all your bills are paid, maybe you don't have any children in jail, maybe you don't want to know God more, maybe you don't need any help. Well I do, I have been struggling all week and I want to talk to the one that can help, so forgive me if I'm a little too loud." Right then and there I cried out with everything in me, "Help me Jesus!" With tears rolling down my face, I began to praise Him with everything I had. I felt like the blind men in "And, behold, two blind men sitting by the wayside, when they heard that Jesus passed by, cried out, saying, Have mercy on us, O Lord, thou Son of David. And the multitude rebuked them, because they should hold their peace: but they cried the more, saying, Have mercy on us, O Lord, thou Son of David. And Jesus stood still, and called them, and said, what will ye that I shall do unto you? They say unto him, Lord, that our eyes may be opened." (Matt 20:30-33). God gave me my freedom and my deliverance as I praised Him. That was the day I decided that I couldn't be like everyone else.

My Three Fathers (the Gifts)

There were some things only God could do for me, and I couldn't get God's attention if I didn't give Him my all. When I pray, I pray and talk to God from my heart. I'm not saying that you must do things like me, but I am saying, please let me be me. This is what it takes for me to get my breakthrough. My deliverance was in my praise, and the enemy was trying to steal that from me.

With everything in me, I tried to hold on to the freedom and joy that had increased in my life during those conferences in Detroit. During those conferences, the power of God manifested itself and we always got to see a miracle or two. There was this one time that Pastor Charles Miles called this lady out to pray for her. I remembered the lady from the night before. She sat at the table with us at the banquet. She never said anything to anyone; she just sat quietly and ate her meal. She would look up from her plate and smile occasionally. I didn't know it at the time, but she couldn't hear. When Pastor Miles called her to the front to pray for her, he told her God was going to heal her, and he stuck his fingers in her ears and prayed for her. When he got through praying for her, she turned and started walking back to her seat. Just when she reached her seat, she began jumping up and down screaming, "I can hear, I can hear!" Pastor Miles then said, "Some were healed as they went." It was moments like these that made my husband's and my faith grow in leaps and bounds.

Loba continued to be a spiritual mentor to my husband and me. There were times when Daniel or I would call him because we were having some difficulties in our marriage. Loba would listen to everything we had to say, and each time he always said the same thing. He would say, "Daughter, the key is death to self. Fasting, praying, confessing and pouring out and laying before God." This was the only way to get my flesh and wrong desires out of the way and to be able to say and mean, "God, not my will but thy will be done." No matter what problem I told him about, this was always his answer.

Daniel and I continued to go to the conferences, but we never took our children with us, and Loba never got a chance to meet Alex and Simone' before I lost them in the car wreck in 1998. After the car wreck, Loba and Lizzie made a choice to come to see me in Albuquerque, New Mexico, in the hospital, instead of going to the funeral. A few months after I started walking on a walker, he and Lizzie came to my house for the first time. He finally got a chance to see my son, Little Mike, but not Jim, because he was still hiding from the FBI. I was so pleased to have him in my home for the first time. Friends and family came over and Loba did what he does best. He talked about his God. Everyone listened with enthusiasm and awe to the things he was saying.

While he was there, I got up enough nerve to watch the funeral for the first time. I felt awful as I watched him see my children for the first time in a coffin. I could tell his heart was as heavy as mine. We didn't watch all the video at that time because company began to come in and out. Somehow, having him in my home gave me comfort despite how horrific the situation was. I had the pleasure of Loba visiting my home one more time in 2003. He had come to Arkansas for a funeral of a friend in Pine Bluff, Mr. Clark. Loba called my husband and me in 2002 to tell us about his friend, Mr. Clark, who had heart trouble and needed a transplant. He asked us if we would go visit with him sometimes and have Bible class with him. For almost a year, we drove to Pine Bluff on Tuesday night and had Bible class with him and his wife. We worked with Mr. Clark until he went to the hospital for the last time. Mr. Clark had gotten his life right with the Lord before God called him home. Loba came to Arkansas for his friend's funeral. He stayed with me while he was here for those few days. I was in nursing school and was unable to spend a whole lot of time with him. This is something I regretted after I found out what he was going through in 2003.

I got a call from Loba one evening after he had gone back to Detroit. After talking and laughing with him for a while, the tone of his voice changed as he said, "I have something that I have to tell you." He then went on to say he had been diagnosed with colon cancer a year or two ago. When he said this, it took my breath away. All I could think about was Mama, and for a few seconds I didn't say anything. Then I asked, "Why didn't you tell me this when you were here?"

His reply was, "I started to tell you." The only person he had told in the beginning was his wife, and he had made her promise not to tell anyone. My mind ran back to when he came to visit the last time, and I was too busy with nursing school to spend quality time with him. When I picked him up at the airport, the first thing I commented on was the fact that he had lost a lot of weight. I didn't think much about it because he was overweight quite a bit and needed to lose weight.

So, I just asked him how he was losing weight. We were trying to get his luggage and I don't even remember if he even answered.

Before I could ask any more questions, he began to tell me the rest of the story. The doctors found the cancer while it was in stage one and wanted to perform surgery to remove it. But Loba had refused the surgery and told them God was going to heal him. He also told them, "When God heals me, you all going to put me on TV."

The doctors replied, "If God heals you, I'll go on TV and tell the story." The doctors then explained to him what would happen if he didn't get the surgery. It was 2003 and the cancer had spread to his liver and lymph nodes and he had started losing a lot of weight. I was careful at this point not to say anything to discourage him. He had already told his brothers, sisters, and his pastor by the time he told me, and their reactions was basically the same as mine. *Why didn't you tell us?* I was just about to finish nursing school and I truly understood the battle he was facing. But I did my best not to let him know how I was truly feeling. During this time, Lizzie was also diagnosed with colon cancer, but she let the doctors do the surgery and was back on her feet recovering just fine. I held myself together and prayed for him, but after I got off the phone, I fell to my knees, bawled and called on God for strength.

My husband had just bought a 2003 Dodge truck and we decided to drive it out to support Loba during this time. So, we prepared to leave for Detroit that weekend. We got there that Friday night and checked into a hotel right off the interstate, not too far from where he lived. When we got up the next morning, the truck was gone. Someone had stolen it. I couldn't believe it. I was angry, but I was trying to keep the right attitude. After calling the police, the insurance company paid some on a rental vehicle and we were able to get transportation while we were there. We finally got that situation out of the way and began to focus on why we were there.

When I walked into their house and saw Loba, I couldn't believe it. He had lost so much weight, he looked sick. My heart just sank as I fought to keep the tears back. I hugged him and told him I loved him. I spent as much time with him as I could that weekend. The police hadn't found who had stolen our truck yet, so we had to drive the rental truck back to Arkansas. We left that Monday morning, and by the time we got halfway home, we received a phone call that our truck was found. Whoever stole it had taken the tires off and it was sitting on bricks. The insurance paid for the repairs and Daniel went back that weekend to pick it up.

I graduated from nursing school December 2003. One week after graduating, I found out that my best friend Polly was dying of colon cancer and the doctors weren't giving her much time to live. This was a hard pill to swallow and deal with. Both of my spiritual leaning posts were sick and having to lean on me. Polly lived one year after she found out about her condition. She left this earth in January 2005. I was hurt about Polly's death, but I had to hold myself together and turn my attention to Loba. About seven to eight months after Polly died, I got a call that Loba was dying. Without any hesitation, my husband and I went to Detroit.

When we arrived, we went straight to the hospital. I walked into the hospital room and Tranice and Lizzie were at his bedside. Tranice was there in the trenches with our father from the time she found out he was sick. I looked at my father and he looked up at me and said, "Hey." It seemed to have taken all his energy just to say that one word. My heart hurt as I looked into his eyes, trying to see the big strong man I had grown to love over the last twelve years. He was skin and bones now and was letting go of this world. The fight had gone out of his eyes and soul. Both were now in agreement with his failing body. There was a time he fought with everything in him to stay on this side, but his body was no longer strong enough to hold such a giant soul. As we sat around his bedside and talked, there were points when Loba looked at his wife and told her he was sorry. She gently stroked his head and told him that he had nothing to be sorry for or ashamed of. "You are a mighty man of God."

Later that night, my husband went back to the room and Lizzie went home, and Tranice and I stayed at his bedside. Tranice and I talked to him even though he was too weak to really talk back. Loba looked at Tranice and said, "I love you, girl."

Tranice responded, "I love you too daddy."

I looked at him with tears in my eyes and said, "It's been a pleasure knowing you, you are one mighty awesome man of God. I'll see you on the other side."

Loba truly was an awesome man of God. He affected the life of everyone he came in contact within a positive way.

The people at Chrysler loved him and the God in him, so they built him a pulpit on the job. He would minister to the people on his lunch breaks. Sometimes the power of God would move, so when he laid hands on the people, God filled them with the Holy Ghost. Lots of times, his lunch break would be over, but the power of God would be still moving. He would leave whoever was crying and pulling on God and go back to work, only to meet them on the next break. Loba had found favor on his job with the people who were over him. Again, I say Loba was one awesome man of God.

Tranice called Robert Jr. and Tracey to tell them if they wanted to see their father, they should come now because he was dying. Robert Jr. soon came walking through the door to be by his father's side. The next day, Loba did less talking than he did the day before, but a phone call from one of his church members made him talk more than I had heard him talk since I had been there. Lizzie was talking on the phone with one of Loba's friends and decided to put the phone up to his ear. Loba eyes opened and he had this strange look on his face. Then he said to the person on the other end of the phone, "You are trying to interrupt my trip!" I don't know who was on the other end of the phone, but they had told Loba that he couldn't go anywhere because he had promised them that he was going to do something for him. This was Loba's friend and he hated to see him go.

On Loba's last day, his friends from the church and family came to see him. Some prayed and some sang to him. He tried to sing with them, but he was too weak, but you could see that he was enjoying himself and it was just what the doctor ordered. Early that afternoon, he heard God's call and answered. I was at both Polly's and Loba's bedside as they transitioned. The things they taught me will forever live in my heart. I can still hear Polly saying, "God will pull you through if you can stand the pull." When things get rough and I can't see my way, I can hear Loba telling me, "Daughter, the key is death to self, praying, fasting, confessing and pouring out and laying before God."

He has been gone for several years now and I have truly found out what the key is for me getting know and grow in God ways. Because I had learn to use the key that Loba taught me about I was able to stand and stay with God during these difficult times, because I knew if God could take me through losing Mama, children, niece, nephew, and stepfather, I knew He had my back through whatever situation came my way.

After Loba passed away, Lizzie finally showed her true face. She showed the side that I had been hearing about from so many of Loba's family. She stopped answering my calls while I was there waiting for the funeral service to take place. I was hurt by this, but not as hurt as I was the day of the funeral. She told all Loba's family that the funeral was going to be at a certain time. It wasn't until the morning of the funeral that we found out the funeral was one hour earlier than she had told us. I was an emotional wreck that morning and was struggling to get ready. All I could do was throw myself together and get to the church as fast as I could. I couldn't believe that this was happening. She was trying not to include us in any of the service. Everyone got dressed and got there on time. As a matter of fact, we beat her there. I decided not to march in with the family and sit on the front bench. She walked in with her sister at her side. She was shocked when she got to the front bench and I was sitting there. Her mouth fell open as the usher asked me to move down. I moved down just enough to leave room for her to sit and the rest of the family that was behind her sat on the other side of me. When she sat down, I spoke to her and she spoke back, but you could tell she was uncomfortable.

Only one of Loba's sisters was on the program to say something. The day he died, we agreed with some of the church members at Loba's bedside that we wanted to send him out with a bang. In other words, we knew Loba wanted us to have some knock-down drag-out service at his funeral, but it didn't happen. I was in such disbelief at Lizzie's behavior and hurt, because he was gone.

The service was over with and the pastor and preachers had come out of the pulpit, shaking the family's hands on the front row, when Tranice whispered in the pastor's ear. The pastor told everyone to stop and sit back down. He escorted Tranice to the pulpit. She had whispered in his ear that she wanted to say something about her daddy. When Tranice opened her mouth, the power of God fell, and people jumped to their feet, clapping their hands and praising God. Lizzie even jumped to her feet to try to play off the wrong she knew she had done. I wanted to say something too but couldn't get past the hurt that I was feeling in that moment. I felt like I had on concrete shoes.

After the service, I couldn't take any more of the division confusion, so I chose not to go to the burial. I asked my husband to take me home and we went back to Arkansas. I learned from Jessie in

2016, after the burial Lizzie told Loba's family not to even come to her house, they needed to go to Jesse's house. It took me some time to let go of the hurt. I couldn't believe this was the same woman I knew before Loba died. I loved her and didn't understand why all of this was happening.

A couple of years after Loba died, Daniel and I decided to go to Detroit for their yearly conference. While we were there, we decided to go by the house to see Lizzie. She answered the door and when I saw her, I hugged her and cried. I told her that I missed her, and my husband did the same. She invited us in, and we laughed and talked like nothing had happened. We soon said our goodbyes and Lizzie gave me her new number. I decided to call after we got back home. She picked up the phone and hung it up after she heard my voice. From that day forward, I never could get her to answer my calls anymore. I finally was able to let it go and forgive her. I realized that life was too short, and I had already been through too much to hold a grudge in my heart. I love her and the rest is between her and God. I'm just glad now that I got the opportunity to know Loba.

After Loba's death, I got to meet his daughter Diane, who lived in California. Jessie had given me her picture and phone number. I had communicated with her over the phone about two years before I went to California. I went to Los Angeles to visit my Mama's brother Jack, and after spending a day or two with him, I gave Diane a call. She didn't hesitate; she wanted to meet me just as much as I wanted to meet her. She gave me directions to her home, and I went to meet her. I couldn't believe it; she looked just like Loba and Robert Jr. Diane introduced me to all her children and boyfriend. We sat down and talked about everything. After we got through catching up, she invited me to stay with her for a few days, and I gladly accepted.

Diane and I talked about more serious things, especially Loba. She never got to know who Loba really was. They met when she was a teenager and the visit didn't go too well. Words were exchanged and they went their separate ways. It grieved my heart that he didn't get to know his wonderful and awesome daughter whom I had grown to know and love. It also grieved me that she didn't get to know the awesome man of God her father was, whom I had grown to know and love.

Yes, I can say that I am a blessed and a better person because of my three fathers. All I wanted was to meet my real father and God heard my cry as a little girl. He not only gave me what I desired, but He gave me more than enough, He gave me three fathers. He has proven to be a God of more than enough, time and time again over the years.

I know some of you have missed the whole point of this story and are wondering, "Which one is her father?" Well, I won't leave you hanging anymore. World, I would like to introduce you to my father, Curtis, Roy, and Robert (aka Loba). They all were my father, and they all contributed to the person I have become. Each one played their part in my life and I'm a product of all three. God did this just for me. Who wouldn't serve a God like that?

I will say this to those whose curiosity is getting the best of them. I never got a DNA test, but I found out from a visit to the doctor that my real father had left me a gift. The doctor had drawn my labs and noticed that some of my lab work was off in places. When he did further investigation, he told me that I had a Sickle Cell trait and it had to come from one of my parents and the trait didn't come from my Mama. The Sickle Cell trait was a gift from my father. I knew who my real father was, but by this time, it didn't even matter to me because I was blessed to have three fathers. It was orchestrated by God, and God is a master at what He does. Tell the Lord, Thank You!

Chapter Nine

Momole

Young Momole (My grandmother)

Older Momole (My grandmother)

Bill (my great grandfather)

Mary Lou (One of my great grandfather Bill's women, who lived in the house with him and his wife, my great grandmother Elizabeth)

Momole was unique and eccentric in a lot of her ways. I often wondered why my grandmother acted and responded to certain situations like she did, but I came to learn in my latter years that a lot of her behavior was because of the things she endured in her lifetime. The things instilled in Momole at an early age not only had a profound effect on her life, but mine also. I didn't understand some things my grandmother struggled with until I heard her life story. When I became enlightened regarding her story, I then began to ponder back on my childhood years when I did not fully understand her struggle.

Viola Howard (aka Vie or Momole), was born to William Bill Howard (aka Bill) and Elizabeth (Spur) Howard in 1915. Momole was one of seventeen children raised in Bill and Elizabeth's home. Their home may not have been fine or elaborate, but it was home. Their home had three large bedrooms with dirt floors, which was normal for many of the black folks' homes back then. An individual passing by on a hot summer day, seeing all the children playing and laughing in the yard, Bill, Elizabeth, and two other ladies sitting on the porch, keeping a watchful eye on the children, would think that this was a normal family. Yes, their family might have been normal for someone standing on the outside looking in, but once you got a look on the inside, you could see that it was far from the norm.

The way Momole was raised and the things she was exposed to influence her way of thinking for the rest of her life. When Elizabeth began to have children, Bill decided she needed help taking care of the house and the children. So, he decided to move his mistress, Mary Lou "Abbie" Milton, to their home to help Elizabeth do the things she was not able to do. Bill was stern in what he wanted and there was no changing his mind about the way he wanted things to be. It wasn't long after he moved Abbie in that he moved another one of his mistresses in to help, and her name was Kate. At this point, the ladies were there more to help him with his needs than Elizabeth's needs. I'm sure Elizabeth may have protested in the beginning, but it was to no avail. Even though it was not easy, she made a conscious decision to stay and accept things as they were.

As the years passed, this became normal for Bill and the three ladies, but not for some of Elizabeth's children. Even though some may have struggled with the situation, they wouldn't dare breathe a word of what they felt out loud. Bill and Elizabeth had eight children together: James (aka Partner), West, Johnny, Viola (aka Vie, Momole my grandmother), Susie (aka Mu), Janie (aka Jane), Francis (aka Fick), and Essay. Bill and Abbie had nine children together: George, Sid (aka Fox), Martha (aka Mott), Eliza (aka Doogah), Manda (aka Dallie), Lula (aka Lu), Suzanne, Albert, and Lucinda. Mrs. Kate didn't have any children. I was told that Abbie already had a couple of children when she came to live in Bill's house.

Francis

Susie

Johnny

Bill ruled his house with a firm hand. Every New Year's he would call everyone who lived under his roof together around the wood stove. He would say, "We got new rules and if you can't follow them, you've got to go." Then he would sternly spout out each rule and everyone did their best to appease him.

At the end of each day, Bill and the family would all gather in the living room. The atmosphere was filled with the different conversations from the children and the three women. Bill sat in his easy chair, eyes closed and resting, but paying attention to every word that was being said. Everyone in the room soon found out that Bill may not have been a part of their conversation, but he was listening closely. He didn't make a big fuss, but he would gently clear his throat in disapproval to something that he had heard one of them say. Silence filled the room, because they all knew all too well what this meant. When everyone's conversations started back up, it would be about something different or whatever mischief was going on ceased in that moment. Bill didn't tolerate confusion among the children or the women in the house. So, when he was around, everything ran like a well-oiled machine.

When the women weren't working in the cotton fields, they all had jobs to do and they would work together to take care of the children, cook and clean. Abbie did most of the cooking and she helped take care of the children. Kate helped Elizabeth keep the house clean. Elizabeth and Abbie were having children back to back. When one of the babies cried and needed to be fed, it didn't matter whose child it was, either of them would breastfeed the child. Sometimes when Abbie cooked, she would get distracted and maybe burn the biscuits. Whenever this happened, a sense of urgency came over her to get rid of the evidence. She would hand the burned biscuits to one of the children and tell them to hurry and throw them out to the dogs before Bill came home. Abbie knew if Bill came home and found that the biscuits had burned, he would get mad and accuse her of having her mind on another man. So, Abbie got rid of any trace of food gone wrong.

The house may have seemed to run like a well-oiled machine to Bill, but there was one problem with his big, happy family, and the problem was with the hens of the house.

Bill and the three women all slept in the same room. The women's beds were lined up in a row and Bill slept on a cot at the end of the beds. The big problem with this harmonious arrangement was the three women had to take turns when it came to intimate time with Bill. The women had assigned nights they would get to feel Bill's touch. Bill slept with only one of the women in a night. If it wasn't your turn, you would have to wait, and this was the part of their arrangement Elizabeth struggled with the most. There would be nights that Elizabeth yearned to feel her husband's touch, but unfortunately, she had to watch him be intimate with one of the other women because it wasn't her turn. To make matters worse, three women were not enough to soothe Bill's burning loins.

There were several shotgun houses lined up in a row, built on the property where Bill and his family lived. Several widows and their children lived in these houses. Bill also frequented these houses when the opportunity presented itself. He took care of everyone who stayed on his property; there was always plenty to eat. Bill always kept a watchful eye and monitored what men came onto his property, and that was very few. Bill did all he could to make sure he was the only rooster in the hen houses. The people who lived in the neighborhood knew and accepted Bill for the way he lived.

Bill had more than one offbeat habit-he hardly ever wore shoes. No matter what time of year; rain, sleet, snow or sunshine, Bill was barefoot most of the time. It didn't matter, the women loved him, and they chose to stay.

Elizabeth was a strong woman to endure the situation she was in. In other words, whatever he said to do was law in his house. Elizabeth grew to love the other two women and she held no animosity in her heart against them. She was a religious woman, and whenever anyone would ask her how she was able to endure the situation; she would simply reply, "If I want to go to heaven, I got to love them all. They'll have to pay for the deeds they've done. I haven't done anything wrong. When I die, I'm not going to suffer, I'll just go to lie down and die." After she said this, it would be the end of that conversation.

To make sure everyone had plenty to eat for the summer and winter months, Bill had a garden, peach, pear trees, hogs and a smokehouse. The women would can all the fruit and vegetables and there was always plenty to eat. Bill didn't allow the children or anyone just to eat off the trees. This was their food supply, all vegetables and fruits had to be canned. If the children got caught eating from the trees without permission, they would soon regret it. But there were occasions when Bill would say to one of the children, "Chap, reach up there and give me a peach off that tree," and he would give each of the children or grandchildren a peach. All the children would sit around with juice running down their mouths and arms, savoring every bite. Yes, this was one of the moments from the good old days that I believe Finnie (Mama's brother) could taste the peach as he told the stories of yesteryear.

Bill's children grew up and he couldn't always keep a watchful eye on them. George and Sid were young boys when they got into a fight with a white boy from the neighborhood. After they beat the boy up, they went home and didn't think too much more about it. That is, until the local white men showed up at their house a few hours later, shouting, "Send those two nigger boys out that jumped on the white boy or we will burn you out." Fear filled the house because they all knew what was about to happen; Bill knew if he was going to save his boys, he had to get some help. He managed to get out of the house without being seen, and he ran and got Mrs. Olen (a prominent white lady he had worked for). Mrs. Olen came with Bill to the house and she told the clan, "I know who everyone of y'all is under those hoods and all y'all owe me money. So, y'all need to go on and leave my peoples alone." There wasn't too much more said after that. They all left Bill and his family in one piece. That would not be the last time trouble knocked at their door.

Darnell (Momole's baby son) told me a story that Momole had told him. One of Bill's daughters got a job as a maid working for a white couple. The man of the house took an interest in Bill's daughter and began having his way with her every chance he got when his wife was out of the house. One day he sent his wife to the store to get groceries, and as soon as she left the house, he took Bill's daughter straight to bed. The wife was almost to the store when she realized she had forgotten the money, and so she went back to the house. When she got to the house, she caught her husband in bed with the maid. Her husband quickly jumped up and told Bill's daughter to leave. Fearing that his wife would leave him, he grabbed the shotgun and went outside. When Bill's daughter came out of the house, he shot her through the breast and killed her. Then he told his wife, "You don't have to worry about that nigger anymore, she's dead." Momole told these horror stories of yesteryear to her youngest children. With bitterness in her heart, she told them the white man never got punished for killing her sister.

Momole and her sisters and brothers were growing up, leaving home, and having children of their own. Momole was thirteen years old when she caught the eye of James Harris. He was a forty-five years old, but this did not deter him from asking Bill for her hand in marriage. Their marriage may have been legal back then, but it would be against the law in this day and time. Momole was a child bride and never got to experience the life of a normal child. She had to grow up quickly, whether she wanted to or not.

After Momole married James, they moved off her father's place and moved to Wynne, Arkansas. It wasn't long after the wedding that Momole started having children. James and Momole had seven children, Freddie, Jack, Billy Louis (aka Louis), John (aka Shaffer), Finnie (aka Brown), Bessie, and Anna Beth (aka Sis or Annie Bess).

James stuck around close to the house when Momole had the first couple of children, but as the children started coming, he started disappearing. James would catch a train in and out of town like a hobo. When Momole got pregnant, he would leave town and come back three weeks before she had the baby. Then he would stick around long enough to get her pregnant again and then catch a fast train out of town.

Momole had a dog named Trailer. Trailer was always the first to know when James was back in town. Weeks before Momole was about to have the baby, Trailer would start barking and howling as he heard the train whistle. Trailer didn't do this all the time, and Momole knew what it meant. She would yell to the children, "Go meet the train, your father is here." They were little boys, but Freddie, Jack, John, and Finnie ran to meet the train. The train track was a mile or two from the house. The boys could hear the whistle of the train blowing as they ran to meet their father. They didn't understand why their father left for months at a time; they were just overcome with excitement and anticipation of their father's long overdue presence. Like clockwork, three weeks before the baby was born, he jumped off the train, greeting his children as if he had just left yesterday. That old dog, Trailer, was right again. The children never got to spend enough time with James to find out who he really was. Sis and Bessie never got to know their father, because they were babies when he died.

Momole and the children struggled to get by as James came in and out of their lives. She always told the children, "We're going to make it by the grace of God." There were many days they were hungry because food was not plentiful. Momole had a milk cow and always told the boys, "Whatever you do, don't let the cow eat bitter weed, or you will not have milk to eat with your cornbread." When food was scarce, there were days Momole would say, "Jack, get your slingshot and go kill us a rabbit for supper." Jack would get his slingshot and go out and sometimes he came home with the rabbit she had sent him for. Momole would smile at him when he brought the rabbit in because she knew this day, they would not go hungry.

When all else failed, Momole loaded the shotgun with buckshot and went blackbird hunting. The farmers tilled the ground, getting ready to plant their crops, and this brought the worms to the surface. This was the blackbirds' and Momole's feasting grounds. She planted her feet and took careful aim while the birds feasted on the worms.

Just as she pulled the trigger, the gun's kick lifted her off her feet and she landed on her backside. She was small and sometimes the gun's kick was a little bit more than she could handle. But this did not discourage Momole. She did this again and again until she had enough for her and the children to eat.

Momole did what she had to do to make sure her children had something to eat. Times were hard back then, but God always provided. While the birds had their fill of worms, Momole and her children had their fill of blackbirds. When Finnie got old enough, killing the blackbirds became his job when times were lean.

Momole took corn to the mill to make corn meal for them to eat, but there were days that the meal barrel ran empty and they had to eat the husk off the corn. As the years passed, they were fortunate enough to have chickens, and occasionally they had chicken for supper. Momole instructed the boys not to kill the rooster or the best hen because they were the ones that laid the eggs and produced more chickens. Whenever Momole got ready to kill a chicken, they didn't have to go outside to get one. The house they lived in sat so low to the ground that you could see through the cracks in the floors and walls. John was the smallest of the boys and was the only one who could fit under the house. Shaffer would remove one of the planks and the other boys would hold his feet while he reached under the house to get a chicken for supper. That was a day of feasting when they were able to have chicken for supper.

Due to hard times and scarcity of food, Momole and the children knew they couldn't afford to be wasteful. As Momole left the house one day, she glanced back and yelled to the boys, "Don't mess with the butter, that's all we have." After she was gone, the boys forgot to close the door behind her. Freddie and Jack were outside when one of the chickens came wandering through the door. The butter was sitting out and the chicken helped itself and ate it all. When Freddie and Jack came in the house, they realized the chicken had eaten the butter. Momole's last words filled their minds and hearts with fear. "Don't mess with the butter, that's all we have." Momole disciplined her boys like her father disciplined her and this was all Freddie and Jack could think about when they saw the butter dish empty. *Mama is going to kill us.*

The chicken had gone under the house. Freddie turned to Shaffer and told him to reach under the house and get the chicken. Without hesitation, Shaffer moved the plank from the floor, grabbed the chicken by his legs, and pulled him into the house. The chicken was squawking and flapping its wings, trying to get away, but to no avail. They held onto the chicken as if their lives depended on it, and in a way it did because they didn't know what Momole was going to do when she found out the butter was gone. When Freddie and Jack got their hands on the chicken, they held the chicken's beak over the butter dish while choking him. It wasn't long before the chicken started choking up the butter. They were able to get most of the butter back, but it did not look the same coming out as it did before it went into the chicken.

The first thing Momole noticed as she walked through the door was the change in the butter. Momole said, "What happened to the butter?" Before anyone could say anything, Shaffer eagerly answered, "The chicken ate it and Freddie and Jack made him give it back." The boys managed to dodge trouble that day.

Momole's boys were quickly turning into young men, and she began to educate them about life. The boys would all gather around and listen to what she had to say. "You got to work. If you don't work, you will steal," Momole said. "Don't worry about what other people think about you or your clothes. You got water and pots out there, just wash them and put them on again." They didn't have the choice of name brand shoes like we have now. All they had was high-top Buster Brown shoes. As she handed them their shoes, she would say, "Don't down yourself, and hold your head up, you look just as nice as anybody else. Be proud of who you are."

Momole would get up early and go to the cotton field. She let the children sleep in a little longer, but she left the boys a pillowcase to put the cotton in that they picked. She had cut a slit in the pillowcases so they could wear them over their shoulders. When the children woke up, they walked through a path to the cotton field that went by Mr. Big Boy's and his wife, Mrs. Dee's house. Mrs. Dee would say to them as they passed by, "Them my boys there." On the way back from the field, Mrs. Dee would always ask them, "How much y'all pick today?" Jack would reply, "A sack full."

Momole and the children would chop cotton all week, and at the end of the week, all the children gave the money to Momole. She put the money in a little red cotton drawstring bag. At the end of the week, she and the children all sat in the middle of the floor and poured the money out and counted it. Momole told the children, "I'll allow y'all children to work four days a week and I'll keep the money for those days. If you all work Friday and Saturday, you can keep the money for those two days," and this was what they all did. Momole went on to tell them, "I'm looking out for your welfare, because one day it's going to rain and get tough and if I don't look out for y'all, you ain't going to have nothing." Momole and the children pooled their resources together and made it through the hard times, since her husband, James was never around to provide for them.

It turned out James had another family in Benton, Arkansas, and this was where he went when he disappeared. James had one son when he and Momole got married that she knew about. His name was James Henry. He left town, and no one ever heard from him again. James (Momole's husband) also had three brothers: Vince, Freddie (aka Hammer), and Jack. When James would leave, Momole had to survive the best way she could. Momole mostly cleaned houses, washed clothes for white people, and worked in the fields, chopping cotton. The white people she worked for gave her parts of the pigs they didn't want; feet, chitterlings, etc., and other things to help her take care of her family.

Finnie was three years older than Sis, and during these three years it took for Sis to make her arrival into this world, James stayed around. When Momole got pregnant with their last child, Bessie, James caught the first train leaving town. The last time James came home, he had TB and was deathly ill. James knew he would probably never see his family again. So, he paid a white man to move Momole and the children back to where he had gotten her from, her father Bill's house. Before James left, he gave Freddie, his eldest son, a pocketknife that had all kinds of different gadgets, and told him to take care of the boys. He told his sons he was going to stay with his brother in Memphis until he got well. He knew if he stayed, he would probably infect his family. Even when he talked to them this time, it was from a distance. This may have been the most decent thing he had done for them. Momole and the children never heard from James again. James had been dead for two years when Momole received a letter from his brother, informing her of his death.

After James died, some of the white people told Momole, "Vie, why don't you put those children in a home for children? You're young and need to go on and live your life." Momole's reply to this was, "I'm not giving my children to anybody, the Lord will make a way."

Momole and all seven of her children had to sleep in the same room at her father's house. Bill had rules for his house, and if you lived under his roof, he expected you to follow his rules. He was a hard disciplinarian; sometimes when he beat the children for something they had done wrong, he drew blood. This was one reason Momole didn't like for him to discipline her children. There was this one occasion that Freddie, Louis, Jack, and Shaffer were playing in a field near the house. The neighbor was growing oats and had asked Bill to keep the children out of his field. Bill had asked the boys to stay out of the field, but they disobeyed him. When Bill saw them in the field, he went ballistic and began crying and screaming at the top of his lungs. Momole was standing beside him and she knew this was not good. He turned and ran into the house and she turned as quickly as he did and was on his heels, because she feared what he was about to do. When Bill emerged from the house, he had a shotgun in his hand and Momole on his back. She was pleading and begging him not to shoot her children. The children heard the gunshot and they ran for their lives. God had spared them that day and they never played in the oat field again. But they continued to get in and out of other mischief.

Freddie, Jack, Louis, Shaffer, and Finnie were walking down the road when they met Jack Coleman (son of Martha, Momole's sister) walking from the opposite direction, coming toward them. Jack C always gave them a hard time, and when he finally met up with them this time was no different. Jack C told them, "Boys, I'm going to spank y'all tails and then I'm going to spit in your booty." So, one by one he began to pick them up and he hit them one time on their bottoms. After Jack C hit them that one time, he rotated them around his shoulder and held their butts up and made a spitting sound like he was spitting on their bottoms. Freddie was the oldest and he stood there patiently watching Jack C pick up each one of his siblings. Jack C glanced up at Freddie and said, "I'm going to get you last, because you think you're grown." Freddie didn't say a mumbling word; he just stood back and waited for his turn to come.

Jack C would soon be sorry he had messed with them. Freddie took the pocketknife out of his pocket that his father, James, had given him, while waiting for Jack C to pick him up. Jack C was unaware of this and he picked Freddie up over his head and began to rotate him around his body. He didn't realize that the whole time he was rotating Freddie around his body, Freddie was cutting him until it was too late. Blood poured from Jack C's body, and he dropped

Jack Coleman

Freddie and said, "This man child done cut me." Jack C took off running toward the house.

When Jack C got to the house and Momole heard the bad news, she knew her father would probably beat her boys within an inch of their lives. Jack C would be okay, but Bill was in a rage. Momole knew she had to get her boys out of there and quick. In a panic, Momole ran down the road toward her children to keep them from coming to the house. When she reached them, she told them to hide in a nearby ditch that had tall grass. She told them, "Don't come out until I come get you." This was one time the boys did not disobey her order.

Bill was furious and he hunted for the boys but could not find them. Momole pretended to hunt for them also. They hid in that ditch for two days. Momole brought them food and water. Each time she brought them food, she reinforced how important it was for them to stay hidden. The boys might have been afraid of the sounds that came with nightfall, but they were more afraid of the repercussions that awaited them if their Grandpa Bill found them.

Two days passed, and the boys were still hiding in the weeds. This proved to be the longest two days of their young lives, but they dared not to show their faces until Momole came to give them more instructions. When Momole finally came, her presence was a welcome sight. But she was not alone. Momole had married William Scott (aka Will) and they had come to get the boys to take them to their new home.

Even though Momole moved on with her life, things remained the same at her father's house for many years to come. Elizabeth stood strong on what she had said over the years when she was asked how she could live with her husband and two mistresses. Elizabeth simply replied, "I have to love them if I want to go to heaven. I haven't done anything wrong and when I die, I'm not going to suffer, I'm just going to lie down and die." That's exactly what Elizabeth did when she passed away. She was sitting on the porch one day with Abbie, then she got up and went into the house. She didn't say a word when she went in the house, she just went in and got in the bed and covered up her head. When Abbie went in the house, she passed by the bedroom and saw Elizabeth's head covered up. Abbie thought this was strange, so she went in the room to check on her. When Abbie uncovered Elizabeth's head, she was dead.

Miss Kate had died some time before Elizabeth. Bill died before Elizabeth, and then Abbie died. Bill was almost 100 years old when he died. After he died, Francis (aka Fick, Elizabeth's daughter) made the statement, "Now I'm going to get my Mama out of this mess."

Elizabeth told Francis, "If you want to leave, you go ahead, but Abbie and I are going to stay together." Elizabeth had grown to love Abbie and they stayed together for years even after Bill died. They continued to sleep in the same bedroom with their beds side by side.

In Bill's later years, the life he had lived brought him many regrets and guilt. Before Bill died, he apologized to Elizabeth and Abbie about the way he had treated them all those years. Bill still slept in the same room with them, but the fire in his loins had long since gone out. Father Time had introduced Bill to old age, and there was no turning back the hands of time.

As Bill reflected over his life, he prayed to God more and more. Finnie recalls the time he heard his Grandpa Bill praying and asking

God to forgive him. Bill's voice could be heard all over the house as he prayed to the Lord for forgiveness. He prayed so hard it sounded like he was preaching. He even joined the church and got on the moaning bench (the front pews in the church where people would go to pray and ask God for forgiveness). Abbie lived many years after they all died. She spent her final years bedridden in a nursing home, praying to God.

Will and Momole lived on the Slim Davis Plantation. Will was from the Prescott and Hope, Arkansas area, but he had moved to Lonoke County. Will loved Momole and he was good to her children, but they continued to get in and out of mischief. Out of all Momole's boys, Freddie stayed in and out of mischief the most. Occasionally, he got up enough nerve to talk back to Momole when she had given him instructions on what she wanted him to do. Well, this day, he talked back to Momole and she wasn't in the mood for it. They were sitting at the kitchen table when he mouthed off at her; she didn't say a word, she just reached up and got the shotgun off the wall. By the time she turned around to aim the gun at him, all she saw was an open door. Freddie got up and ran for his life; he knew he had gone too far. By the time Momole made it out the door, Freddie was a mile down the road. He waited until he thought Momole had cooled down before he came back to the house. Momole might not have had trouble out of Freddie in this area anymore, but it sure didn't stop him from getting into more mischief.

There was this white boy who lived near Momole, and he would come and play with Freddie and his brothers from time to time. The boys were sitting around on the porch, idle, with nothing to do, when Freddie got this crazy idea. Freddie's mind gave new meaning to the statement, "An idle mind is the devil's workshop." Momole had stored cotton in a bin on the porch. The bin had quite a bit of cotton in it. Freddie dared the white boy to touch the bottom of the bin. So, the boy took the dare and dove into the cotton bin headfirst, with his feet flapping in the wind. By the time the boy got started, Freddie grabbed his legs and feet and held onto them. The boy was unable to move up or down. He kicked, trying to work his way out of the grip Freddie had on him. The harder he kicked; the tighter Freddie's grip became. It wasn't long before the kicks got slower and slower until there was no movement at all. The boy was unable to breathe and was dying, but Freddie still held onto his feet and didn't pull him up for air. This scared Finnie half to death when he saw the boy's feet had lost their vigor. He ran in the house to tell Momole what Freddie was doing. This was not a moment too soon. Momole didn't understand all Finnie was trying to tell her until she finally made it to the porch and saw what Freddie was doing. Freddie was so focused on what he was doing, he didn't see Momole when she made it to the porch.

Without saying a word, Momole picked up a big piece of wood from the nearby wood pile. She held onto the piece of wood with both her hands, drew it back with all her might, and hit Freddie so hard in his back that it sent him flying off the porch. Momole immediately turned her attention from Freddie to the lifeless feet sticking out of the cotton bin. She quickly pulled the boy's lifeless body from the cotton bin so he could get some air. When she got the boy out of the cotton bin, he was not breathing, and his color was gone. Momole's heart dropped because she knew the trouble the boy's death would bring to her house. Before the horror of the boy not breathing could really sink in, the boy took a deep breath and his color began to return. As soon as the boy woke up, he regained his composure, jumped to his feet, eyes wide and heart racing. Without saying a word or looking back, the boy ran home, never to return to play again.

After the boy left, Momole's attention turned to Freddie and she yelled at him, "If you had killed that boy down here, I would have had to kill you." Momole's heart raced as she pondered the situation in her mind. She understood the trouble that would have come to all of them if Freddie had killed this boy, even if Freddie didn't understand.

Momole raised her children with a firm hand. She had to, because she basically raised them by herself up until she married Will. Will and Momole had six children together: Nathaniel (aka Nay), Will (aka Gabby), Mary (aka Helen my Mama), Mattie, James Ray and Christine (aka Stine).

Will was a good man and did what he had to do to take care of their thirteen children. But he was not without faults. He liked to go out on the weekends and hang at the Juke Joints from time to time. On some weekends, Will went out with Momole's brothers; Sid (aka Uncle Fox), West, George, and Albert (aka Fugga). Momole was no longer a child; she had grown to be a strong young woman. She was nothing like her Mama, Elizabeth; she was more like her father and she didn't tolerate too much nonsense. She let Will and her brothers stay out for a little while, but after a while her imagination would get the best of her. The thought of what they might have been doing made her spring into action. Momole grabbed her pistol and headed for the juke joint, but not before making a detour to pick up her brothers' wives, Octavia (Albert's wife), Elma (Sid's wife), Bert (George's Wife) and Carrie (West's wife). Octavia and the other wives entered the club first. Momole's brothers spotted their wives coming in the door and this made them panic. They panicked, not because their wives had shown up but because they didn't know if their sister, Vie, was with them. They went over to their wives and asked them, "Is Vie with y'all?" Octavia responded, "Yes." They then replied, "Oh hell, I'm getting out of here, because it's going to be some [expletive] if Vie is out there. She's gone come in here shooting." They grabbed their wives and left the Juke Joint running, because they knew their sister, Vie, was crazy enough to kill somebody if she felt it necessary. No one died that night, but there were other nights they had to leave the Juke Joint running.

With all the drama Momole caused, this didn't deter her husband, Will, from going out. One weekend Will decided to stay out all weekend. When he came home, he was greeted by a wife who was glad to see him, but angry and trying to keep calm. Momole calmly asked him where he had been. Will didn't answer her persistent questions. He just sat at the table with his eyes hiding behind his sunglasses. He let her continue her inquiry for a few minutes, then he finally interjected, "If you going to keep this up, I'm going back where I came from."

Will was just playing around when he got up and went to the door. Momole was angry and this was no time to be playing. She looked at him and told him, "Don't put your hand on that doorknob." He was still teasing her and reaching for the doorknob. She repeated her first statement, "Don't put your hand on that doorknob." By this time, she had gotten the shotgun. He grabbed the doorknob and went out the door and closed it. He didn't leave; he was just on the other side of the door, pretending to be gone. This made Momole so angry, she raised the shotgun as soon as he closed the door and pulled the trigger. The buckshot from the gun blew a hole in the door and hit Will in the face and chest.

Blood was everywhere, and with tears in her eyes, Momole stepped over Will and went to Sid's (her brother) house and told him, "He's dead, I killed him." Sid jumped up without asking Momole any questions and they ran to her house. When they got there, Will was lying on the porch bleeding, but still alive. West and Sid (Momole's brothers) lifted him off the porch and rushed him to the doctor. It took the doctor a while to pick the buckshot out of Will's face and chest. The only thing that stopped Will from getting shot in the eyes was the shades he had on. Those shades saved him from being blind for the rest of his life. Will stayed with Momole and the children even after this incident.

Momole had watched her Mama be the submissive wife all her life and endure things no woman should have to endure. She was the total opposite of her Mama. In fact, she went to the extreme in the other direction. There was no middle ground when it came to her husband cheating with another woman. Momole was not going to take it lying down. Will didn't leave her; he stayed by her side despite her eccentric ways. I believe this was one of the reasons he loved her, although they continued to have their ups and downs.

I don't know what Will had done, but he made Momole mad. She chased Will out of the house with a butcher knife in her hand. He ran out of the house and ran around the house with her right on his heels. She got close at times, but Will always kept her just out of reach. Their children stood back and watched in amusement as their parents ran around and around the house. Will finally took off running down the road and Momole was right behind him with a knife in her hand. When she realized she couldn't catch him, she fell in the road and kicked and screamed like a child throwing a temper tantrum. As Will ran on down the dusty road, she made so much commotion that people came through the fields and bushes to see what was going on. When they saw who it was and what was going on, they went back to their tasks at hand. Will waited until he figured she had calmed down some and decided to return home. After he came back down the road, Momole was still lying in the road, crying and screaming. Will bent down and gently picked her up and carried her home, and that was the end of that.

Will loved Momole until the day he died of lung and stomach cancer. Momole's son, Shaffer, said the week of their stepfather's death was the week she vowed never to go to church again. She believed in God but not church folk. The church folk had left a bitter taste in Momole's mouth that would never wash out. Will and Momole believed in God but did not attend church often. This caused a problem when it came to making Will's funeral arrangements. There was only one church at the time where they lived, and it was St. James. The pastor and the church members didn't want Will's funeral at the church because he was not a member. Momole was already grieving from the loss of her husband and worrying about how she was going to take care of her children. She had a graveside service for her husband. That day, Momole lost her faith in church folk, but not God. She never attended church again after that day. This church hurt caused another layer of hardness around an already hardened heart.

James, Will's youngest son, remembered the day he saw his father lying in a coffin. To this five-year-old, his daddy looked as if he was sleeping. Because he was too short to see his father clearly, Momole picked him up to get a better view of his father. James took one look at his father and said, "Daddy, wake up and let's go." Momole looked at James with tears in her eyes and said, "He can't wake up."

Finnie was a young lad when Will died, but old enough to take on the responsibility of working. Will had worked for this white man driving tractors, and before he died, he asked his boss to give his job to Finnie. Will knew Momole would need financial help after he was gone. He also knew Finnie would take the money he made home to give it to Momole. Finnie took the job and did just as Will had told him to do until she remarried.

Some of the children who were old enough worked in the cotton fields and corn fields. After Will passed, they didn't go to the cotton field or corn field the next day. They stayed home with Momole. She had fixed them supper and they were all sitting around the supper table when Slim Davis, the owner of the house they lived in, knocked at the door.

Momole replied to the knock at the door by saying, "Who is it?" The heavy voice heard on the other side of the door replied, "Mr. Davis." Slim Davis was a tall, big man, and when Momole opened the door, his body frame filled the doorway. Slim's presence was intimidating. He carried a gun in a holster on his side and he had a club in his hand whenever you saw him. He looked down at Momole and the children sitting at the table and said, "Vie, the next time you don't send these nigga boys to the field, someone's going to pay. I want to see these nigga boys in the field tomorrow, understand?" Momole simply replied, "Yes sir, but I want my children to go to school sometimes."

Boss Man Slim replied, "It doesn't matter what you want. As long as you live on my land, these nigga boys will do as I say." Momole didn't say another word. Her first seven children didn't get to attend school much because of this. The children rode on the back of a wagon that was being pulled by a mule. They picked the corn and threw it on the back of the wagon as the mule moved up and down each row.

After the Boss Man Slim Davis left, Momole had made up her mind to move out of his house and off his land. After everyone finished eating, Momole and the children got busy moving. They moved just a few miles away in a house on the Teague's land. The only thing they had to move the furniture with was a little red wagon; she and her boys moved the cooking stove, kitchen table, beds and all with that little red wagon. The Teague land was where Momole's brothers, Albert, Sid, West, George, and their families lived. Momole's father lived on this land also at that time. Their houses were all in a row and Bill lived at the end.

Boss Man Slim was not a nice man. There were times Will would drink excessively and get falling down drunk. When he did, Boss Man Slim would catch him by himself in the woods and beat him. Will called him a coward, because Slim would wait until he caught him drunk to beat him.

Finnie, the oldest living sibling at this time, talked about how good their stepfather, Will, was to them. Now that Finnie was grown and doing well for himself, he thought about his stepfather often. Finnie wished he had lived long enough to show his gratitude for the way Will took care of them when they were children.

Momole was alone again, and this time she didn't have seven children to take care of, she had eleven. Freddie and Jack had gotten married and moved into their own places. But there were still plenty of mouths that had to be fed. Momole didn't have time to lie down and grieve for the loss of her husband, Will. She had to take a deep breath and grieve as she moved forward in her life. Now was not the time in her life that she could quit. Even with thirteen children, Momole would not stay single for long. Stine was Momole's baby when she married her third husband, Sam Nellum (aka Cooter). Cooter and Momole had four children together: Sam (aka Mack), Charles, Troy (aka Darnell) and Darlene. Darlene was Darnell's twin and she died at birth.

Sam

Cooter & Momole

Charles

Darnell

Momole was a tower of strength and she did what she had to do to take care of her family. When Momole loved, she loved hard, but when she hated, she hated just as hard as she loved. So, I for one, was glad to be one of the ones who felt her love. Momole was unique in many of her ways and misunderstood by so many. I came to learn in later years some of the reasons behind her eccentric behavior. As I learned more about her past and the things she had to endure in her lifetime, I began to understand why she did some of the things she did. Momole had seventeen children; she had to be a strong woman. Her life was not a life that a weak woman could survive. At that point in Momole's life, she realized all white people weren't the same and some would become her lifelong friends.

I don't remember my other two grandfathers, James or Will, but I got to spend many years with Cooter. Many years later, Cooter told me how he and Momole met. I listened and laughed as Cooter told me that Momole's hips had caught his attention. She was in the juke joint, standing in front of the jukebox, shaking her hips to one of her favorite songs that was playing. That image of Momole in a Juke Joint, shaking her hips to music, was hard to imagine. But it was not as hard as when James and Bessie (Momole children) told me about the times when Momole would make hooch (moonshine) and invite over her two sisters, Francis and Susie. Momole, Susie, and Francis would crank that old record player up and let the good times roll. They would laugh and dance the night away, while the children all sat around and looked and laughed. At those moments in time, they didn't have a care in the world -- all the troubles of past days took a back seat as time stood still for a little while, as they enjoyed their moments of relief.

Finnie was thirteen years old and left home after Cooter married Momole. Finnie left because he felt it was not right for Momole to be marrying again. Finnie was crazy about his stepfather, Will, and didn't want anyone taking his place. But Finnie grew to love and respect Cooter as the years passed. Cooter was an awesome man, but he was just as eccentric in a lot of his ways as Momole was. "Opposites attract" is what comes to my mind, when I think of my grandparents. Cooter was laid back, easygoing, and a man of few words. Cooter always started or ended his sentences with "thee." Cooter would say things like, "Thee doing alright today" or "thee grandma in the house." Cooter and Momole understood one another, no matter how strange their relationship may have seemed to others. Cooter had learned to love and accept Momole just as she was and dealt with each day's obstacles as they came.

When Cooter and Momole married, Stine was the baby. Momole had thirteen children and Cooter had one daughter from a previous relationship. It takes a great man to take on this kind of responsibility. Mattie (Momole's daughter) had this half smile on her face as she reminisced about the good old days. She talked about how good Cooter was to them and how he treated all of them the same. Cooter and Momole didn't have a car when they first got married, so Cooter walked to the store every day, and the store was not around the corner. It didn't matter what Cooter would buy, he always got enough for all the children. Whether it was bologna, peppermint sticks, cookies, etc. All the children gathered around Cooter, eagerly awaiting their turn to receive whatever goodies were being passed out. Cooter would talk to them as he made each one of them a bologna sandwich. He had settled into the role of being father, he was a hard worker and did what he had to do to take care of his family.

Money was scarce and times were hard. To make ends meet, Cooter would sometimes go to the cotton fields after the cotton pickers had picked all the cotton and he would glean the fields like Ruth did in the Bible. He took a sack and picked the cotton that was left behind in the fields. When he got a sack full, he took it to the cotton gin, and they paid him for it. Cooter continued to come up with creative ways to take care of his family. He wasn't an educated man, but he was a wise man. He'd bought this old blue Ford car, but he desired a truck. Well, one day when we went to go get into his car, it was no longer a car, it looked like an El Camino. Cooter had taken the trunk top off the car, cut the opening all the way up to the window and then placed wood planks on each side. The planks were there to keep whatever object he was hauling from falling out. He had made himself a truck out of his car. Cooter may not have been an educated man, but he was a smart man. He made money hauling things and junk around from place to place.

While Momole and Cooter were out trying to make a living for the family, the younger children were at the house, fending for one another. When Momole and Cooter were away from the house, the older children had the responsibility of taking care of the younger children. As the children got a little older, they got in more mischief.

Whenever Cooter and Momole left home, they instructed the children to stay away from the pond, which was a deep ditch. The pond was near their house, and this was where they went to swim whenever they got a chance. All the children heard Momole's instructions clearly, but they would be almost holding their breaths, waiting for Momole to walk out the door so they could do just what she had asked them not to do. As soon as Cooter and Momole disappeared, Bessie, Sis, Nay, Gabby, Mary, and Mattie would grab the babies, James and Stine, and head for the pond. They played in the water for hours until their hearts were content. The little children didn't go down to the pond without the bigger children most of the time. But one day, Mary (my Mama) and Mattie decided to go down to the pond and play. They didn't get in the pond; they just stood on the bank and threw sticks in the water. They didn't throw the sticks too far out, just far enough so they could reach in the water and retrieve them.

Mattie had thrown her stick in and was trying hard to get it back, but it was just out of her reach and she fell in. Mary, not knowing what to do, went home and walked in the house but didn't say anything. The look on her face got the older children's attention. Louis, John, Bessie, Sis, Nay, and Gabby were sitting around talking when Louis looked up and saw the expression on Mary's face. Louis knew something was wrong and he asked, "Where is Mattie?" Mary replied, "She fell in the water." Louis jumped up and ran to the pond with all the other children behind him. When he arrived at the pond, Mattie was nowhere to be seen, she was at the bottom of the pond. Louis dove in the pond and swam to the bottom and when he emerged, he had Mattie in his arms. Mattie was still alive only by God's grace and mercy. Momole had no idea about the things the children would do when she left home. The children gave new meaning to, "When Mama's away, the children will play."

Momole had to work hard to make ends meet to feed her family. Even after she had a baby and was having difficulty getting around, she would sit in her rocking chair and tell the children how to cook and clean. As soon as she was able, she was back in the cotton fields. She knew her children had to eat and sitting around wasn't going to do it. Momole use to mail order her chickens from a catalog. The mailman would deliver a crate full of small chickens. She raised them so they could have chickens to fry and eggs to eat.

Torturing and sometimes even killing a chicken or two were another form of mischief some of the children got into. The children would wait until Momole had a lot of chickens before they messed with them. This way, Momole would have a hard time telling if one of the chickens were missing. Some of the children did cruel things to the chickens. For instance, stick corn cobs in the chickens' behinds and then watch to see if they could walk. If the chickens couldn't walk, the children would then take the cobs out. If one of the chickens accidently died during these escapades, they buried the chicken so Momole wouldn't know.

Mattie, James, and Stine were the youngest of the bunch at this time, and they picked up the bad habits of their older siblings. Stine and James would get sticks and knock the little chicks out. As soon as the chickens were unconscious, they picked them up and blew in the chickens' mouths to bring them back to life. This worked sometimes but not all the time. The younger children were only imitating the things they had seen some of the older children do. They got away with doing these things for a while, but it soon caught up with them.

Momole had just gotten another order of chicks. Right after Momole left for work, Gabby's mischievous wheels started turning. He came up with a scheme to trick Stine. Gabby placed the baby chicks in a Kroger sack and convinced Stine to take the chickens around in a circle over her head. He told Stine if she did this, it would make more baby chicks. Stine eagerly did as she was told, anticipating more chickens. She stopped swinging the chicks around and eagerly began to open the bag, and to her surprise the little chicks were dead. Stine's heart dropped as she looked at the chicks' lifeless bodies. After the older children found out about the chicks, the thought that passed through their minds was, *Mama is going to kill us when she finds out her chicks are dead.* Will and Stine had killed too many of Momole's chicks to hide. Sure enough, when Momole came home and found out that the chickens were dead, she hit the roof and grabbed her gun. All the older children took off running for their lives. They ran to a nearby field and ducked down and hid in the tall weeds. Momole came out of the house looking for the children with the gun in her hands, but nobody was in sight. This didn't slow her down. She took aim at the field and fired the gun. She may not have known exactly where the children were, but she knew they were out there. She wanted them to know she meant business. The children were too scared to come out of the field, so they stayed until dark, waiting for Momole to cool down. After firing a few more shots at the field, she went in the house.

When Cooter came home and found out all that had taken place, he called the children out of the field to come in the house. Momole might have been calm enough not to shoot them, but she was still steamed up enough to give them a lashing they would not forget. When she got ready to give a lashing to the children, it was with whatever she could lay her hands on at that time -- piece of wood, belt, extension cord, etc. The children might not have liked the punishments Momole handed out, but it still didn't stop them from getting into more mischief.

Momole moved on to Burgess land not to long after marrying Cooter. Burgess had a son named Little Burgess. Nay and Gabby went to their house every day to play with Little Burgess. Well, they got this bright idea and built a fire in the yard, and when they got through building the fire, Gabby and Little Burgess began baiting Nay. They told Nay, "You're Superman and you can jump over the fire without getting burnt."

After a while, Nay believed what they were saying and got up enough nerve to jump over the fire. Nay backed away from the fire to get a running start. He ran toward the fire as fast as he could and jumped as high as could. But it was not high enough. His pant leg caught on fire. Gabby and Little Burgess managed to put the fire out on Nay's pants, but not before severe damage was done. Nay had third degree burns to his leg and had to stay in the hospital for months before he recovered.

Momole had put the fear of God in some of the children, but not all of them. Gabby was still up to his old tricks. Momole had a pet cat, and while it was walking across the yard, Gabby took the notion to throw a stick at him. Gabby threw the stick hard, hitting the cat in the head. The cat immediately fell and died from the blow to his head. Gabby realized the cat was dead, but seemed unmoved about the trouble he was in. Gabby strolled into the house as if he had not a care in the world and said, "Bessie, Mama's cat is dead."

Bessie's eyes got big as she went into panic mode. She yelled, "What you mean, Mama's cat is dead?" Gabby replied, "I just hit the cat one time and he ran and fell dead." Bessie said, "Mama's going to kill all of us, you fixing to make me get a whooping for something

I didn't know anything about." Gabby responded, "No, no, no Bessie, a cat got nine lives and by the time Mama gets to that bridge, the cat is going to be alive."

Bessie believed her brother and sat there on the porch, holding Stine and watching the cat, waiting for it to take a breath. After a while, Bessie saw Momole walking toward the house. She yelled in the house, "Gabby, here comes Mama!" Gabby replied, stuttering, "He, he going to be alive when Mama gets here, don't worry about it, you're not going to get a whooping." Momole stepped on the porch and the first thing she saw was her dead cat. With her voice filled with anger, she screamed, "Who killed my cat? Go get me some limbs." Bessie replied, "I ain't going to get any limbs because I didn't do anything."

Momole told her, "Oh yes the [expletive] you are." Momole stormed off the porch and went to the bush and began cutting limbs from the bushes to beat them with. Bessie and Gabby realized they were about to get the beating and took off running toward the cotton field. Momole went in the house to retrieve her gun and shot out across the field a few times. Bessie was fine until a skunk came walking by her. Fear of the critter took precedence over the fear of what Momole would do to her. Bessie started crying and told Gabby, "I'm fixing to go home; something just walked past me." Gabby told her, "If you do, Mama going to kill you." Bessie didn't care about what Gabby was saying; she ran and hid in the outhouse. Gabby stayed in the field and Bessie stayed in the outhouse until she heard Louis' voice inquire about where she was.

Louis said, "Where's Bessie?" Momole replied, "She got her [expletive out there in that cotton field because I'm going to kill their [expletive] for killing my cat." Louis yelled out, "Bessie, come on in this house. Mama ain't going to whoop you." Bessie eagerly came out of her hiding place and went in the house with Louis. Bessie sat near Louis while keeping a watchful eye on Momole.

Momole stared at her and said, "Ain't no sense and you sitting there looking like no [expletive] fool, Louis ain't going to be here every day." Gabby was on the porch listening and was scared to come in the house. Bessie yelled out to Gabby, "You might as well come on in here, cause Mama going to whoop us both together." Louis interjected, "Mama ain't going to whip you because you ain't done anything but sit here and rock this baby all day." Bessie asked,

"Mama, why I got to get a whooping every time somebody else do something wrong? I don't move; I just take care of Stine." Momole replied, "Yes your [expletive] do move and I'm going to whoop all y'all [expletive]." Bessie was able to escape Momole's wrath that day, but Gabby didn't.

Cooter and Momole had been married about four years when they had their first child, Sam (aka Mack). Cooter, being the man that he was, decided to work a few extra hours to help take care of the family needs. He worked for Burgess plowing the fields. It had gotten dark and Cooter was hard at work when he thought he heard a baby crying. So, he turned off the tractor and listened closely. Sure enough, it was a baby crying. This baby's cry was not just any cry to Cooter. He recognized the cry and began to walk toward the distressed screams. When he finally made it to the baby, his fears were confirmed -- it was his son, Mack. Momole, in a fit of anger, had driven out to the field where Cooter was working and left Mack in the field. She had done this because she didn't want him working nights; she wanted him home to help take care of the children in the evening. Cooter picked up Mack and consoled him and came home and never worked nights again. He understood the point Momole was trying to make, even though it was to the extreme. Momole was one of those people who felt, "I can show you better than I can tell you." Momole had gotten older and had her last two children at forty-five years old, and her patience had gotten thinner.

Momole's last two children were Charles and Darnell. She was tired by this time and the older girls took on the responsibility of taking care of the last three children. Mary (my Mama) took care of Mack, Mattie took care of Charles, and Stine took care of Darnell. These were their babies and they were responsible for taking care of their needs while Momole and Cooter worked. Even though they were responsible for taking care of the babies, they were only children themselves. When it came time for Mary and Mattie to bottle feed Sam and Charles, a lot of times they would lay Mack and Charles on the counter while they sat on the floor to suck the milk out of Mack and Charles' bottles. They would eventually get fed, but not before Mary and Mattie had their fill of milk. If Mack was crying, Mattie would look at Mary and say, "Your baby is crying." Mary would get up and take care of Mack. Then in return Mary would do the same thing to Mattie when Charles would cry. Charles was a little harder to take care of than Mack because he was forever having diarrhea. It was almost impossible for Mattie to keep enough clean diapers.

After Mack started walking and talking, Momole made Mack these little suits and dressed him up on the weekends. Mack loved his little suits and always liked to keep his clothes nice and clean. Momole did her shopping and visiting on weekends. This was the time she took all the children with her. The children's hearts were filled with excitement as they all piled in the car. The children knew while they were out they would probably get a piece of candy or some clothes from the second-hand store. They all piled in the car like sardines, stacked on top of one another. At this time, the cars didn't have air conditioning and the only breeze that could be felt was from the car windows being rolled down as you traveled. By the children having to stack on top of one another in the back seat, it was impossible for them not to touch one another.

This situation was hard for Mack to understand. All Mack knew and understood was that the other children were touching his new suit, and this was a problem. Mack would scream and cry because whoever was sitting beside him was touching his suit. While screaming and crying, Mack would pause long enough to say, "Y'all stop touching my suit, y'all messing up my clothes. Mama, tell them not to touch my suit, they are messing up my suit." Like most children, some days they would go the extra mile to irritate Mack even more by deliberately touching him. This was not funny at all to Mack back then -- but they sure got a laugh out of reminiscing about it later when telling me the stories. Mack always has liked his clothes to be clean and neat, and this trait has followed him until this day.

Even though most of the older children had moved away and had their own families to take care of, there were still plenty of children left at the house. Finnie moved his family to Lonoke in 1960. Behind their house was about an acre of land that was for sale. Cooter and Momole bought the land and decided to move the family to town. Finnie helped them purchase a house that was located down Highway 31 and they moved the house to Lonoke in 1965. I was born in 1963, and by the time they moved to Lonoke, Mary (my Mama) had married Curtis. The children who still lived in the house with Cooter and Momole were Will, Mattie, James, Stine, Sam, Charles, and Darnell.

By 1968, Momole had tragically lost three of her boys. This was a horror that no Mama wants to ever experience. This was hard on her, but she managed to keep moving forward with her life. She knew she had the other children to take care of, and this was not the time to give in to life's trials. But the hurt of losing her third child made her fall to her knees and talk to the Lord. She said with tears rolling down her face, "Lord, I don't want to live long enough to see another one of my children die."

Some of the children still living at home were old enough to live on their own but were not financially ready. Momole decided to build a house on the left side of her house. The two houses were separated by her garden. She built the house for her children who wanted to move away from home but not too far from home. The chicken coop and outdoor toilet were just a few feet in front of the garden, but not facing the garden. Mattie and Stine were the first of Momole's children to live in the house that she built. At one point, after Stine got married, she and her husband lived in the house. Charles was the last one of Momole's children to live in the house.

Louis' wife, Amy, and her children lived in the house on the left side of the house that Momole had built. Nay and his family lived in the house on the left side of Amy's house. Sis's house was in front of Nay's house, with about a half-acre of land separating them. Nay and Annie lived in a housing addition that the citizens of Lonoke referred to as 'the hole.' The hole was simply a circle. If you traveled to the hole by road, there was only one way in and one way out. Some of the best times of my life were in the yard of these houses. I'm almost sure most of my cousins and other children in the neighborhood would say the same thing. Momole babysat me and a lot of my cousins. Most of Momole's children were living in Lonoke or near Lonoke; Finnie, Shaffer, Sis, Mary, Mattie, and Stine all lived in Lonoke and Momole was the babysitter for their children most of the time. Sam, Charles, and Darnell were still at home currently. Amy babysat me and my siblings on occasions. Bessie and James lived in Pine Bluff and Jack lived in California.

Momole was the strongest woman I knew. Whatever she set her mind to do, she did it. She didn't wait on anyone who may have been dragging their feet. I never saw Cooter mow or rake the leaves off the yard. Momole always did this and made the children help. I will never forget those long fall days when we raked the leaves. Momole had several trees in her backyard, and in the fall, this caused quite a bit of work. The leaves were so deep they came to our knees. As we raked the leaves, we picked up the pecans that had fallen from the pecan trees. We would eat a few and pocket the rest. There were days that we played more than we worked. Some days, Momole would let us get away with this, and then there were days we had to work more than we played. After raking the leaves in piles, we'd run through them and throw leaves at one another. After Momole felt we had the leaves piled high enough, she burned the leaves and then we spent what seemed like hours running through the smoke and eating pecans. The pecans we didn't eat, we saved so she could roast them in the wood stove.

Momole had built this wooden bench that sat against the wall near the wood stove. The smell of burning oak, roasting pecans, peanuts Cooter roasted, or a pot of brown beans with fat back permeated the air while cooking on that old wood stove. My mouth is watering now as my mind and senses recall the tastes of those pecans. My aunts and uncles would laugh and tell jokes that would make me laugh so hard until I almost peed in my pants. Momole had a black and white TV, but she didn't let us watch it too much. So, we entertained one another. Most of the time we got to watch TV on a Saturday when the westerns came on. Christine would cry every time a western came on and someone got killed. I didn't realize it then, but I do realize now that those were some of the best times of my life. At the end of the day when we went home to our parents, we would smell like burning leaves in the winter and fall months.

The hog pen was behind the house that Stine and Mattie lived in. We helped Momole slop the hogs, feed the dog, cats, rabbits, chickens, and Smokey the horse that Momole had bought for Charles. We also helped her tend to the garden. The garden was one of my favorite places to be. I spent a lot of time in the garden because of the tomatoes. There's nothing like the taste of a juicy, red, meaty, homegrown tomato. I ate them every chance I got. Standing in the middle of my grandmother's garden with a tomato in hand, I would block everything and everyone out as I took my first bite. Nothing else was more important to me than that tomato. Standing there with juice rolling down my chin and arms, I didn't even care about the trouble I would be in when I got caught. A whooping was a small price to pay because my stomach was full of one of the things that I loved most in the world, a garden tomato. When I wasn't eating tomatoes, I was eating persimmons from the tree that stood next to the hog pen. The persimmons were as large as a child's fist. In the summer, we enjoyed the persimmons until the worms took over the tree. These were small things that I didn't think much about at the time, but that was some good eating and my mouth is watering and longing to taste them just one more time.

Like I said previously, my grandmother was a strong woman, and whatever she set her mind to do, she did it. One day she decided that she needed a storage house. So, she went and bought all the materials she needed to build it and had a truckload of dirt delivered to the house. We all called it a smokehouse when she completed it. Finnie, Cooter, and the children who were big enough to help her, helped. We had the pleasure of spreading that pile of dirt over the yard, and of course we played in the dirt more than we worked. This didn't bother Momole because the dirt still got leveled out. I remember looking up, seeing my grandmother on the rooftop of the framed storage house, hammering away. I don't know too many women who had the tenacity my grandmother had. These weren't just any old storage houses-One had three rooms and was good enough to live in. Momole fixed it up with a bed and furniture at one point and we would hang out there on many days. Later, she also built a couple more smokehouses (storage houses).

When we got thirsty, we didn't go in the house to get water; we would all drink from the water hydrant that stood in front of her house. We never gave a thought to all the dogs, cats and other animals that put their mouths on the same hydrant we drank from. It never crossed our minds until we grew up and we didn't get sick or die from it.

Momole's house was a little distance from the road. We had to walk through a path that was in front of her house to get to Brown Street, which was one of the main streets on our side of town. There were several trees and tall grass along this path and a fence that separated the path from her land. My grandmother was one of the last people in town to have an outdoor toilet, and she lived in the city limits. She had an indoor toilet, but I don't remember being given permission to use it but twice.

Most of my fun was had with Charles and Darnell. Mack was older and involved with sports and the girls. I spent what seemed like hours trying to get on Charles' horse, Smoky. I would run and jump on the horse, only to land on the other side. Mattie started calling me

Annie Oakley. I eventually got it right and rode until I got tired or the horse bucked me off.

Mattie and Stine had gotten married and moved away from home. Mattie left her first two children, Kendrick and Katrina, with Momole, and Stine left her firstborn son. A lot of my other cousins and I spent a lot of time with Momole because she was our babysitter. While we were at Momole's house, it didn't take long before her yard would be filled with our cousins and friends. We would play until our hearts were content. Around about lunchtime, we would all gather on the floor on the front porch, waiting for lunch. It wouldn't be anything elaborate, but just enough to get us through the day until our parents picked us up. I was all right with the days that Momole fed us potted meat, crackers or lunch meat. But the days we had to eat Vienna sausages and crackers were the worst. I hated Vienna's, but I didn't dare tell Momole that. I hurried and gulped down a couple of them just to say I ate. Another reason I didn't complain was because I knew we would get a cool pop or ice cream cone for dessert. In the summertime, Momole sold frozen Kool Aid in a cup and ice cream cones to the neighborhood children and grownups. The cool pop or ice cream cone always made eating Vienna's worth it.

Momole babysat so many of us, she needed a little help sometimes with the smaller children. Charlie (aka Monk) would come over to help her babysit. Monk was a kind-hearted, loving person. But he stood out because of his disability, and sometimes the younger and older children would tease him and give him a hard time. Monk's right hand and foot were withered from birth and this caused him to walk on the side of his foot, which caused him to limp. He held his right arm and hand near his body and had to manually move it to different positions. Monk's disability didn't stop him from rocking those babies. When one of the children was crying, Monk rocked whoever was crying while Momole took care of the rest of the children.

Cooter didn't like Monk hanging around all the time. People in the neighborhood knew about Momole's jealousy, but they didn't realize that Cooter was just as jealous as she was. Cooter accused Momole of having a relationship with Monk. She explained to him tirelessly that Monk was just helping with the children. Besides, Monk's girlfriend, Malva Lee, lived in the house in front of Momole. This still didn't soothe Cooter, but he knew she needed the help with the children, so he let it go.

Monk spent most of his days between Malva Lee's house and Momole's house. Monk and Malva Lee would sit on the front porch of her house watching time and people pass by. Occasionally they would steal a kiss. Whenever we caught them kissing, we would tease them for most of the day. All the children playing in the yard would start singing, "Monk and Malva Lee sitting in a tree, K I S S I N G." Before we could get the rest of the song out of our mouths, Monk would jump to his feet and chase us. We would scream and run for a while, knowing that he couldn't catch us. He would do this until he got tired. There would be days that Malva Lee would come over with Monk and help Momole babysit. Malva Lee always had to be on the lookout when she came, because Momole had this dog named Shorty that would always sneak up behind her and try to bite her. One day he was successful. After that, Malva Lee was always on the lookout whenever she came to Momole's house. Shorty never barked at her; he just would sneak up behind her before she knew he was there.

There were days that Momole's jealousy of Cooter got the best of her and she would load all of us in the car and we would follow Cooter to work. When it came time for him to take his lunch break, she would go to his job and follow him to the store. Momole would sit in the car and watch Cooter sit outside, eating a banana, banana caramel candy, and drinking a Barge banana soda and whatever else he bought. Cooter would get back in his car and go to work, with Momole following close behind. We would go back home, and when it was time for Cooter to get off work, Momole would load us up again and follow Cooter home from his job. I didn't understand, as a child, why she did this. After I got grown and was told about her father and the two women he had in the house with her Mama, I understood. Momole had watched her Mama share their father with two other women and she had no intention of sharing her man with anyone if she could help it. She may have taken it to the extreme, but the situation she grew up in was extreme.

A lot of people have told me down through the years that I was a born hustler. I even had one of the missionaries from my church to tell me, "Girl, I believe you can sell boiled water." Well, I believe I came about this honestly. One of my fondest memories of my grandmother is of her selling ice cream cones, cool pops, pickles, and pickled eggs in the summertime. This would draw most of the children and grown-ups in the neighborhood to her house. The backyard would be full of young men playing basketball. The presence of the young men would draw a lot of the older girls to watch them play.

The younger children would be playing games like Red Rover, a game with two teams facing one another and team members holding one another's hands as tight as they could. One of the teams would start chanting, "Red Rover, Red Rover send Jackie right over." I would run as fast I could to try to break the other team's grip. If I broke the grip, I joined their team. If I didn't, I was out. This went on until one of the teams had no one left. We played croquet or we would use one of Momole quilts to toss one of the children in the air as high as we could. There would be times that the person being tossed in the air would miss the quilt. That was our cue to stop the game. These were simple games that kept us occupied and having fun.

We got along most of the time. If trouble started, Charles would always be in the middle of it. Charles would sooner or later get in an altercation with someone and start a fight. He hated to lose. This would be the end for basketball playing for the day. Momole always took Charles' side, whether he was right or wrong. She would make everyone go home. But they always came back the next day, knowing how the day would end.

Then there were those lazy days that we'd make pallets under the trees with the quilted blankets. I would lie there under trees, looking at the clouds in the sky, trying to make out the figure that the clouds had formed. Sometimes I would fall asleep watching the clouds and enjoying an occasional breeze, without a care in the world.

I don't think anything could have topped the days that Momole decided to kill one of the hogs. It was a grand experience. Momole would let the hog out of the pen and we would chase it and ride the pig while they got things ready. I remember these big black pots sitting on an open fire. One filled with cooking oil and the other with boiling water. They were sitting next to the hog pen. After a while, we would hear Momole holler, "Y'all get back!" We all knew what this meant.

As soon as everyone was clear of the hog, she would raise the shotgun with a careful aim and shoot the hog. It would only take one shot and down he went. We stood back and watched as the dark red blood poured out of the hog. The men would come get the hog and string him upside down on the tree near the hog pen and boiling pots. We continued playing as they worked. My favorite part of the hog at that time was the skins. Momole placed the hog skins in a big paper bag after they had cooled off. She would set the bag on the countertop in the kitchen. We would eat those skins for days. Every time we walked by that greasy paper bag; we would grab a handful of hog skins. They were seasoned to perfection and the fat part would just melt in your mouth. The taste of those fresh hog skins was second to none. The chitterlings were also a treat. Fresh hog guts don't smell good while they're cooking, but they sure taste good if you can just get past the smell. Food doesn't taste like it used to.

When I went home, we ate eggs from the store, but when I was at Momole's house we went to the chicken coop to get eggs right out of the chicken's nest. The eggs were white or brown. When you cracked the brown eggs, they had this dark yellow yolk. The egg taste and smell were strong. Most people couldn't stomach a real egg this day and time because they have become accustomed to the store-bought eggs.

Being at Momole's house in the wintertime was just as fun as being there in the summertime. I used to follow Cooter outside on those cold winter days to watch him chop wood. Darnell and I would bundle up together against the fence, trying to keep warm. We'd laugh and play while watching Cooter chop wood. Some days he would even let me try to split a log or two. Sometimes we would tie Charles' horse to the post near where we would chop wood. Darnell and I followed Cooter outside as usual. Charles' horse was tied to the fence post. Darnell and I sat down against the fence, laughing and talking. I don't know what spooked the horse, but it began to kick and buck. The first kick hit me in my mouth. The pain was excruciating, but not so bad that I didn't move out of harm's way, screaming and crying. I had a big lip for a few days, and I had learned a lesson. I never sat behind that horse again.

Strong and determined, Momole faced life's ups and downs head on. She struggled most of her life, but God brought her though. Momole didn't care too much for white people. Oh, she never disrespected anybody and always communicated well with them if they didn't make her mad. But she didn't truly trust white people. I always wondered why, but I came to understand why as I heard some of the things she had to endure as a young black woman coming up in the South. Most parents and grandparents, when they rock their children to sleep, they would sing "Go to Sleep Little Baby," but Momole sang another song to me while she rocked me to sleep.

"What you gonna do when the well runs dry, um hum, hum? What you gonna do when the well runs dry, um hum, hum? Gonna sit on the fence and watch the white folks die, die, die, die, die, die, die."

I didn't understand what this song was all about until I was older, and by that time some of her struggle had become my struggle. However, I didn't understand fully what the struggle was all about.

Most little girls get the enjoyment of playing with dolls while growing up. Momole didn't get to enjoy this part of her childhood for long. She had to grow up quicker than any child should have to. She was a child having to be a grown-up. I believe therefore this was why she collected so many dolls in her adult years. For years, I watched her collect dolls. Every Saturday or Sunday morning, she would drive to Pine Bluff, to a flea market, or the Goodwill in North Little Rock. Momole went to these places hunting for one thing, and that was dolls. My cousins and I would load up in the back seat of the car, hoping in our hearts that we might get a toy or some type of clothing. Cooter and Momole loaded up in the front seat. The heat from the long summer days was stifling, but we didn't care; the reward would be worth the trip. We never knew the direction we would be going, but we were just glad to be moving. All the windows would be down and the breeze from the window was hot, but it felt a lot better than sitting still. When we went to North Little Rock to the Goodwill, most of the time Cooter stayed in the car. He would park the car under the shade tree and open all the doors. I hated this, because sometimes Momole would make us stay in the car with him until she got through shopping. Momole would probably be in the store for about thirty minutes, but the heat made it seem like a lifetime. So, I was glad when Cooter didn't come with us because she would have to take us in the store with her.

The store and booth owners were used to Momole coming and looking for dolls. Some of them would even save dolls for her. They would say to her, "Vie, I have a surprise for you." The clerk would pull this doll out that they had been saving for her and Momole's eyes would light up and this crooked, unforgettable smile would stretch across her face. My cousins and I were just as excited and pleased as she was, as we looked up at the doll in her hand, desiring to play with it. But we all knew that this would never happen. Sometimes the flea market personnel would give her the dolls and not even charge her for them. After Momole got her dolls, we would look around a little longer and she would buy us all a little trinket, but never a doll. We had gotten used to this and didn't mind. We were just glad to get whatever she bought us, whether it fit or not. There were several times we got shoes that were too small for us, but we would squeeze them on our feet anyway. Carla and I laughed as we talked about the time Momole bought Phanie these too-little shoes. Phanie wore the shoes proudly; she walked down Brown Street on her tiptoes like she was stepping on thumb tacks. The shoes may have looked good, but the expression on her face let us know they didn't feel good. Phanie wore the shoes a few days, but soon realized she couldn't take the pain anymore.

Momole took the dolls home and put them all in this one bedroom. There was a sewing machine in this room, and she would go in there for hours, sewing clothes for these dolls. The dolls were all sizes, shapes, and had different functions. Some talked, walked, wet themselves, and some just stood there or lay there. As a little girl, all I wanted to do was play with Momole's dolls, but we were not allowed to. When Momole died, there were over a hundred dolls in this room lined up along the walls, bed and floor. Now that I'm grown, I understand what the room was all about. This was Momole's retreat to the childhood she never had.

The years seemed to fly by, and now all Momole's children were grown and gone. They were all caring for their own families. Momole and Cooter were now babysitting Darnell's children from time to time. The last of her grandchildren she babysat was Darnell's son and daughters.

Cooter and Momole had been married forty-three years before she passed away from ovarian cancer. God heard and honored Momole's request not to see another one of her children die, and she never buried another child. The early part of their marriage was rocky, but they held on. Their later years were much easier, and they had gotten comfortable with one another. They were like an old pair of shoes that were too tight in the beginning, but as time passed the shoes became more comfortable and now those shoes were old faithful. Cooter lived several years after Momole died and he was eighty-nine years old when the Lord called him home. Mattie had gotten some of us together to go see him on his eighty-ninth birthday. The mobile home he lived in was too small to hold all of us, so we celebrated in his front yard. I remember him saying, "I'm old now and I probably won't see another birthday." I responded by saying, "Cooter, you'll be around many more years." Cooter was right -- he didn't make it to his ninetieth birthday.

His grandson, James Jones got a chance to say something at his funeral. He talked about the good man who took on the responsibility of a woman and her thirteen children. As James stood there and reflected over the past, he shook his head and said, "What a man, what a man, what a mighty good man." Then he went on to say, "He was a better man than I am." Cooter called James "Rocky" whenever he saw him. The next words out of Cooter's mouth would always be, "Where Betty Jean at?" This was James's oldest sister. We all laughed as James talked about the only grandpa he knew. It was hard to believe that the patriarchs of our family were gone. Momole and Cooter may be gone, but they will never be forgotten.

Chapter Ten

Momole's Children

All Momole's children have a story they could tell. But I wanted to go into more details about the first seven children who grew up with her, and a few from her second set of children. Momole was a child having children at thirteen years old. She fought and struggled to make her way in this world, and she made it the best way she knew how. She did what it took to take care of her children. The children who are still living are now grown, making their own way in this world and taking care of their own families. Momole's first set of children father was in and out of their lives. The only adult men they had to look up to and follow were their mom's brothers, Sid (aka Fox), Albert (aka Fugga), West, Johnny, and George. Most of Momole's first set of children followed in their footsteps -- drinking, gambling, and fighting, and this was what the Harris's were best known for.

Freddie Harris

Freddie was Momole's firstborn, and he had a bit of a mean streak that didn't get any better as he got older. He and Momole would even fight like cats and dogs. Freddie, Jack, Louis, and John (aka Shaffer) finally started driving, and took turns driving Momole's old '49 Chevrolet. Freddie drove the car the most and he made sure that it stayed this way. Whenever Freddie came home with Momole's car, he would disconnect a part of the car and this kept it from running. This would frustrate his brothers at first because they couldn't figure out why the car wouldn't start. Their frustration soon turned to anger when they figured out that Freddie was behind the car not starting. Freddie wasn't concerned about what anyone thought about him. He just wanted the car to be there whenever he got ready to go party, or to see the young lady who had captured his heart.

Sennie Mae Williams was the young lady who had captured his heart and soon became his wife. Sennie Mae had one child before she and Freddie were married, but she soon gave birth to her second child, Stanley. This was Momole's first grandchild and they eventually had four more children. When the children or anyone talked about Freddie, there were no pleasant memories. They didn't remember him spending a lot of time with them, and he wasn't an affectionate man. There was no hugging or kissing or 'I love you.'

Sennie Mae Harris, Freddie's wife

When Freddie was home, he was verbally and physically abusive to Sennie Mae, and all of this was done in front of the children. Freddie was an angry man and it seemed as if he was mad at the world all the time. He was abusive to his family even when he was sober, but more so when he was drinking. Whenever Freddie would drink in excess, Sennie Mae knew she had to be careful about whatever she said or did. The least little irritation Freddie might feel led to an argument and the argument led to her getting beaten. A couple of times, Sennie Mae got enough nerve to leave Freddie. She escaped to her parents' house, hoping to find refuge under the one roof where she had felt safe for so many years. Sennie Mae was barely at her parents' house long enough to tell them of her plight before her father loaded them up and took them back to Freddie. Sennie Mae had no one and nowhere else to turn to, and felt her only option was to stay with Freddie.

You would think you could at least have a little peace when Freddie and his family went to dinner at Mama's house, but this was not the case. It was even more chaos. Before the visit was over, the entire family would end up fighting. Freddie would be cursing Momole out and she'd be cursing him out while chasing him with a butcher knife. Sennie Mae's nerves were worn to a frazzle as she sat there shaking, because she knew the fight was not going to end there. It would continue when they got home.

The children not only saw all of this, but there were times that they were the victims of this abuse. At the age of five years old, Patricia recalls Freddie beating her until her nose would bleed. Sennie Mae felt helpless as she begged Freddie to stop beating their daughter, but it was like talking to a brick wall. Patricia thought this was a normal way of life. So, while she was at school, the teacher asked the class what they wanted to be when they grew up. One by one the children answered her questions. One would say a nurse, a police officer, a doctor and a teacher. But when it came Patricia's time to answer the questions, she said, "I want to be a wife, have a lot of kids and have a husband that beats me." When the other children laughed, Patricia felt shame, but didn't realize what she had said wrong. The teacher was in shock and questioned Patricia about the answer she gave. Patricia didn't really realize that this was abnormal until that day.

Living under these circumstances got the best of Sennie Mae. She was a nervous wreck in and out of Freddie's presence. Sores broke out on her legs that wouldn't heal. When she went to the doctor, he advised her to leave Freddie. Sennie Mae heard what the doctor told her, but she didn't have the strength to leave. Things had gotten so bad, she had a nervous breakdown twice and had to be admitted into a mental institution. She eventually got better and went back home to her family, but nothing had changed.

Freddie bought himself a 1956 Bellaire, green and white, and he was proud of his new car. Sennie Mae very seldom got to drive it and was nervous when she did. One day while driving Freddie's car, she got stuck in the mud. Fear gripped her heart as she desperately pushed the gas pedal and prayed for the car to come out of the mud. The children were in the car with her, and as small as they were, Sennie Mae made them get out of the car to help push the car out of the mud. All Sennie Mae could think about was what Freddie was going to do to her. The children scrambled around picking off leaves, rocks, and sticks to go under the tires of the car to make the car gain traction to get out of the mud. It's amazing the strength that fear gave her and the children in this situation. If only it had given her the strength to leave. They finally got the car out of the mud.

Freddie having easy access to all the moonshine (hooch) he wanted didn't help matters. Sometimes he would sneak in and take his Uncle Louis Sutton's (husband of Momole's sister, Susie) hooch. Freddie would get so drunk until he just lay in his Uncle Louis' yard after getting his fill of moonshine. Louis and Susie would see him lying in the back yard many days, but they never bothered him. They knew he would sleep it off sooner or later and move on to his next venture.

There was a fight in every bottle Freddie drank. That was the main problem with him drinking; the drinking made an already mean person worse. It made him throw any caution that he might have had to the wind and do whatever came to his mind. The alcohol made him meaner than a junkyard dog. Not only did Freddie love to drink, he also was a lover of gambling. His drinking coupled with losing his money was like throwing gasoline on an already out-of-control fire. Unfortunately, there came a weekend that his love for both vices changed his life and his love ones' lives forever. He got into one of his drunken weekend brawls while gambling with an acquaintance, Sammy. Freddie was losing and this didn't sit well with him. He didn't like the fact that things were not falling in his favor. So, as usual the fussing, cussing, and fighting began. As things heated up, Sammy pulled out his pocketknife and put it to Freddie's throat and threatened to kill him. Freddie was drunk, but not too drunk to realize that the odds were against him in that moment. The altercation ended with no one hurt, but Freddie's pride and ego had been bruised. He was angry enough to spit bullets and refused to let it go. In a drunken rage, talking to himself, he jumped into his car and headed home to get his gun. Freddie was drunk and speeding down the highway toward his house with one thing on his mind.

    Sennie Mae was startled as Freddie burst through the door yelling, "Where's my gun? I'm going to kill that nigga." Sennie Mae tried to calm him down as he staggered back and forth, ranting and raving about the knife that had been pulled on him and the money that he had lost. The children were standing around the wooden stove, trying to keep warm when their father pulled out his penis to urinate. He was so drunk; he missed the container he was trying to urinate in and urinated all over them. Sennie Mae was unable to calm Freddie down, and when he got his pistol, she left him alone. Fear gripped her heart as flashes of past abuse she had suffered at Freddie's hand crossed her mind. Freddie began shooting the pistol in the air before he got into his car. Sennie Mae realized there was nothing she could do to stop her husband from leaving when she heard the squealing tires.

    With tires squealing, he was on a mission to take someone's life. But little did he know that his own fate had been sealed and the time he had left in this world was not long. Freddie entered a curve that was known as 'dead man's curve' at a high rate of speed and lost control of his car. The car flipped four times before coming to a stop. He was taken to the hospital, badly hurt. There was a hole in his head and several other things wrong. When Sennie Mae went to see him, Freddie was very apologetic for the way he had treated her all those years. He asked for her forgiveness. Freddie recognized Sennie Mae the first day she went to see him and was very aware of what had happened. But the next day she went to see him, he didn't even know who she was. He called her Mama, because he thought she was Momole. Freddie's head wound got infected and he lived about a week after the wreck. Freddie was thirty years old and it was 1962 when his life ended so abruptly. He left a wife and six children behind, and his youngest daughter, Dorine, never knew her father. As the children grew older, the longing and void of not having their father only grew bigger. To make things even worse, there were no pictures of Freddie to be found.

Sennie Mae eventually got on with her life, remarried and had more children. She became a pastor over a church in Muskogee, OK. She was well known and loved by many. Patricia and Stanley talked about the awesome work she did for the Lord. Patricia also talked about some of the people God surrounded her with in her ministry. A lot of the people were murderers, rapists, child molesters, wife abusers, and other violent people. The very people who had done things that seemed unforgivable and unimaginable, Sennie Mae loved and led them to the God who forgives even when man won't. God had put a special ministry down in Sennie Mae. Not everyone is equipped to do the type of work she did for the Lord. It takes a person with a forgiving heart to do this, and this was the heart God had placed in her.

The things Patricia remembered about her daddy affected her life for years to come. After she was grown, she attracted men who were just like her father. If they weren't beating her, she was fighting them. She had grown up to be just what she said she wanted to be, minus a whole lot of children. Patricia was so angry and didn't understand why she was like she was. She was so angry, she just wanted to kill. One guy she was with hit her in the head so hard, it was several days before she knew who she was or who he was.

For years, her life spiraled out of control down the wrong path. Patricia finally came to the end of herself and trouble had driven her to her knees. She began to talk to the God her Mama had introduced her to so many years ago. Patricia told God she was tired of the way things were and she wanted a better life for her son. She was tired of the fussing, cussing, and fighting. When she got off her knees, she had made up her mind not to take the same path. She stayed away from men who wanted to argue, fuss, and cuss. There are some things only God can give you the strength to change and let go.

Whenever Patricia came to Lonoke, she always went to see Momole. She thought Momole didn't like her because she never showed any affection towards her. Momole never really held much of a conversation with her while she was there. About six o'clock in the evening, Momole would tell her she had to go because she was going to bed. After I heard these stories, I explained to her that Momole was like that with everyone. She was not the kissing, hugging, and 'I love you' type of person, but she loved her family in her own way.

Jack, aka Big Jack

Upon the death of his father, Jack Harris, Momole's second-born child was given part of the responsibility to help provide for his Mama and younger siblings at a very young age. Jack loved to drink and party, and when he wasn't doing this, in his spare time he was playing horseshoes, singing, or making some contraption he could play music with. He was pretty good at the horseshoes and there weren't too many people in the neighborhood who could beat him. Singing and making music was what he loved the most. He loved it so much, whenever he got ready to do some serious singing, he would make a guitar out of whatever he could find. When Jack had a tune, he had to get it out. Doing it without music was not an option. Jack grabbed a hammer and went to work. He nailed two nails in a tree, tied some thin wire around those nails and hooked the wire to

Jack & Pearlie Mae

two bottles. Jack's makeshift guitar might not have been fancy, but it made the noise he needed to get out the tune he had ringing in his soul. Jack would pick that makeshift guitar and sing until his heart was content. Jack wasn't quite as bad as Freddie, but he loved to drink that hooch and gamble. Yes, he would fight, too, when he deemed it necessary.

After working all week long in the cotton fields, Jack was glad to see the weekend. He would catch the first ride he could get going to England, Arkansas to gamble and get his 'drink on.' Once he made it to England, he headed straight to Buster Dodson's house. Buster's house was the place to be on the weekends. Jack had just got paid and was ready to let the good times roll. He would drink that hooch, gamble and party all night long. If he couldn't catch a ride, he would strike out walking and sooner or later a ride would come along. Sometimes the night ended with an altercation that landed Jack in jail a time or two. But then there were a few times that he didn't do anything, and it landed him in jail.

One of these times, he was attending a baseball game. He rode to the game with his friend, Essie Shepherd. When they arrived, one of the first persons he saw was his Uncle Fox and he was so drunk he was staggering all over the place and talking loudly. Fox talked so much noise until he finally got under someone's skin. This argument led to a physical fight and Uncle Fox reached into his pocket and hit the man in his head with his brass knuckles. After the man fell to the ground, Fox threw the brass knuckles away in the grass. Jack knew Fox would be in a lot of trouble once the police showed up, so he suggested his uncle get in his car and go home. Fox seemed to have taken Jack's advice and headed to his car, but he didn't go quietly. He cursed and talked loudly all the way to the car. When he got to the car, he was so drunk he couldn't get the key in the lock to open the door. When Jack looked up, Fox was on his way back to the field, talking loud and staggering. After saying a few words, he turned and went back to his car, but before he could get in the car, he went back to the field in the same manner he had left. Jack realized there was nothing he could do to deter his uncle, so he jumped on the back of his friend Essie's truck and they left the ball field.

Jack didn't leave soon enough. The police caught up with them and took Jack to jail. A lady known as the neighborhood snitcher had lied and told the police that Jack had a gun at the baseball field.

Jack didn't have a gun, but he had a pocketknife. The police put Jack and Fox in the same cell. Fox tried to tell the police that Jack didn't do anything, but they wouldn't listen. Jack and Uncle Fox worked for the same man, Mr. Riley. Thanks to Mr. Riley, they didn't stay in jail long. Mr. Riley got the news that Jack, and Uncle Fox were in jail, and he paid the jailers a visit. He wasn't concerned about what they had done; all he wanted was for them to be at work on Monday morning. Mr. Riley walked in the police station and went up to the desk, and said, "Y'all have to let Fox and Jack out of jail by Monday morning, they have to go to work." Just as Mr. Riley turned to walk out, he looked back at the policemen and said, "If y'all don't let them out, y'all going to be in trouble." Sure, enough when Monday morning came, they were out of jail and back at work.

Jack continued to go out and gamble and drink with his friends on the weekend. This weekend, he was with his brother, Louis. Louis had gotten into an altercation with a young man called Preacher Dodson. He wasn't a preacher at the time; everyone just called him this because he looked like a preacher. Well, Louis had gotten the best of Preacher Dodson and this made him mad. So, while Dodson was gambling with Jack, he talked crazy to Jack. Jack looked at him and said, "Don't be talking to me, this is between you and Louis." Dodson didn't listen and persisted on giving Jack a hard time. He took it as long as he could, but the situation soon got the best of him. He balled up his fist, drew his arm back, and hit Dodson with all his might. His feet left the floor and he landed flat on his back. He was out cold for a while, and for a moment Jack didn't know whether he was dead or alive. Fear gripped his heart before finding out that Dodson was going to be okay. Jack knew he couldn't continue living the way he was living. He was growing tired and was ready for a change, but the change didn't come at that time.

Growing tired of running around and the life he was living, Jack began to think about settling down. The young lady who had captured his heart was Pearlie Mae Bryant, but there were a few problems with this situation. Jack was friends with Thoriace (Pearlie Mae's brother) and he knew Jack well. Jack was a little nervous about asking for Pearlie Mae's hand in marriage, so he talked to Thoriace about it before going to their father. He told Thoriace, "I think I'm going to pop the question." Thoriace looked at Jack and told him, "If you do, Daddy going to pop you." This didn't scare him off because the love he had for Pearlie Mae in his heart left no room for fear. Thoriace had a couple of concerns about Jack marrying his sister. He was a lot older than Pearlie Mae; she was only sixteen and Jack was no choir boy. He took the chance, not knowing what would happen, and went and asked Pearlie Mae's father for her hand in marriage. Mr. Bryant gave Jack his blessing.

Once Jack made up his mind to make Pearlie Mae his wife, he knew he had to have money to put his plan into action. So, Jack went to the only person he knew would have money for him to borrow. He went to Mr. Riley, his boss and said, "Mr. Riley, I need to borrow twenty dollars." Mr. Riley started laughing and asked, "Why you want to borrow twenty dollars?" Jack replied, "I'm going to get married." Mr. Riley simply said, "Get married, okay then." Without any more hesitation, he reached in his pocket and handed Jack twenty dollars. At age twenty-three, Jack proudly marched up the steps of the Lonoke County Courthouse with his bride-to-be, Pearlie Mae Bryant. After he got the marriage license, he paid Judge Hamilton to do the ceremony. Jack and Pearlie Mae left the courthouse and went to the grocery store and bought a loaf of bread and bologna with some of the money they had left. Pearlie Mae's father gave them a cow and some groceries and told them, "I want to help you all on your way. You're on your own now."

Jack and Pearlie Mae went back to the cotton field the next day. Even though their parents were okay with them getting married, they soon found out that everyone wasn't happy for them. As Jack and Pearlie Mae walked in the cotton field, they could hear different ones whispering about their union. Jack listened as he heard someone say, "I don't know why Mr. Bryant let Jack marry Pearlie, he's too old for her and he can't take care of her. All those Harris boys are no good." Black and white people talked bad about their union, but Jack never responded to the things that were being said. He loved his wife and treated her the best he knew how.

Jack and Pearlie Mae continued to go to the field, but there were a lot of days Pearlie Mae was not able to work because she was sick. On those days, she went to Jack and with a slow, southern twang said, "Jack, my head hurts." Jack told her, "You go on to the house and I'll pick enough cotton for us both." Pearlie Mae did as Jack had ordered and went home. Jack did as he promised and would pick 300 pounds of cotton a day. Pearlie eventually stopped coming to the field and never returned to the workforce. Jack picked cotton or plowed the fields until it was lunch and supper time. Jack wouldn't say a word to anyone, and when lunch or supper time came, he just headed for his house. Everyone around him was trying to figure out how he knew when it was quitting time to go eat. They never figured it out and Jack never told them. When it was time for Jack to come home to eat, Pearlie Mae would hang a diaper on the porch. Jack would look up and see that diaper and head for the house.

Jack knew his life was headed nowhere fast. He needed something or someone to slow him down. He felt the Grim Reaper nipping at his heels even though he was a young man. Before Jack got married, he would often tell his friends that he didn't think he would live to be twenty-three if he didn't stop drinking hooch. After marrying the girl of his dreams, this slowed his pace some, but not completely. The love he had for Pearlie Mae was strong enough to slow Jack down, but it didn't make him quit all of his habits. Pearlie didn't let that worry her. She knew a God with all power, and she continued to pray for her husband.

Jack rode from time to time with some of his friends to go out, but he stopped drinking. God was working on him. One time, he hitched a ride with some friends, and they were headed to England to blow off some steam. Freddie, Pattie Moore, and Junior Miller were some of the young men in the car with him. Everyone was drinking but Jack. The car they were in resembled a hearse and the way Junior was driving, Jack was afraid they were on their way to an early grave. Junior was going eighty miles an hour when he hit the curve just past Henderson Store. Just as they entered the curve, Jack yelled, "Everybody hold on because something is fixing to happen!" The car turned over three times and landed upright on the bank of a ditch, still running. They all survived with a few bumps and bruises and were able to tell the story.

The next day, Jack went to Henderson Store as he often did to play horseshoes for Barge sodas. While Jack stood in the store, the owner was talking to another customer in the store. The store owner said, "I woke my wife up in the middle of the night and told her, honey you know a car done turned over out there?" His wife replied, "It ain't nothing but a carload of niggas and I hope they all got killed." Jack didn't say a word. He just got what he came for and left the store.

Jack and Pearlie Mae prayed to the Lord and asked the Lord to give him strength to quit his ways. God soon gave Jack the strength he had asked for. Jack was singing a new tune and Big Jack was now a gentle giant. The things he used to do; he didn't do them anymore. Jack and Pearlie gave their whole hearts to the Lord. Every opportunity they got; they would tell someone about the goodness of God. Jack and Pearlie Mae witnessed in the cotton fields to friends and family about the love of God. Many of those family members they witnessed to accepted Jesus as their personal Savior and are still saved this day. Some of the family members were a little harder to reach than others, but that didn't stop Jack from trying.

Jack recalled the time when he went to visit his Uncle Fox (Momole's brother Sid) to tell him about Jesus. He approached Fox's house with light feet and a happy heart. Fox was sitting on the porch. Jack started the conversation off with little small talk, but quickly moved on to what he had come for. Jack said, "Uncle Fox, what you going to do when the world catches on fire?" Fox quickly replied, "Run like hell and holler fire, fire, fire!" Jack was serious about his God and didn't find this funny at all. Jack knew this was not the day he was going to get to his Uncle Fox, so he left him alone for the time being.

Thoriace (Pearlie Mae's brother) had moved to California and was trying to get Jack and Pearlie Mae to move there. They were indecisive about moving for a time period. Jack was sharecropping and basically working for slave wages. No matter how many crops he managed to grow, at the end of the season, he never broke even or made a profit, and this was what Thoriace wanted to get him away from, so he would be able to take care of his family.

Thoriace decided to drive back to Arkansas. He made up his mind and said to himself, "I don't know who, but somebody is coming back to California with me." Thoriace knew they could have a better life in California than they were having in the South.

Jack talked with his Mama to let her know he was moving to California, and she was not happy about this. Momole told him, "If you get sick, you're going to be too far away for anyone to get to you." Jack heard what his Mama said, but he chose to do what he thought was best for his family. In 1961, he moved his family to Los Angeles, California. Within the first week, he joined the Greater Good News Church of God in Christ and began construction work with the Local

300 Laborer's Union. His brother-in-law, Thoriace, was the foreman at the construction job and was able to assist Jack in getting hired.

Jack and Pearlie Mae eventually had six children and his family was only second to God. He often reflected on times past growing up in Arkansas and enduring the injustices as far back as when he was a child. In the era of sharecropping, Jack was forced to forego formal education at a very young age. There began the making of a man who would possess enormous strength and character. He passed that down to his children and grandchildren by the lessons he taught and the life he lived. His wisdom surpassed his education by far. He saw to it that his children attended school every day until they graduated, and that they were equipped to become productive citizens and would have a choice whether to endure hard physical labor for a living, as he had done.

Jack was part of an inseparable union bound by God and by the love between him and Pearlie Mae. Really, who says Jack without saying Pearlie Mae, Daddy and Mamma, or Pawpaw and Grandma, Uncle Jack and Aunt Pearlie Mae? They indeed became one when they were joined together in marriage. Their children, grandchildren, and great-grandchildren are the joys of their hearts. On his children's birthdays, even in their later years, he still gave them a dollar for each year. Just last year Jack said, "I may not be able to do this again." After all, the children were getting old and those dollars were adding up.

Each of Jack's children held a special place with him. Velma is his firstborn, Lorenzo his first boy child, Martha was born on the same day as the love of his life, Tanya is and always will be his baby girl, and Jack Jr. was his namesake and youngest son. His daughter, Carolyn, counted it to be the highest honor and the best birthday gift ever that her daddy went to heaven on the anniversary of the day she first met him, fifty-eight years before. On April 28th, Jack's name was written in indelible ink in the Lamb's book of life.

Lorenzo (Jack's son) reminisced about some of the life lessons he learned from his father. Jack Jr. had gotten into a fight with one of the neighborhood boys. After the fight, Jack Jr. went home and prepared to go out. The fight had long since left his mind, but the young man who lost the fight was still angry. He went to some of his friends and talked with them and they decided to go to Jack Jr.'s house and get revenge. When they got to the house, they stood outside, talking loud and cursing, trying to get Jack Jr. to come outside and fight. They didn't realize that Jack Jr. was not at home. Jack finally got tired of the young men being so disrespectful, so he went outside and asked them to get away from his house with all that cursing. Well, instead of leaving, the young man continued cursing, and then he did the unexpected and hit Jack in his mouth. This not only shocked Jack, but the young man realized the mistake he had made and turned and walked off.

Jack sat down on the curve after the young men left and cried. He didn't cry because he was hurt, he cried because of his love for God and thanking God for where He had bought him from. Jack realized that years ago he would have handled the situation so differently. Lorenzo sat on the curve beside his father and listened as he talked. Jack told his son, "I could have seriously hurt that young man and cut him up really bad." Lorenzo knew all too well that his father always carried a pocketknife in his pocket. This was the knife he used when he was at work. Then Jack went on to tell his son, "How would it look for the preacher to be in the streets fighting? All of my witnessing to the neighbors, trying to lead them to the Lord, would be in vain."

Lorenzo understood and respected what his father was saying. There were many life lessons that Lorenzo learned from his father. Lorenzo is a minister now and cherishes those life lessons. He struggles some days to be the man of God that his father not only taught him to be but showed him how to be. So, he holds on no matter what life may bring.

One of the things Jack hated to hear the saints say when he greeted them was, "I'm hanging in there." Jack felt as if God never leaves any of His children hanging. If you're just hanging in there, you are going to fall. So, if you got on, you can hold on. God will come see about you. He never leaves anyone hanging. Jack held on until God called him home.

Billy Louis Harris (aka Louis)

Louis was Momole's third child, and nine months later John (aka Shaffer) was born. Susie (Mu), Momole's sister, was married to Louis Sutton, and at the beginning of their marriage they were having some difficulties having children. Momole was the total opposite; she was conceiving children back to back. When Momole got pregnant with her third child, Susie had a plan to help them both out. Susie wanted to raise the child Momole was pregnant with and name him after her husband, Louis, if it was a boy. With all the struggles Momole was having with her husband coming in and out of her life, she accepted her sister's proposal. After the baby was born, Momole did as she promised and named him Billy Louis Harris.

Louis Sutton was a sharecropper and made and sold hooch (moonshine) on the side. They spoiled Louis by showering him with everything he wanted. Louis S. taught his son how to make a living as a farmer and a few other trades. This knowledge Louis S. passed on to his son gave him the skills to make what was considered good money back then. One of the major problems with this was that Louis S. was not a good steward over his money. The fast life got the better of his heart, and by the time he had started realizing that life was not just about him, it was too late.

When Louis got old enough to work, he lived back and forth between Susie and Momole's house. Susie and her husband spoiled Louis until neither they nor Momole could do anything with him. Susie used to say, "I know he ain't any good, but he still my baby." Louis loved fast living and everything that came along with it. At a young age, he began drinking, gambling, chasing the ladies, and never missed the chance to engage in a good old fight. Louis and his brother, Will (aka Gabby), were a lot alike and would fight at the drop of a hat. Many people feared them because of this. They may have lost a fight or two on occasion, but that was very rare. Louis did whatever he had to do to win the fight: kick, bite, or pick something up to finish the job. There was only one person that could truly give Louis a run for his money in a fight, and that was his brother, Gabby. Louis was the only one of the brothers who could defeat Gabby. They didn't tangle but a few times, but each one of them left the fight with some evidence that they had been in a brawl.

This one fight they had engaged in over God knows what: Gabby grabbed Louis by his testicles and squeezed with all his might. This caused Louis a lot of pain, and all he could think about was what he had to do to loosen Gabby's grip. He hit Gabby with all his might until Gabby finally let go of his testicles. He went home wounded enough to go to the doctor, but he refused to go. It would be years before Louis completely recovered from this fight.

Louis was wild and couldn't be tamed. He finally ran into one young lady who calmed him some but was unable to tame him. Louis stole Amy Gooden's heart at first sight. He loved her also, even though he didn't always show it in his actions. She had fallen in love and soon realized that Louis was not the knight in shining armor she thought he was. But it was too late; Amy had fallen for Louis and had fallen hard. Just as hard as she had fallen for him, her sorrows would be just as great.

Their relationship escalated, and she conceived their first child, Louis Jr., who died at birth. They would never see or feel the joy of watching him grow into a man. Although this was a great hurt and disappointment, it did not discourage them from conceiving their second child, Birtie, who was named after one of Louis' girlfriends. One year after Birtie was born, their son Robert made his way into this world. Louis and Amy were not married at this time and not until nine children later did Louis conclude it was time to do the right thing by his family. Amy had another miscarriage around her fifth pregnancy. She was doing her daily chores when she tripped and fell out the back door while throwing out leftover scraps from previous dinners. Immediately following the fall, excruciating pain surged through her body, taking her breath away. Time seemed to stand still for those moments as Amy gathered the strength to get off the ground. She knew something was terribly wrong. She survived the fall, but the child she was carrying, unfortunately, did not. The children didn't understand what was happening to their Mama while she was miscarrying, but they knew something wasn't right because she stayed in bed crying a lot. When Louis and Amy first started their family, they didn't have a house of their own, so they moved in with Louis and Susie. No matter how many children Amy had, Louis' lifestyle never changed. He kept living the life he loved.

Back then, a lot of the black people who now live in the city limits of Lonoke lived down Highway 31, which is the rural part of Lonoke County. The black people may not have had much, but they made it and they believed in being a help to their neighbors. After the families worked hard all week long in the cotton and corn fields, they were looking for an outlet to relax or burn off some steam. A lot of them would gather at the local bootleggers and gambling houses in the neighborhood. Those who had rides would frequent the nearby juke joints in England. Either way, there was a good time to be had.

The chatter of the people, Blues and R&B music filled the air -- BB King, Jackie Wilson, and Muddy Waters, as people drank, gambled, or held on to their partner dancing in the middle of the living room floor. There was money to be had and money to be given away as the dice were rolled and cards were played. Everyone was trying to forget the turmoil and troubles from the week. Many times, this was where Louis could be found, letting the good times roll while Amy was at home with Susie and Louis S., taking care of their children.

None of the black people who lived in the woods down Highway 31 had electricity at that time. They had coal oil lamps to light their houses, outdoor toilets, and wood stoves for heat and cooking. Life was simple and hard at times. When electricity finally made its way to the homes on Highway 31, Louis S. and Susie were one of the first black families to get a television. The children in the neighborhood would all migrate to Susie's house because of the TV. She didn't turn them away, she just invited them in.

When Susie cooked, she cooked enough for all who were in the house. She didn't have a store-bought table. Her table resembled a spool that held thread. Only this spool was people-sized and left behind by the electric company workers. The spool used to hold the electric wire that had been strung up to give them lights. The table sat in the middle of the floor and the children stood around this table at suppertime and ate. There were no chairs around the table, but the children didn't care; they were glad to be eating. Technology was making its way to the back woods, but there was no running water. Most people had well or pond water. The Bryant's were one of the first families to have running water, and they had a hydrant outside. They were nice enough to let their neighbors fill up their buckets with water to take to their houses. Some of the neighbors would travel a mile or two to carry water back to their houses. In those days,

Aunt Susie's wire spool table

neighbors looked out for one another. No one really had much, but everyone 'made do' with what they had. Times were changing and those who could afford it were changing with the times.

Louis and Amy's family stayed with Susie and Louis S. for quite a spell. But around 1960, Louis and Amy finally moved into their own house. It was a little shotgun house located not too far from Susie's house. The house didn't look like much, but it was home. Louis was a lot like his father, James. Sometimes Louis would leave home and be gone weeks at a time. There were times when he'd come home from a night of partying in a drunken rage. Amy hated and dreaded these times, because they always ended with her being beaten. Birtie, Robert, and the other children who were old enough to remember would lie in their beds with fear in their hearts as they listened to their parents fight and wishing it would stop.

Louis was in and out of their lives, stopping in long enough to get Amy pregnant. Robert, Louis's oldest son, recalls some of the times Louis would come home and stay for a few days. They weren't good times or good memories. The children had to be quiet in the house and couldn't play. When Louis was home, he didn't spend much time interacting with the children. Most of the time he came in the house fussing and cussing, and when he wasn't doing that, he just sat in the corner in his easy chair, unwinding from the day's work or all-night partying.

Many times, Louis and Amy got in an altercation over small things, and this would turn into a big fight. This would lead into an all-out fight. Of course, Amy would lose. Robert felt helpless in these situations. He wanted to save his mom, but he realized he was too small to do anything about the situation. The last time Louis jumped on Amy was in 1966, and Robert's frustrations got the best of him. With all his bottled-up emotions, Robert overcame his fears for that moment in time. He walked up to his father and looked up at him and said, "When I get big, I'm going to get you for what you have done to Mama." Robert disregarded what his father Louis might do to him for speaking his mind. He was a child, in a hopeless situation he could do nothing about for the time being, but he had hope for the future.

Robert, being unable to do anything about the circumstances at that time, developed a relationship with what others would call an imaginary friend. But this friend was not imaginary to Robert, he was very real. His friend was not a helpless child but was grown and big enough to take on anyone who caused Robert trouble. This helped him cope with a lot of things he was going through. Just as Robert finished telling his father what he was going to do to him, his friend told him, "Don't worry about it, I'll take care of him." Louis looked down at his son and told him, "Boy, you got a lot of hell in you and it ain't going to get you far. You can't let your hate for me and wanting to kill me get the best of you. If you do this, you're going to wind up like me." Robert looked at him and asked, "What you mean, I'm going to wind up like you?" Louis replied, "You ain't going to have [expletive] and you ain't going to ever be able to do anything but whoop somebody's [expletive], and that's not good."

Louis and Amy slept in different rooms in the house, but this did not keep the children from coming. After every altercation, they managed to make up and meet up. Louis was not only having babies by Amy, he had other women pregnant at the same time she was pregnant. Some of the children Amy knew about and some she didn't. Although she knew about the other women, she made a conscious decision to stay with Louis.

Louis loved the fast life, but he wasn't afraid of working. He put to use the trades that Louis Sutton taught him. He could build anything, farm, and work on cars, and these trades helped him make a lot of money even for those times. He would work all week and sometimes he came home with $1,200 to $1,500 in a week. That was good money back then. The only problem with that was that he blew a lot of the money he made in the streets, and this caused his family to suffer hard times they shouldn't have. Louis had a good heart, but had his priorities mixed up. If Louis liked you, he would give you the shirt off his back, but he didn't have the same conviction for his family until it was too late. This was one of the biggest things that he and Amy fought about. Their fights started when Amy told him the truth about himself, because he couldn't stand to hear that truth.

One of the things that upset Amy, which she confronted Louis about, was the time he picked up John Jr. (aka Junior, his brother John's son, aka Shaffer). The problem was not with him picking up Junior, the problem was that before he brought him by the house, he took Junior by the store and bought him a toy. Junior had no idea about the trouble that was about to come over the gift he had received. He was excited and played with his new toy until his little heart was content. Louis looked down at Junior with pride and was pleased the boy was pleased with his toy. Louis said to Amy, "See that toy, I bought him that." This upset Amy and she replied, "You mean to tell me that you bought a toy for someone else's child and won't buy any toys for your own kids?" Louis couldn't handle hearing the truth, so he reacted the way he always reacted to most situations, and that was with violence.

Even though Louis made a lot of money, he didn't put much of it on the places where he moved his family. They moved around a lot, from one shotgun house to the next. The houses they lived in were too cold to heat in the winter, and too hot to cool in the summer. They had to move around a lot -- not because Louis couldn't afford to pay the rent, but he refused to pay the rent, or he would get into an altercation with the landlord and this led to them getting evicted from their home. The older children got frustrated about having to always move from place to place. The children never got any notice when they had to move. There were days they came home and got off the school bus like always, thinking they would go in the house and do their normal routine. But when they walked in the house and saw just about all the furniture gone, their little hearts got heavy. The children sat down, waiting, and wondering where they were moving to now. Hungry and tired from a long day at school, they sat wondering when someone would be back to the house to pick them up. Later, rather than sooner, someone always showed up to get the last of the things in the house, and that included the children.

There was a time Louis and Amy were renting a house from Art Lester, Amy's uncle, for $5 a month. After a time, Louis refused to pay the $5, and this refusal eventually led to yet another eviction. He tried to get over or get by with whatever he could. When he was confronted by the person he wronged, he would cuss, fuss, argue and fight if necessary, as though he was in the right. Louis didn't get along with too many people because he always wanted things his way and he would do whatever he had to do to get his way, no matter who it hurt.

Louis had a temper, and on occasions, Robert happened to be on the receiving end of his wrath. He was doing some repairs on his vehicle when he asked Robert to get behind the wheel of the car and push the gas pedal. Robert's foot couldn't reach the gas pedal, but he was doing his best to follow his father's instructions. Louis became frustrated and lost his temper. He came from under the hood of the car and snatched the boy from behind the steering wheel. Robert landed on the ground beside the car. Caught up in his frustration, Louis punched and kicked Robert in his back, all while cursing at him about what he had done wrong. The pain from his father's kicks made every nerve in his body hurt. But that would be nothing in comparison to the emotional trauma he suffered from this incident.

In the last year of Louis's life, the scales came off his eyes and he began to realize how important his family was to him. He had stopped moving his family from place to place and decided to build them a house. He was so excited about building the house and drew the plans on a piece of wood. He not only drew the house, but he added finishing touches such as blue skies, sun and flowers around the house. He had a vision and bought the lumber to complete it.

He also planted a garden with different kinds of vegetables so his family would have plenty to eat. Louis woke Robert up early so they could work in the garden. Robert hated doing this and Louis knew it. Going to the garden with the boy was more than just work for him. This was the time he took to talk to Robert and tried to instill something positive in him. Louis talked to him as they worked in the garden. Robert couldn't appreciate it then and didn't understand. Now that he is grown, he looks back on the conversations that he and his father had and realizes the significance of the things his father was trying to convey.

Louis told Robert, "I know you don't like doing this, so you need to go to school and get your education, so you don't have to do this." He went on to tell him, "When you get grown, get a job, wife and children, take care of your wife and children. If you don't do the things you're supposed to do in life, you're going to have to pay for it. If you don't make any money, you ain't going to have [expletive]. You see how my sisters and brother are right. All we do is what?"

Robert replied, "I don't know what you all do."

Louis answered, "We can't get along and all we do is fight." He wanted Robert to be a better man than he was and had been. So, Louis began to instill in him the things it would to take to be a better man. When Robert did something wrong, Louis took the time to tell him, "Boy, don't do that," and tell him why he shouldn't do it. Robert managed to hold on to some of the good things about his father during all the bad. He realized later in life that his father had a good heart underneath all his struggles.

Robert believed his father wanted to get along with people but didn't know how to. Louis had come to his senses and realized all he had done and the time he had wasted. He was trying to make up for lost time. It was 1967 and Louis was thirty-three years old. He struggled with an infirmity in his body. Sometimes Louis would be working or just around the house and got so dizzy and weak he had to sit down for a while to gather his composure. Sometimes when he had these spells, he passed out. He was afraid to go to the doctor because he was scared, they would tell him he had cancer. What Louis and everyone else around him didn't know was that his time was about to run out.

Shaffer (Louis's brother) filled Robert in on the missing details about his father's death years later. It was a Friday evening in 1967; Louis had just picked up his check. He got in his work truck to go deliver a load of lumber. Just as he went to cross the train tracks, a train hit his truck and dragged it for quite a distance. Louis was still alive, but his body was in bad shape. His neck was broken; his jaw was cut from the front of his mouth all the way back to his neck, and the bottom of his jaw was lying on his neck. He was bleeding internally. Louis died about nine o'clock that night, from massive internal injuries. Robert believes the reason his father didn't see the train coming was because he passed out like he had done several times before.

At the time of the train wreck, Robert was on the school bus headed for home. He heard bells and whistles in his head. After the bells and whistles stopped, his imaginary friend said, "I got him." Robert sat there, wondering what in the world his friend was talking about. The bus finally made it to their stop for them to go home. About three-thirty or four o'clock, Mr. Williams and his wife (Louis's boss) knocked at the door. When Amy answered the door, they informed her that Louis had been in a wreck. The Williamses were kind enough to take Amy to the hospital. When she got to the hospital, she made it to the door of the room Louis was in. Then one of the nurses stopped her and told her she could not go in the room. Amy had to go back to the waiting area and wait for news of her husband's condition. When someone finally came out to tell her some news, it was not good. Louis was gone and she had to go home and tell her children their father would not be coming home again. Amy's youngest child was only a few months old. This was a hard burden and task she had to do, but there was no way around it.

When Robert heard the news, he was numb and didn't feel a thing. All he could think about at that time was how Louis had mistreated his Mama. Robert began thinking about his imaginary friend and wondering, "Is this real?" Lying in his bed one morning, he heard a voice ask, "Do you want to see your friend?" He responded, "Yes." Robert opened his eyes slowly and there stood his imaginary friend. It was a big guy who favored his Uncle Finnie, but he was a lot bigger. Robert didn't tell anyone about this at that time. Even though Robert's father had started to make a change, the anger and bitterness that had built up in his heart against his father for the things he had done had gotten the better of him. All of Louis' hopes and dreams died with him. The lumber he bought to build his family a house laid waste in the backyard for years. For years, the children kept the piece of wood where Louis had drawn their dream house. Occasionally, they looked at the picture on that piece of wood and dreamed about what could have been. For the younger children, this was all they had left of their father, plus the picture their Mama had hanging on the wall.

The children who were old enough to realize what happened were traumatized, and no one thought to ask them how they felt. Amy had just had her last child and was still healing from that. It would be years before the children could forget the image of the man in the coffin who looked nothing like their father. Louis was a light-skinned man, but his body had been through so much, his face was disfigured, and his skin was dark black. That image caused some of the children to have a lot of sleepless nights, but they all eventually moved on the best they knew how.

Robert was now the little man of the house, but Birtie (Louis' oldest daughter) was the boss. Robert thought Birtie was more like her father than any of them. She was stubborn and hardheaded when it came to her obeying what their Mama told her to do. All the children who were old enough had chores to do. Robert and Gwen (Louis's third daughter) got up early and started their chores. They had to wash the white clothes and rinse them twice. Then they hung them on the clothesline. Birtie would lie in the bed until about one o'clock. When she got out of bed, she was faced with doing her chores. She would tell Robert and Gwen, "Y'all going to help me?" When they refused, she started beating them. Robert grinned as he remembered the beatings they got from their sister, Birtie, like it was yesterday.

Robert said, "Boy, that Birtie, she used to beat us like slaves. I used to be so sore from those beatings. She used to beat us until we could hardly walk." He was able to laugh, but it was not funny then. This went on for quite some time until Robert and Gwen put their heads together and started double teaming Birtie. Robert and Gwen came up with different gags to pull on Birtie. Gwen was the mastermind behind the plans and Robert implemented them. They both knew Birtie loved to run and jump in her bed. So, they started putting wood, sticks, and bark from off the trees under her covers. When Birtie ran and jumped in the bed, it would hurt. This worked a few times, but they soon had to come up with another plan.

There was a tire swing in their backyard, and they would all race to get to it when it was time to play. Robert and Gwen outran Birtie most of the time to get to the tire swing first. The tire swing had so much wear and tear, the rope was about to break. So, Robert and Gwen said to one another, "Let's let Birtie have it now." She made it to the tire first and she began to swing, unaware of her siblings' plot. They stood back and watched as Birtie swung higher and higher in the swing. Just when the swing got as high as Birtie could swing, the rope broke. Robert and Gwen took off running into the house and locked the door because they knew Birtie was going to kill them if she caught them.

That plan worked out so well for them, they had to come up with another plan. The next plot Gwen came up with was even more devious than the others. They took hot ashes out of the stove and put them under the chair Birtie was to sit in. She came bouncing into the room and headed straight for the chair they had booby-trapped. When Birtie sat in the chair, it didn't take her long to realize they had gotten her again. With her butt smoking, she jumped out of the chair, screaming and running. Robert and Gwen took off running because they knew once the smoke cleared, they would be in a world of trouble. Birtie soon got the picture and stopped beating them, because she feared what they might have plotted against her.

Amy chose not to marry again, even though she had a few suitors. I asked Amy why she chose to stay with Louis after he had treated her so badly for so many years. She had no answer. Back then, a lot of black women didn't have an education and depended on the men to take care of them. This alone made them put up with things they wouldn't have normally put up with. Down through the years, she gave her heart and soul to God and she raised her children in church. She taught them right from wrong. Whenever one of the children got in trouble or wanted to fight, she would tell them, "Don't be like your father." When they got old enough to drink and go out, she reminded them not to be like their father. All the children are now grown and have their own families. Despite what they have been through, they have managed to go on and do well in life.

Years later, after Amy had got to her golden years, Robert fulfilled her dream of having a new home. He built his Mama a house from the ground up with his own hands. Amy still resides in Lonoke, enjoying her new home, going to church, and fishing.

John Harris (aka Shaffer)

Shaffer was Momole's fourth child, and he had made his arrival in this world a year after Louis was born. Just like Shaffer's siblings before him, he didn't get much schooling; he only completed the third grade. The man Momole worked for felt if her kids were old enough to go to school, they were old enough to work, so they worked. Shaffer missed school to pull corn or pick cotton. Just knee high to his mom, Shaffer stood on the back of a wagon as it moved up and down the rows of corn and pulled it off the stalks. He grew up with a hate in his heart for white people, just like his Mama. It was only because of the way the white people treated them when they were growing up. As he grew up, he often thought of the times his family had to move from place to place in the middle of the night because the boss man put them off his land for some reason or another. He could never forget the hurts they put his Mama through, knowing she was raising seven children by herself. Shaffer saw his Mama suffer and take many things that no woman should have had to. That's the story of a lot of black folk in those times, but they did what it took to survive and that's exactly what Shaffer did.

Shaffer was growing up fast, and the man he knew as his father had passed away. After William's death, he watched his Mama struggle with the way the church folk had treated her. The only church down Highway 31 at that time for black folk had refused to let her have the funeral at the church because her husband wasn't a member. Junior said his father told him that it rained that day and his father's coffin was on the back of a wagon in the rain. They had a graveside service and put him to rest. When Momole went to church again, it was for her three sons. Other than that, she never went to church again, and she would often say, "Them church folk." She was so put out with church folk until Mary (my Mama) invited her younger siblings to church, and Momole would tell her, "Leave my children alone. Go get somebody else's kids and leave mines alone." Shaffer could see the bitter taste the church folk had left in his Mama's mouth and heart.

Momole remarried and had more children. The house was too small for all of them and the children fought all the time. At the age of thirteen, Shaffer got tired of fighting with his siblings and decided to move in with his Aunt Fick (aka Francis, Momole's sister). He moved out of fear that one of his siblings would eventually make him mad enough to kill them. Someone always got hurt when they fought one another. Shaffer knew if he stayed, this would be inevitable. Aunt Fick loved Shaffer like he was her own son, and had named him after her husband, John Henry Goss. Momole was not happy about Shaffer's decision, but his heart and mind were fixed on making his own way in this world.

Shaffer continued working in the fields on the Teague's land. Whatever money he made; Shaffer always gave Momole some to help with the children still living in the house. He stayed with his Aunt Fick for a while, but eventually moved into his own house a couple of years later. He was fifteen years old and was his own man and could come and go as he pleased. Shaffer started hanging out with his uncles, Momole's brothers, from time to time, drinking and gambling and taking the ups and downs of life as they came.

Shaffer was a hard worker and didn't mind working if he got paid. He went to work as he usually did and was just trying to make it to the end of the day, when he had a difference of opinion with one of the Mexican guys he was working with. They started fighting and Shaffer got the best of the gentleman and had him down on the ground, but he wouldn't stay down and kept coming at Shaffer. He stood looking down at the Mexican, hoping he would stay down. But when he looked into the Mexican's eyes, he knew he had to kill him or be killed. The man called Shaffer's name as he refused to stay down, and this sent chills through Shaffer as he begged him to stay down.

He realized he had to kill this man, because if he got up, he wasn't going to let it go until he was dead. Shaffer pulled his gun out and shot the Mexican gentlemen. Shaffer stared at the lifeless body of the man he had just killed and said, "He wouldn't stay down." The look that the man gave Shaffer just before he shot him would plague his mind for the rest of his life. Shaffer went to jail for a short period of time at the Lonoke County Courthouse. Fortunately for him, he didn't have to stay long. The white people he worked for stood up for him, so he could be released. After being released, Shaffer went back to work. Shaffer had learned that all white people were not bad. Life was not the same for him after that, even though he went on with his life.

The house Shaffer lived in was blown down by a tornado and he was not ready to give up his newfound freedom and move back home. So, he and his friend, Ceil Cardwell, decided to get a house together and split the cost of everything. This made it easier for both financially. On the weekends, Shaffer's older brothers, Freddie and Louis, came by their house to hang out. They laughed, drank, and talked as they got ready for the ladies and a good time. Sometimes Ceil bought himself new clothes or had his clothes pressed and laid out on the bed until he got ready to get dressed to go out. There was only one problem with this: Freddie would bully Ceil a lot of times when they were visiting. Sometimes Freddie got Ceil's clothes and put them on. Freddie strutted around the house like a peacock in Ceil's clothes, and they all laughed at Ciel's expense. Ciel wasn't happy about Freddie being in his clothes, but he was too scared to say or do anything about it. He knew he was no match for Freddie, so he just found something else to wear. Shaffer and his friends all loaded on the back of Louis's truck and headed to England for a good time.

When Louis and Freddie weren't around, Shaffer would catch a ride with his other friends who had a car, Abraham Woodard Sr. (aka Sugar Boy) and Frank Carson. One way or another, Shaffer was going out on the town. He was a good-hearted person and would give you the clothes off his back. However, when he was drinking, he would be mean as a junkyard dog and wanting to fight. But when you caught him in the right frame of mind, you could get anything from him. When Shaffer got to England, a lot of times he hung out with his uncles and gambled. One night, he was hanging with his Uncle George, drinking and gambling. Uncle George and Shaffer were cut from the same cloth and they both were crazy when they got enough alcohol in their system. This night, things got out of control. While gambling, they disagreed, and the argument got heated until George pulled out his pistol and shot Shaffer. Shaffer almost died that night. The doctors were unable to remove the bullet, and later in life this bullet caused him a lot of pain. George was Momole's brother and was sorry for shooting Shaffer, but Momole wasn't hearing it. She was furious as she cursed him out, telling him, "You tried to kill my son." It was a long time before Momole spoke to her brother. It took time to heal the hurt she was feeling. Eventually she forgave her brother and let it go.

Shaffer, like his brothers, loved the ladies and they loved him. He had four girls by different women. He intended to marry one of the ladies, but Momole stopped that before they could get wedding plans off the ground. Mrs. Hosiana Robinson was one of Shaffer's friends who stayed in his life no matter who came in and out of it. However, he did eventually fall in love and marry Bobbie Ford. Bobbie and her sibling had moved to Lonoke from Montgomery, Alabama, because their parents had died. They moved in with their Aunt Emma Lime. Bobbie caught Shaffer's eye, so he began courting her. It wasn't long before they were married. Their marriage was tested from the beginning. Bobbie had one son already when she got pregnant with twins. It was time for the twins to arrive and everyone was excited, but their excitement soon turned to sadness. The twins were stillborn. It took some time, but they were able to move forward. In 1959, Bobbie was pregnant again, and in 1960 she gave birth to another son and they named him Junior.

Marriage and family didn't slow Shaffer down. He continued to drink heavily and hang out with his friends and the ladies. Many weekends he would get drunk and start shooting and fighting. This would always end with the police being called. When the police got there, Shaffer never went with them willingly, and when they got him to jail the police would always beat him bloody. This went on for years and was another reason he harbored so much hate in his heart against the police. The police never messed with Shaffer if he was sober. They would always beat him when he was drunk.

Bobbie got tired of the different struggles she and Shaffer were going through and decided to leave him. She moved to Chicago and took the children with her. Shaffer wasn't happy about this and decided to pay someone to take him to Chicago to get his family.

When he arrived, Bobbie refused to come back. Shaffer couldn't get his wife back, but he refused to leave his son, Junior, and he brought him back to Arkansas. Junior slept most of the trip back but woke up for a little while and looked around. His father and his friend were in the front seat, drinking and talking, so he just laid back down. By the time he woke up again, they were in Lonoke. Junior was a little boy and didn't understand all that was going on, but he loved his father.

Shaffer moved back in the house with Momole and she took care of Junior while he worked. Momole cooked dinner, and most of the time she cooked some form of hog meat because this was what she raised and had plenty. She would cook pig feet, ears, chitterlings, and hog maws (stomach of a hog) and almost everyone in the house was happy about the meal. When she got through cooking and fixed Charles' and Darnell's plates, they would dig in and eat like it was their last supper. You couldn't hear anything but lips smacking and fingers licking.

Junior sat there and stared at his plate a while, and then stared at Charles and Darnell. He couldn't believe they were eating this stuff. He didn't even know what it was. Junior looked up at Momole and then down at his plate and said, "I can't eat this." Momole understood that Junior wasn't used to eating food like that. So, she told Junior she would fix him something else. This made Charles and Darnell mad. They looked at Junior, hit him on his head while Momole's back was turned, and told him, "You making my Mama fix you something else with your spoiled [expletives]. Talking about you can't eat this. Yes, you can." Momole heard what they were saying to Junior and told them, "Y'all leave Junior alone, he not used to eating this kind of food. I got to fix him something else to eat."

Junior loved staying with his daddy, but it wasn't long before his Mama showed up and took him back to Chicago on the train. Before Bobbie and Junior could get settled, Shaffer was back in Chicago to get him. For about three years, Junior was back and forth from between Lonoke and Chicago. The last time Shaffer went to Chicago, he tried to live there, but was unable to make it in the city because he didn't know how to read or write. So, he loaded Junior up for the last time and brought him back to Lonoke.

Junior was finally old enough to go to school. His father would leave for work before they went to school. Every morning that Charles, Darnell, and Junior woke up, they looked in the window seal to see what Cooter had left them. Cooter left change in the window every morning. He left fifty cents apiece for Charles and Darnell and left Junior thirty-five cents. As soon as they ate breakfast and got dressed, they headed to Beatum's Store to buy candy before going to school. At night, Momole made them a pallet on the floor to sleep on. Some of the best times of Junior's life were at Momole's house.

Charles and Darnell were the only two children in the neighborhood who had minibikes and a horse. They rode the minibikes and horse in the field between Uncle Nay's and Aunt Sis's house. Junior would be right with them, having just as much fun as they were. They would all be in their own little world, taking turns riding the bikes and the horse. Darnell never got so engrossed in the fun that he didn't see the two neighborhood bullies coming. Rob and Bob lived not too far from Momole's house, and Charles and Darnell were terrified of them.

As soon as Darnell spotted them, he would stop what he was doing and take off running toward the house. While he was running, he'd yell, "Charles, come on, here comes Rob and Bob!" Junior would take off running too, but Rob and Bob weren't after him, they wanted Darnell and Charles. Junior was running with all his might, but Rob and Bob would run right past him and go after Darnell and Charles. Rob would yell to Darnell and Charles, "When we catch y'all, we're going to comb your hair." While Darnell and Charles were running, they would be hollering, "Momole, Momole, Rob and Bob!"

Momole heard their cry and rushed out of the house to help her sons. As soon as she made it to the side of the house, she would pick up a plank and start swinging it at Rob and Bob. They were no fools, they knew Momole meant business. Momole would swing that plank and say, "Get away from here with y'all bad [expletive]." Of course, Rob and Bob would run away, only to return another day.

In the summertime, Momole would wake up early in the morning and raise all the windows. The fresh summer breeze would flow through the house as everyone slept and relaxed. Most Saturdays, all the children loaded up on the back of Momole's pickup truck and headed to Pine Bluff to see Bessie. A trip to Pine Bluff wouldn't be a trip unless they stopped at Miss Brown's Store down Highway 31. She sold any and everything, and even if you didn't get anything, it was fun just to look around.

In the wintertime, when Charles, Darnell, and Junior woke up, they would put a pan of water on the wood stove to wash their faces. Those times may have seemed hard to Junior as they were happening, but now that he is grown, he realizes they were just good times.

Shaffer and Junior finally moved out of Momole's house into a tan, one-bedroom shotgun house across the street from the skating rink in Lonoke. It wasn't much, but it was home. When Junior wasn't at Momole's house, Willie Jean (the Mama of one of John's daughters) or Amy (Louis's wife) babysat him.

Shaffer drank excessively sometimes, but he was still a functioning alcoholic for a while. After getting drunk at night, he went to work the next day. None of the utilities ever got cut off. There was always food in the house and he always cooked for Junior. Junior bragged about how good his father could cook. One of his favorite dishes was his father's rice pudding. Junior said, "Shaffer could cook anything, and he could cook just as good as any woman." Shaffer took care of his son the best he knew how and never brought any women to the house to stay all night around his son. Most weekends, Shaffer gambled, and he always gave Junior some of his winnings. He gave Junior fifty dollars at a time, and as soon as he got a chance, Junior went back and forth, walking to get candy at Beatums' Store. On one occasion, Junior gave it to one of Shaffer's lady visitors. Even though he was just a little boy, he was in awe about how pretty she was. So, when she asked him to give her his fifty dollars, he didn't hesitate to give it to her. When Shaffer asked him where the money was that he had given him, Junior told him, not realizing the trouble he was in. Shaffer gave him a whipping he still remembers to this day.

Shaffer was an alcoholic, but there would be times he had the willpower to go weeks without taking a drink. Then out of the blue he would tell his son, "I think I want a drink." Shaffer would drink Echo Springs Whiskey for about three weeks, day in and day out. Junior sometimes emptied two five-gallon buckets a week that were filled with empty Echo Springs Whiskey bottles. Sometimes Shaffer was able to stop on his own, but there were times he was unable to stop, so they would take him to Benton, Arkansas, to a facility for alcoholics to let him dry out.

Shaffer drank, trying desperately to drown out past hurts. No matter how much he drank, he couldn't get rid of the voices and faces of the past that tormented his mind. One of those things was how he killed the Mexican man. He would tell his son, "Junior, the way that man looked at me, I didn't want to kill him, but I had to. If I didn't kill him, he was going to kill me." Sometimes he talked about how the white people treated them when they were growing up and how he hated them. Shaffer was trying to drown out the ghosts of his past but couldn't. On the weekends during these drinking binges, he went to Walter Holloway's house. He was one of the local bootleggers and he had enough to carry everyone through the weekend.

The times when Shaffer tried to stop drinking or couldn't get a drink, he went through delirium tremens (aka DT's) and would shake so bad his feet came off the floor. He would hallucinate. This was when things were bad for Shaffer, and they would have to load him in the car. One or two people had to ride in the back seat to hold him down to keep him from jumping out of the car during the trip.

Later that year, Shaffer and Junior moved to another house that they shared with Jake and his family. Shaffer and Junior lived in the back of the house, and Jake and his family lived in the front.

In 1966, Shaffer went to work for the mayor of Lonoke. Bobbie came back to town and they decided to get back together. Shaffer purchased a house across the tracks on Eagle Street. Even though Shaffer and Bobbie got back together, he was unable to quit his ways. He continued to drink heavily and hang out with his friends. One weekend, Shaffer and his friend, Frank Carson, got stopped by the police. They had been drinking as usual and Frank was very aware of the things the police would do to Shaffer every time, they caught him drunk. He decided to run. The police told Shaffer to stay right where he was while they went after Frank. Well, Shaffer decided to go home and go to bed instead.

About three o'clock in the morning, there was a knock at the door and the voice on the other side of the door said, "It's the police, open the door or I'll kick it down." They had so many searchlights pointed toward the house, it seemed as if it was daylight. Junior was frightened and decided to open the door. As he walked to the door, he heard his father say, "Don't open that door." At that moment, the police kicked the door in and four other police followed the first. They went to the bedroom where Shaffer was. He had made up his mind that he was not going in peace. He had sobered up some by the time the police arrived at his home. They didn't know it wasn't going to be easy as it usually was for them to whoop him. Shaffer started throwing blows; he was not going in peace. Shaffer was whipping the police when he yelled, "Help me, Junior!" Without any hesitation, Junior jumped in the fight. Before he could get started good, one of the policemen pulled a gun on him. Bobbie grabbed Junior and pulled him into the kitchen. The police finally dragged Shaffer out of the house that night and took him to jail, and of course they gave him the usual beating.

A few years after that, they beat Shaffer until they almost killed him. When Finnie came to see Shaffer in jail and saw the shape he was in, he decided to get a lawyer. It wasn't until then that the Lonoke police stopped beating Shaffer.

Life was full of ups and downs for Shaffer, and 1967 brought news that took him to an even darker place in his life. Shaffer received news of his brother, Louis, getting hit by a train. Barely able to hold himself together, Shaffer rushed to the hospital to see about his brother. When he got there, he was the only one allowed back to see Louis. Shaffer wanted to see him, but almost wished that he hadn't. Louis' face was so torn up he was unrecognizable, and this image haunted Shaffer for years to come. This was one more ghost that would join the other ghosts of his past. After getting the news that his brother had died, Shaffer cried as they handed him Louis' bloody possessions. When Shaffer got home, his wife and son were there. With tears in his eyes, he walked into the house, holding the bloody bag of clothes. Through his tears, he looked up at his son and said, "He was torn up, you couldn't hardly recognize him." Shaffer sat down and did the only thing he could do, he sobbed uncontrollably. Shaffer loved Louis; they were close and there would forever be a void in his life for his brother and friend.

Struggling to move forward in his life after losing his brother, Shaffer got some more bad news about a year after Louis died. Gabby and their brother, James Ray, had borrowed Shaffer's car to go out on the town to party. Shaffer didn't know as he watched his brothers pull out of the yard that only one of them would be coming back. Gabby died that night from a gunshot wound to the head. One emotional blow after the other. Shaffer struggled to keep his head above water. He was not always successful; he drowned his sorrows often in alcohol.

This also was the year that Shaffer's long-time lady friend, Hosiana, conceived his child. But unfortunately, the baby was stillborn. Hosiana was there for Shaffer no matter which crooked turn his life took. She accepted him just as he was with all his weaknesses and strengths. There were a lot of days that Shaffer got drunk, then get his gun and start shooting it aimlessly. Momole had a hard time calming him down. Most of the time she was unsuccessful, so she would take Shaffer to Hosiana's house, hoping she could help, and she did. Hosiana and Shaffer's brothers would load him in the back seat of her car and take him to the rehab facility. His brothers had to ride in the back seat and hold him to keep him from jumping out of the car the entire trip. Hosiana had to do this on numerous occasions. When she got him to the facility, she didn't just abandon him, she went back and forth to see about him. One time she went to see him, Shaffer walked out of the facility and got in her car and told her to take him home. She did as he asked and soon found out she had made a big mistake. Shaffer picked up where he had left off before going to rehab. Hosiana was such a fixture in Shaffer's life, when he called her one night when his wife was sick and asked her to take him to get her medications, she didn't hesitate, she did as Shaffer requested.

Junior didn't know about his father's relationship with Hosiana in the beginning, and Shaffer did what it took to make sure he didn't find out. Junior would ask his father if he could ride his bike to go play with his cousin across the tracks. He told him he could go, but he had to be home before dark. When his father caught him on that side of the tracks and it was getting dark, he yelled at him, "Boy, get your tail home!" Junior didn't argue with his father; he simply peddled his bike as fast as he could and headed for home. Years later, Junior found out that it wasn't about him being home before dark. Shaffer wanted him home before dark because he didn't want Junior to see him at Hosiana's house at night. When Shaffer wasn't drinking, he had a heart of gold, and this was what Hosiana knew and loved about Shaffer. Therefore, she stayed his friend until the end.

After working for the mayor for a few years, Shaffer left that job and went to work as a cement truck driver. He drove the cement truck for years. About 1977, he began having pain in his back. The bullet that was left in him after being shot by his Uncle George had worked its way next to a nerve in his back. The pain was a constant reminder of that night. The pain was so bad, he was unable to work. He would work for a while, then have to quit because of the pain. His wife, Bobbie, worked at the courthouse and Junior worked the summer program for the Lonoke Highway Department during eleventh grade to pay for the food stamps that helped keep food in the house.

Shaffer finally applied for disability, but it would be awhile before he would receive it. He knew they had to survive some way until then. Junior was in the middle of his senior year in school and he was on the basketball team. Shaffer tried to figure out what to do about the situation -- the solution he came up with was to tell Junior he had to quit the basketball team and get a job to help pay the bills. This situation hurt them both, but Junior sacrificed for his home team (family) and didn't hesitate to get a job. Junior informed his basketball coach that he would not be able to play basketball anymore because he would be working at Walmart in the evenings. Shaffer refused to just give in to the pain and not do anything. So, he would rise early in the morning and get in his truck and go different places, picking up cans and hauling scrap iron to have some income. Shaffer did this for years and started making a pretty good living with it. He was a survivor despite his struggles.

Junior continued to work and try to find his place in this world. He started running with friends who would lead him to nowhere good. He finally met a young lady and they had three children. Junior eventually moved to Jacksonville, with the young lady, and they stayed together for nine years, on and off. During that time, Junior went back and forth from Jacksonville to his father's house. He finally moved back home. Shaffer and Bobbie weren't getting along, so he bought some land on the other side of the tracks. He built a shop and started living in it. Junior stayed with his Mama to help her out. Bobbie and Shaffer never got back together after that.

About 1988, Shaffer came to grips with his demons and overcame his drinking after several more visits to the rehab in Benton. It was the nineties and Junior was using drugs and alcohol. His father continued to spend money to get him out of the different situations he found himself in. Shaffer would have continued to spend money to save his son if it hadn't been for his lawyer. The last time Junior got in trouble; he was facing prison time. The lawyer Shaffer had hired for his son time and time again spoke to Shaffer and told him not to spend another nickel. "Let him go down there, that's the only way he's going to learn."

That was one of the hardest things Shaffer had to do, but he took the lawyer's advice and let his son reap the repercussions of his actions. Junior went to prison but came out a better person from the lesson that was taught. Only time would tell the end results. Shaffer had to deal with the death of his Mama and sister along with the trouble Junior was in, but he was able to hold himself together and not take a drink. He stayed strong and dealt with whatever came without reverting to his old habits. Junior finally came home from prison and he looked better than he had looked in a long time. Time did pass and Junior turned over a new leaf. He let go of all the things he used to do and became a productive citizen. After going through many more changes in his life, he finally met Hannah, the true love of his life. Hannah loved Junior unconditionally, and he, too, learned to relax and love.

Even in Shaffer's latter years, he never stopped giving Momole money. Every Christmas like clockwork, Shaffer gave Momole $500. In 1998, when Shaffer's health started to fail him. His sister, Mary, was living in Vegas, dying of breast cancer. He was supposed to travel with some of his sisters and brothers to Vegas to see Mary, but it never happened. He had pain in the back of his neck and a wet cough he couldn't get rid of. Shaffer told Junior, "I don't think I'm going to be able to make that trip, I'll just give them some money and let them go on." Junior took his father to the doctor to try to find out what was going on. The doctors were unable to determine why he had the neck pains.

July 1998, Junior went to see his daddy on a Friday. Shaffer was working out in the yard and tidying up his shop. Junior left his job and came over to see his father on his lunch break. It was hot that day and he was concerned about his father being in the heat. Junior looked at his father as he moved around the shop in the heat and said, "Daddy, you need to get out of this heat until they find out what's wrong with you." Schaeffer replied, "I am, I'm going in the house and I'm going to rest and sleep all day and I ain't going to do nothing tomorrow." Shaffer went and played cards with some of his friends that night but had to leave early because he wasn't feeling well. He went home and got in the bed and went to sleep, just like he had promised his son. He died in his sleep that night.

Junior came by that Saturday morning to check on his father, but when he knocked, there was no answer. He left and it was dusk dark by the time he went back to check on his father, and there was still no answer to his knock at the door. Junior thought, "Maybe he's with his friend that he goes gambling with sometimes." Junior finally contacted his father's friend, but he had not seen Shaffer. Junior knew he wasn't with his brother, Finnie, because they had just gotten back from Vegas, visiting their sister, Mary. Junior contacted Hosiana and she hadn't seen Shaffer all that day. Robert (Louis's son) lived next door to Shaffer, so Junior decided to check with him to see if he had seen his father. When Robert told him no, they knew something was wrong. So, they both went over to Shaffer's house and started looking in all the windows. Junior had done this earlier, but didn't see anything. The window of Shaffer's bedroom had a shutter on it, and this prevented seeing inside the bedroom. They had just about given up when Robert decided to go get a ladder so he could see above the shutter on the window. That's when Robert saw Shaffer lying in the bed against the wall. That was why they had trouble seeing him at first glance.

Robert told Junior, "He's in there." Junior then asked Robert what he was doing. Robert replied, "He looks dead." Without any hesitation, Junior ran to the door and kicked it in. Sure, enough his father was dead.

Shaffer must have known he was dying when he went to bed that night. He had placed the deeds to his properties and other important business in a paper bag and then placed that bag in a chair so Junior could find it. Shaffer died a couple of weeks before his sister, Mary (Mama), passed.

When Finnie and his sisters were leaving Vegas, Mary told them, "You all need to check on Shaffer when you all get home." Mama knew something was wrong. Finnie and his sisters had just gotten home the night Junior found his father taking his final rest. I was in Vegas at this time taking care of my Mama, Mary.

Robert said that on different occasions over the years Shaffer had told him that he coughed up a lot of blood. In 1982, Shaffer went to the doctor. After the doctor ran several tests, they found a spot and scar tissue on his lungs. The doctor then told Shaffer he needed to stop smoking. Shaffer tried for a few days and told Robert, "I just can't do it." In 1998 Shaffer told Robert he was sick and didn't know how much longer he was going to be around. Shaffer knew that his days in this world were few.

Finnie Harris

Finnie was Momole's fifth son, and he was fortunate to go to school a little more than his older siblings. Momole depended on Finnie for a lot of things. After his father died, he was a child trying to fill a man's shoes and was doing pretty good. Finnie was thirteen years old when he started working his deceased stepfather's job. When he got paid, he gave Momole most of the money to help take care of the other children. Finnie didn't have any struggle with doing all he could do for his Mama, and he tried to do as she told him. He was the little big man of the house, but he couldn't be a husband to his Mama. Momole had gotten lonely and decided to marry again. She knew she had to tell her children and didn't know how they were going to take it. When she informed Finnie of who she was going to marry, it didn't set well with him.

He pleaded with his Mama, "Mama, please don't marry him, you can't tell him nothing."

Momole replied, "Well that's all right, I'm going to marry him."

Finnie pleaded some more, "Mama, please don't, if you marry him, Mama, I've got to leave."

Momole replied, "I'm going to marry him."

The next day, Momole and Cooter (Sam) went to England and got their marriage license. They didn't know Finnie was following them and watching every move they made. When Momole said "I do" to Cooter, Finnie said, "Mama I'm gone." Even though Finnie moved out, he still was always there for his Mama whenever she needed anything.

After James (Finnie's brother) had grown up, he would get a little jealous and mad when Momole needed something and she'd call Finnie. Whenever she called him, he always came and James would say, "Aww yeah, you gotta call your white son, every time you get ready for something, you got to call your white son and here he come."

James referred to Finnie as white because of his fair complexion and freckles. Ironically, James was also fair-skinned with freckles. Nevertheless, Finnie was there for his Mama and sister, Stine, even when they were on their deathbeds. Mattie would call Finnie at three o'clock in the morning sometimes to tell him about things that were going wrong with his Mama or sister. In less than an hour, Finnie was there, trying to do whatever he could do. After Momole died, Mattie would say, "I know Finnie is a man, but since my Mama died, he's my Mama."

Finnie was a little different from his siblings in that he didn't do a whole lot of drinking alcohol and fighting. Sure, he had fights with his brothers and sisters, but never an all-out brawl in the streets. He tried to drink, but it made him sick. No, Finnie wasn't a fighter, he was a lover, and his choice of indulgence was the ladies. He had one addiction and the only thing that could fix his craving was a woman. He loved the women and they loved him. When he was with a lady friend, he would get drunk on her love and it was like drinking the finest of wine. The ladies were his drug of choice and sobriety was the farthest thing from his mind. Finnie was more like his grandpa, Bill, in more ways than one. His hands were used for working and taking care of the ladies. In 1955, Finnie decided to slow down just a little, so he got married his first wife Joan. They had nine children, including two boys who died after only having lived a few months in this world. Finnie had his oldest daughter from a previous relationship.

In 1955, Finnie not only got married, he joined a male gospel group called the Zion Five. Finnie was tall, good-looking, and could sing, and this made him even more of a woman magnet. The Zion Five were a big hit back in the day, and everyone loved them. Everybody in Lonoke was talking about the Zion Five. One of the songs they were most known for was "Walking up the King's Highway."

Any marriage would have its struggles with raising seven children and trying to make ends meet without any outside interference. But Finnie's love for the ladies and their love for him put even a bigger strain on his marriage. The women were coming out of the woodwork and it was hard for him to say no. Joan couldn't take the struggles they had to face in their marriage anymore. In 1969, without any warning, Joan left him and filed for divorce the same day she left. To add injury to insult, she used his money to file for the divorce. Finnie was at work, unaware of the events that were taking place. In just a few hours, he realized his life was turned upside down and things would never be the same for him.

When Finnie came home from work, the children were in Momole's backyard, playing. When he went in the house, he realized his wife was no longer there. She had left all the children for Finnie to rear. After a few years, Joan got their youngest son and raised him. This situation knocked the wind out of Finnie, but not the drive to keep moving forward. It took some time, but he gathered his composure and accepted the situation for what it was. The only thing left for him to do was to keep working and take care of his children. Finnie was so proud of his two oldest children because they stepped in and did what they had to do to make sure the house and the younger children were taken care of. They cooked, cleaned, combed hair, and kept the house running like a well-oiled machine. He was able to work without worrying about the children, and this took a big load off his heart and mind.

In 1970, Finnie remarried, and He moved to Little Rock with his wife Sandra. Their union eventually yielded thirteen children under one roof. They bought a house to accommodate their growing family. They were married for several years and Finnie loved Sandra. She had his heart, but the problem was he was still sharing the rest of himself with the ladies. Finnie was fertile and not only was he sharing, he was leaving a little of himself with the ladies he was having a relationship with. One of the ladies even gave him her son and he raised him along with the rest of his children.

Sandra soon grew tired of the different struggles they were having in their marriage and decided to move to California. Even though they were struggling with their relationship, they still parted as friends. Sandra even wanted Finnie to move to California with her, but Finnie refused. He bought Sandra a ticket to California and the children all stayed with him. After a time period, Sandra came back to Arkansas to get some of the furniture she wanted out of the house. She also decided to take three of the children with her. Finnie bought the plane tickets so the children could go with their Mama. The other children didn't want to go and chose to stay with their father, and he did what he had to do to take care of them. The children who went to California with their mom didn't stay long. Soon they were ready to come back to Arkansas with their father. Sandra sent them back and it wasn't long before she moved back to Arkansas also. Finnie loved and wanted his wife, but he was not and would never be a one-woman man. In his own way, he respected his wife and never let her see him with another woman.

Finnie eventually had thirty-four children, give or take a few. Nine of his children were either deceased at birth or only lived a few months in this world. Many people are shocked and awed by the number of children Finnie had, as though it was a bad thing. One thing that could be said about Finnie was that he was not a deadbeat dad. In 2016, Finnie and his children, grandchildren, and great-grandchildren had a Father's Day celebration for him. I videotaped as each one of the children talked about their father. I'll never forget what one of the girls said. She said, "My daddy is a strong man, and he has a lot of children, but he took care of all of them." Another one of his children said, "He took me in, took care of me, and he did something for me that I can't talk about, but I will never forget. My daddy is the best man I know." One by one, each of his children expressed their love and gratitude.

I met a cab driver from Arabia who had been in Atlanta, Georgia one year, and he said something so profound that I will never forget. He said, "In our country, you are considered rich if you have a large family." Well, if that's the case, Finnie is the richest man in this book and the richest man I know. In his later years, he was surrounded and loved by his children, grandchildren, and his great-grandchildren.

Finnie and Sandra never divorced. They stayed married but lived in separate homes. They are the best of friends and talk to one another daily and see one another several times during the week. Whenever there is any event that is important in either of their lives, she is there for him and he is there for her. They both have learned to love one another despite their individual shortcomings. She accepts all his children and loves them just as much as he does. Their relationship may be strange to someone else because they don't live together, but they are together. Finnie said he will never marry again; Sandra has been there for him through the years and is still there for him. She accepts him for who he is, and he accepts her, and they have an understanding that people may not understand, but they understand and that is all that matters. Even though Father Time may have slowed Finnie down, he still sings with the Zion Five and is a deacon in his church.

The holidays are the grandest at Finnie's house. The love, laughter and holiday spirit fill his home as the children, grandchildren, great-grandchildren, friends, and other family members gather at his home. Finnie's heart is overcome with joy as he prepares the meal for his family. His daughters all have certain dishes of food they all bring, but none can compare to Finnie's famous oxtail soup and lemonade tea. When his sister, Mattie, arrives, she has a carryout bowl in her hand and heads straight for the pot of oxtail soup. Everyone gets along fine, there is no fighting or fussing, and past hurts are left behind. Finnie's first wife Joan is also in the house, enjoying all the festivities. Yes, I say it again: Finnie is one of the richest men in the world, to be surrounded by so many people who truly love him and accept him for who he is.

Finnie & his family

Annie (aka Sis)

Annie holds the number six spot among Momole's children. Annie grew out of some of her mischievous ways and got her mind on boys. Thelma Heard had moved down Highway 31 from the Dumas and Gould, Arkansas area. When she first moved there, she didn't have her children with her. But later, Freddie and his brother joined her. Freddie was only living there a few days when Annie caught his eye. Within two weeks, Freddie and Sis were married. They got married in 1954. Sis was only sixteen years old, but they lied on the license and said she was eighteen years old. Annie's real name on her birth certificate is Annabeth, but all her life she was called Annie Bess or Sis by friends and family. Freddie and Annie lived down Highway 31 for a while, but moved to Kerr and from there to Lonoke. They finally had their dream home built in Lonoke in a place known as 'The Hole.'

Every couple has their ups and downs without any outside help, but Freddie and Sis's marriage was tested to the limits because of outside interference. Their marriage stood the test of time despite all the obstacles that came their way. When Freddie and Sis moved into their new home, they became bootleggers and sold alcohol and hosted card games for a cut of the profits. The house was full most of the time with family, friends, and enemies. On the weekends, Freddie and Sis's house was the place to be in Lonoke if you wanted to party.

Thick smoke from the cigarette smokers, blues music, and the chatter from different conversations filled the air. BB King was singing his blues when someone felt what he was saying and yelled, "That's my jam, turn it up." They did this all while holding their drinks in the air and their bodies swayed back and forth to the beat of the music. Someone would jump up from their chair to join the individual on the floor because they understood and felt the same thing. For just a moment, the couple got caught up and took the journey to wherever BB King took them. They forgot about their troubles and got lost in the groove.

Freddie and Sis had seven children at this time. Those who were big enough to help with the family business did so. The children got the beer out of the cooler or refrigerator, gave it to the customer, collected the money and gave it to their mom. This way Sis could play cards or keep an eye on everything else that was going on. Sis also knew her customers would eventually want something to eat and she was also ready for that. Annette, and Sis's other daughters who were old enough, would fix food for the hungry drinkers, gamblers, and weed smokers. The food wasn't free, but anyone in the house could have a plate for a price. Yes, the money was coming in and the good times were rolling. Sis did most of the entertaining. Freddie was quiet and sat in the living room in his easy chair as the activities took place. He smiled and greeted and talked to anyone who came through the door. When they got through chatting with him, they would head straight to the kitchen where all the festivities were taking place.

As good a time that everyone was having, there was a storm brewing. Mixing drinks, weed, cards, and music with women and men is a homemade recipe for trouble. But Freddie had already laid down the rules. He told everyone who came in, "If you act the fool, I'm going to act the fool with you." Freddie might have looked all sweet and innocent, but he was always packing some protection in his blue jean overalls. He was the true regulator of the house. Most of the time there was no confusion that wasn't easily handled. Sis handled most altercations without any problem, but Freddie was ready just in case.

One-night things got out of control. This incident altered many lives, and they would never be the same. The year was 1974. Freddie and Sis had planned a party for their anniversary and had to cancel this party two weekends straight because Freddie was sick one weekend, and one of the children was sick the next weekend. All obstacles were out of the way and the party was on for that Saturday night. Just about everyone who hung out at Freddie and Sis's house planned to go to the party. All their neighbors and friends were aware of the big bash. However, Freddie and Sis were not aware of the storm that was brewing.

It was April and Bell (Sis's first cousin) made her arrival at the party. Her husband, Harley had left her for another woman, and he was sitting at the table playing cards. Bell decided to leave the party and go to the club in Little Rock because of the tension between her and the other woman, who was also at the Party. Before the night ended, Harley was shot and killed in Freddie and Sis's house, by a friend who had just come back in town that same day. This friend was also the ex-boyfriend of the woman he was dating. Bell was left to raise two boys by herself. Harley's death cast a shadow over Freddie and Annie's wedding anniversary for years to come. Annette (Sis's oldest daughter) had sneaked out of the house this night to meet her boyfriend, who eventually became her husband.

After Harley's death, Sis and Freddie continued to run the bootleg house. The police didn't shut them down, but business was slow for a couple of weeks. It wasn't long before everything was back to normal and business was hopping and popping again. This wasn't a normal situation for children to be raised in, but it was normal for Sis's children. As a child, Annette said she always wondered why other children, or her cousins couldn't come to their house. Most of the children they played with met in the field between their house and Uncle Nay's house. But no children ever came in their house. She didn't realize the reason why until she got older. The children's parents would not allow them to go to their house because of the bootlegging, gambling, and other things that went on in their house.

Regardless of the rumors or truths about Freddie and Sis, they stayed together. Some of the rumors everyone else guessed and pondered about, Freddie, Sis, and the children knew were true, but they stayed strong. Freddie had to love Sis from a place in his heart that no one else understood because they had eight children, and only two of the children were his. One child into their marriage, Sis had an affair. The affair alone was enough for Freddie to have to endure, but the heartbreaker was the person with whom she had the affair. Sis crossed a moral line and had an affair with Freddie's stepfather.

The situation didn't get any better when Freddie's stepfather fathered four of Sis's eight children. Sis continued with different affairs and had two other children by two other men. It was no secret to anyone, not even the children. As they got old enough, Sis told each one of the children who their father was. She was adamant about telling her children who their fathers were and told each of her children they needed to know who their folks were.

Freddie knew all but chose to stay with his wife and helped raise their children. Freddie took his vows to Sis seriously, and they were married forty-nine years before Sis died of an aneurysm of the brain. Before she died, she had given up many of her ways. She loved Bingo and would play weekly. She joined St. Paul Baptist Church in Lonoke. She was president of the mission's department, sang in the choir and loved being an usher. Freddie lived several years after Sis died. Freddie moved out of the house into a smaller apartment where his daughter, Annette, was the manager. Annette took care of her father until he died in 2014. He was buried in his favorite blue jean overalls.

Bessie

Bessie was Momole's seventh child, and most of Momole's children were delivered by midwives at home. Some of the midwives could barely read or write, and their recordkeeping skills were awful. Bessie found out how awful those skills were years later. She had come to the age where it was time for her to receive her social security and disability benefits. So, she went to the Vital Statistics Department to get a copy of her birth certificate, and they had trouble finding it. When they finally found it, they saw immediately what the problem was. Bessie didn't attend school long enough to learn to read or write well, so Betty (Bessie's oldest daughter) read the birth certificate to her mom. The certificate had "infant child" where Bessie's name was supposed to be, and this upset Bessie. Betty continued reading and saw where the midwife put Bessie's daddy's sister down as her Mama. At this point, the tears began to stream down Bessie's face. Betty laughed, but she consoled her Mama and told her, "Mama, stop crying, you know that Momole is your Mama. You look and act like Momole more than any of her children."

Freddie, Sis's husband

Bessie soon stopped crying and told the person assisting them that her Mama named her Elizabeth. The individual then informed Bessie that they could not go back and put Elizabeth on her birth certificate, she would have to use the name she had been using on her social security card. So, they placed the name, Bessie, in the place of infant baby. She had some doubts in her mind about Momole being her Mama when she was growing up because of some rumors she had heard, that Momole was raising three children that weren't hers. Now she was grown, and this situation brought the rumors to her mind. When she was a child, she talked to her Aunt Susie about the rumors and Susie told her, "Child, shut your mouth about that foolishness; Vie is your Mama." She never thought any more about it after that, at least not until she got her birth certificate.

Bessie didn't know it when she was born, but she was born into a world and family that would require her to be tough to survive. Bessie was only a few months old when Momole walked out of her bedroom and asked Sis to watch her and not let her fall off the bed. Sis was about three years older than her. Bessie was born with a hairy mole on the right side of her jaw. Sis thought it was a hairy worm and she was determined to get rid of it. So, while Momole was out of the room, Sis decided to kill this hairy worm and get it off her sister's face. She grabbed the hot poker iron out of the fire from the stove and placed it on the hairy mole on Bessie's face. Bessie let a squeal out that let Momole know something was terribly wrong.

Without hesitation, Momole ran back into the room. She was thinking Sis had let the baby fall off the bed. But when she entered the room, she saw it was much worse than a fall. Sis had left the hot poker on Bessie's face long enough that it burned to the bone. Momole grabbed Bessie off the bed, trying to quiet and comfort her from the pain of the burn. She looked down at Sis and asked, "Why did you do that?"

Sis replied, "I was trying to kill the hairy worm that was on her face." This was a day Sis would never forget. Momole beat her within an inch of her life. Bessie survived the ordeal, but the scar on her face was a reminder of that day for the rest of her life. But looking on the bright side of things, the hairy worm was gone, never to return.

By the time Momole had child number thirteen, Bessie was old enough to babysit. Babysitting and cooking were her jobs. She took care of Stine and James because they were the babies, while the older children went to the cotton field. Everyone who lived under Momole's roof knew when you got old enough you had to go to the cotton field. Bessie and Stine were the only ones of Momole children who didn't have the pleasure of going to the cotton fields. Most of Bessie's day was spent rocking and feeding Stine, with James nearby. Wherever Bessie went, she had Stine on her hip and James followed. They had gotten so attached to Bessie, they called her Mama. Just about any time you saw Bessie, you saw Stine on her hip or back. Bessie carried Stine on her hip and back so much, some of the older people in the community used to tell her she was going to have a hump in her back when she got older, from carrying Stine on her back.

Bessie would reply, "I'm just going to have a hump in my back then, because Mama told me not to put her down." Momole had warned Bessie if anything happened to her baby, what the consequences would be. Bessie took Momole at her word and would not let Stine out of her sight. When Bessie went to the bathroom, she took Stine with her, and James followed.

Each morning before everyone left for the cotton fields, Momole started supper, and gave Bessie orders to complete it. If she put on a pot of beans, she would tell Bessie she better not let them burn. The sun was be shining through the kitchen window and Momole marked the floor and told Bessie, "When the sun gets to this line, put the bread in the oven." The oven was above the stove, so Bessie had to stand on a five-gallon bucket to reach it. Momole would always give her a warning after her cooking instructions to be careful and not to fall on the stove.

Growing up with so many fighting brothers, Bessie had to fight whether she wanted to or not. With so many of them in the house, if they weren't fighting one another, they were fighting some of the other children who lived in their neighborhood. Gabby and Nay had gotten into an altercation with Gear and two other boys at school. Gear and the two boys told Gabby and Nay they were coming by their house to beat them up. So, Gabby and Nay told Bessie she was going to have to fight Gear because they couldn't beat up the three of them when it was only two of them.

Bessie told them, "No, I'm not going to fight." They didn't argue with Bessie, they just waited until Momole left the house the next day to confront her. Gabby and Nay surrounded Bessie and asked, "Are you going to fight?" She replied, "No." When she said no, they pushed her back and forth between them, and this went on most of the day. Bessie finally got tired and started fighting them back.

While she was fighting them back, Gear and his two friends walked in the yard, ready to fight. Bessie never said a word; she stopped fighting her brothers and lit into Gear with all her might. She whipped Gear until his shoes came off. Gabby glanced over at Bessie occasionally, to make sure Gear wasn't getting the upper hand. Gear took all he could take from Bessie, so he took off running, leaving his shoes behind. Bessie put her hands on her hips, reared back and laughed with all her might. After Gabby and Nay finished whooping the other two young boys, they all had a laugh. They were victorious once again.

None of Momole's first seven children got to attend school much because they had to work in the fields. Bessie didn't work in the fields, but she didn't take to school much, either. The times she did go to school, the teacher made it unpleasant for her. Each morning before going to school, Momole made each of the girls wash up in the number nine tub. She would yell from the other room at the girls and tell them to be sure and wash their feet and puss. Stine sat in the rocking chair and watched each one of them as they washed up. When everyone finished, Stine would grunt as she got up out of the rocking chair and say, "Well I guess I'll wash my feet and puss." The children who were old enough, went off to school.

After getting to school, Bessie sat about the middle of the class between two of her friends. One day, the teacher looked over her glasses with her nose snarled up and called Bessie by her last name. "Harris, you didn't take no bath and you stink." Bessie quickly replied, "That ain't me stinking."

The teacher then told Bessie to come up front and sit. When Bessie went to the front of the class, the teacher continued to tell her she was stinking. The situation made Bessie so mad, she reached over the desk and grabbed the teacher's arm and twisted it while saying. "You're a [expletive] liar. I did take a bath. My Mama makes me wash my puss and feet every morning, that ain't me stinking." Bessie twisted the teacher's arm so hard she broke it.

Bessie got in trouble, but she never had any more trouble from that teacher. But she did have trouble with the children teasing her about the way she walked and talked. She was pigeon-toed, and when she walked it looked as if she was going to step on her own feet. Bessie would fight at the drop of a hat at this point, and she did what it took to stop the teasing. Bessie made it to the seventh grade, but still didn't learn to read or write.

Many black families who lived down Highway 31 had a lot of children, and some of the children would congregate at Momole's house to play. The family of Mr. James and Fannie Jones lived on the lane down Highway 31. Jun, George, Frank, and Bert were their children and they all would hang out at Momole's house. Bert was sweet on Louis, Jun was sweet on Annie, and George was sweet on Bessie. Bert even got pregnant by Louis, and this upset her parents, so they sent her away to Chicago to have an abortion. Unfortunately, Bert was unable to bear any more children after this.

George rode his bicycle over sometimes to see Bessie. While George hung out with the other children, Mattie rode his bicycle until her little heart was content. Bessie wasn't interested in George, but George was interested in her. Bessie saw him as just one of their childhood friends coming over to hang out. Bessie was crazy about Buddy Heard (Sis's husband Freddie's brother). Bessie was a teenager, but she had problems with her bladder and was still wetting the bed. She had to take her bed mattress outside every morning to let it air out. Since Buddy was sweet on her, he came over every day to help her take her mattress outside. One day after Buddy got through taking Bessie's mattress out, he decided to steal a kiss. Bessie was leaning up against the dresser when Buddy gave her a kiss on her lips. Just when their lips touched, Momole walked in. She was furious, and Bessie desperately tried to tell her nothing was going on.

Momole wasn't hearing it. She made Bessie pull off every piece of clothing she had and beat Bessie like there was no tomorrow. She told Buddy, "After I get through with her, you can have her."

When Momole got through whooping Bessie, Buddy told Bessie, "Come on home with me, you can sleep with Thelma." When she got to his house, he told his mom what was going on. Bessie was still crying when Thelma told her to come sleep in the bed with her, "Ain't nobody going to mess with you." Bessie couldn't sleep, she just kept crying, waiting and hoping that Louis would come get her soon.

Later that night, Louis came over to Momole's house and the first question out of his mouth was, "Where is Bessie?" After Louis was informed of the situation, he went to pick Bessie up and brought her home. Bessie cried all the way home. When they made it to the house, Louis told Momole, "I don't want you to ever whoop Bessie again unless I'm here." I don't know what it was about Louis that made Momole humble down when he asked her to do something, but she did.

George continued to come to Momole's house, awaiting the opportunity to get to know Bessie better. One day, George drove his car to Momole's house. The children there were all listening to music and dancing. George told everyone he had a record at the house he wanted them to hear. George then asked Momole if Bessie could ride with him to his house to get the record. Momole trusted George and didn't give it a second thought when she told him yes. Momole soon found out this was a big mistake. George's hormones were raging, and he had other plans on his mind. George and Bessie went into his house and got the records. After getting the records, George's hormones took over and he grabbed Bessie and began kissing and feeling all over her body. George was all hands, and before Bessie could get George off her, he had her panties down. Bessie was a virgin and didn't have a clue as she struggled to get George off her.

George whispered to Bessie, "Come on, come on." Bessie's heart raced. Trying to push George off of her with all her might, she said, "Come on what?"

George whispered to Bessie in a desperate tone, "Just let me touch it, I'm not going to put it in." George didn't put it in, but he ejaculated in Bessie vaginal opening. This was a day that changed the rest of her life. They went on back to the house as if nothing had happened.

A few months later, Bessie began gaining weight. Momole didn't notice and neither did Bessie. Bessie was thirteen years old, and her life would never be the same. George had stolen Bessie's innocence, and this was just the beginning. One of the ladies from the neighborhood was visiting Momole when she noticed Bessie's weight gain. She said, "That girl done swallowed a watermelon seed." That was her way of saying that Bessie was pregnant.

Momole quickly came to Bessie's defense and said, "What are you doing, talking about my child? My child ain't swallowed [expletive]." Then Momole looked at Bessie and said, "Girl you big, did you get a baby in yo [expletive]."

Bessie replied, "No, I ain't got no baby in my [expletive]." She started looking down at her behind, trying to figure out what they were talking about. Bessie was seven months pregnant and didn't have a clue about her unfortunate situation.

Momole told Bessie, "I'm going to whoop yo [expletive]." Momole whooped her like she wasn't pregnant. Bessie had no one to talk to who could explain to her what was going on. She was still a virgin and pregnant and didn't know what to do next. Bessie didn't recall even having her period before this time.

Momole stayed mad at Bessie for the rest of her pregnancy and she was even angrier at George, because he had betrayed that trust she had in him. She never talked to Bessie about the facts of life, so Bessie was still confused about her situation and had no idea about what to expect. Louis and Finnie gave Bessie some of the money they made in the cotton fields on Saturday, so she could get what she wanted to eat while she was pregnant. They knew she loved peaches, so they would both bring her a couple of cans of peaches and Pet milk home to her when they got paid. Bessie didn't have any idea about how bad the birth of her child was going to be. Getting pregnant and Momole finding out that she was pregnant was the easy part. The hard part was yet to come.

One day while in the cotton field, Gabby and Nay had loaded up the cotton sacks on the truck. They then yelled at Bessie to get on the back of the truck and sit on the cotton sack. They didn't know Momole was about to pull the truck forward. Just as Bessie got positioned on the cotton sack, she pulled forward and Bessie didn't have a grip on anything. She fell off the cotton sack to the ground. She was hurt but didn't realize how bad until later that night. After everyone went to bed, Bessie's water broke, and she began to bleed. She didn't understand what was happening and was too scared to say anything to Momole. She left trails of blood and water as she went back and forth to the outdoor toilet with diarrhea. The time had arrived for Bessie to have the baby and she was scared, crying and moaning from the pain, while Momole lay in the bed in the next room, never saying a word. Momole knew what was happening but she was so angry about Bessie getting pregnant, she didn't care. She wanted to show Bessie she was on her own with the mess she had made.

Louis came home about three o'clock in the morning. When he walked in the house, he could see the trails of blood. In shock, Louis asked, "Where did all this blood come from?"

Momole replied, "Bessie probably having that baby."

Louis said, "Somebody got to take her to the doctor."

Momole said, "I ain't taking her anywhere, she can have it outside and let the dog eat it for all I care."

Louis was too tired to go anywhere, so he woke Finnie up and asked him to take Bessie to the hospital. Momole had one final thing to say before they left, "I hope you sit on the mold of his head." On the way to the hospital, the baby started coming out in the car. Bessie didn't know to lean back or lay down, she did just what Momole hoped she would do -- she sat on the baby's head. The baby lived for a short period of time, but not for long.

Louis took Bessie to live with Aunt Susie after that. Bessie accepted George as her boyfriend, and they continued to see one another. When Bessie was sixteen years old she got pregnant by George again. Jack (Bessie's brother) wasn't too happy about this and decided to have a talk with George and Bessie. Jack told them if they were going to continue to see one another, they needed to get married, and Momole agreed with Jack. George and Bessie agreed and were married.

After George and Bessie got married, her siblings used to give her a hard time and tease her because she was still wetting the bed when she got married. Bessie's second child was a little girl and they called

Bessie

George

her Betty. Bessie was a child bride and a child having children. Just like her Mama, she had to learn as her life went along. Instead of life getting better for Bessie, she soon found out that she had jumped out of the skillet into the fire. Bessie got pregnant a third time and lost that baby also. George and Bessie were hurt about the children they had lost, but this didn't deter them from having more children. They eventually had seven children while they were married.

Momole lived on the Simpson land at this time. Bessie lived in an area down Highway 31 that was called Richwood, and this was a pretty good distance from Momole's house if you had to walk it. Bessie went to her Mama's house some days to pick up her little brother and sister, James and Stine. She would carry them on her back to her house and carry them back home the same way.

James and Stine stayed at home while the others worked. They both had to grow up quickly. Stine was a little girl but had been taught to cook at a young age. Momole would put a pot of beans and meat on the stove for them to watch while everyone else was working. They had to watch the food to make sure it didn't burn. When Momole came home and she sat down to eat and if the food tasted burnt, they would get a whooping. After a few burnt meals, it wasn't long until James and Stine got the cooking down pat. James remembers Stine as a little girl standing in a chair in front of the stove, cooking just as good as any grown person. After Momole had Mack, it was James and Stine's job to watch him while Momole was in the cotton fields.

Bessie and George decided to move to Pine Bluff to go in the wrecking business with his father. The only child Bessie had at this time was Betty. George was handy when it came to working on cars, so the wrecking business he and his father embarked upon was the perfect job for him. He made decent money, but had a problem holding onto it due to his compulsive gambling. George's gambling put a big strain on their marriage, because at the end of the week he would lose his entire check gambling. When he came home, he didn't have any money left to pay bills or buy food. This left Bessie trying to figure out how to feed the family. To make matters worse, the children were still coming. Bessie was having children almost every year or two. Their son, Barry, was born shortly after their move to Pine Bluff.

When they moved, George's habit didn't get any better, but worse. George not only gambled his money away; he loved the women and would sometimes bring them to the house. George would come in the room where Bessie was taking care of Barry and tell her to get up and entertain the women he had brought over. Bessie didn't have a baby bed for Barry; she used a box, and she placed a lamp and blanket over it to keep him warm. When Bessie came in the room, George and the women would be talking, laughing, and drinking. She had done this several times for George. Bessie was only seventeen years old, but she decided to stand up and fight for what was hers. She started fighting the women George brought by the house. He was well-endowed and this was what the women were after and one of the reasons Bessie stayed.

Sometimes the ladies would sit on George's lap and tell Bessie, "You don't know what to do with this." Bessie was young and hurt by the situation, but her response would be, "I don't care, and I don't want him anyway, you can have it."

She had grown tired of fighting the other women. She didn't care about them messing with George; she just wanted them to stop coming by her house. They stopped coming to Bessie's house, but sometimes they would drive by and shoot in the air, trying to scare her. She earned the name Bigfoot Bessie, and she didn't take any stuff from anyone at this point.

Bessie didn't really start fighting the ladies and wanting them to stay away from the house until Grady (Bessie's soon-to-be boyfriend) whispered in her ear. Grady told her, "It's not right for George to bring these ladies to your house, especially since he has children by one of them." Grady didn't necessarily tell Bessie this information to benefit her, he was trying to get in for himself and eventually he did.

She tried to be a good wife to George. She stayed home, cleaned house, and took care of the children the best she knew how. She had three children on a bottle at the same time. When it was time to fix their bottles, she fixed them all a bottle, including one for her, and they would all sit in the floor and drink their milk. When they finished, they would all take a nap on a blanket that she had laid in the floor. As the children got bigger, she went outside to play with them, making mud cakes.

There were times Bessie would load up the children and go to see her sister, Sis, in Lonoke. This one time, Sis had a son who was a few months old at this time. When he was born, his skin was so scaly he looked like a fish. So, they started calling him Tadpole. When Bessie saw him, she decided to bring him home with her for a while. After getting home, she was standing in her doorway, looking outside, when she saw a pan of oil that George had drained out of one of the cars he was working on. In her mind, she thought about the fact that they put that same oil on dogs when they had the 'mange' and it cleared up their skin. Why not try it on Tadpole? So, she took him outside and dipped him in the oil, and sure enough, minutes later she was able to get some of the scaly skin off him. For three days straight, she dipped Tadpole in the oil, and the third day his skin was completely clear. When Bessie took Tadpole back to his Mama, she couldn't believe that was her baby. She was so excited, she wanted to know how Bessie got her baby's skin clear. They laughed as Bessie told her the story.

After a while, more times than not, the hard times in Bessie's home outweighed the good times. It became harder for her to take care of the children's basic needs due to George gambling his check away. Bessie was lonely and lost, trying to figure out how she was going to take care of the children and make ends meet. She had grown weary of sitting at the house, weekend after weekend, waiting for

George to come home. So, she decided to take the children to Mom Fannie's house (George's Mama). Lost and alone, Bessie walked down the narrow dark streets to the house. The children were all in a line behind her, trying to keep up. Some of the children started to cry and she picked one up while Betty grabbed the other. She arrived at Mom Fannie's house frustrated, hurt, and tired as she sat and stared into space, trying to figure out what to do. After sitting at the house for a little while, she left the house to look for George, hoping she could find him before he gambled away his check. She returned a few hours later the same way she had left, frustrated, hurt, and tired, because she couldn't find George. Bessie got her children and went home.

This was Bessie's ritual for a few weekends, but things soon changed. When George came home, Bessie would tell George that the children were hungry and his reply would be, "What you want me to do about it?" Bessie didn't find George when she went searching for him on the weekends, but what she did find was a good time and a release from all the pressure that life had brought her. She stopped returning home to the children and started hanging out just as much or more than George. When Betty got a little older, Bessie left all the children at the house with her to babysit. Bessie would charge sandwich meat during the week at a local mom and pop store, hoping George would pay the bill at the end of the week. But he didn't, so the owners of the store stopped letting her charge anything. She realized she had something that men and women wanted, so she set the price. This was one of the oldest professions in the world and Bessie was good at it.

She left the children at the house by themselves when she couldn't get in touch with James or Stine to babysit. Bessie had gotten a taste of the street life and no one could convince her to go home and be the dutiful wife and Mama again. George would come home after a long night of gambling to find his wife gone and the children fending for themselves. This made him very angry, but not enough to make him stay home and take care of the children himself. George wanted his wife home with the children, but it wasn't going to happen. A sleeping giant had awakened in Bessie and there was nothing he could say or do to turn things around. He tried to turn Bessie back into that innocent little girl he had married and make her stay home while he went out. She resisted on every hand, and this turned their home into a battleground almost daily. They both were selfish, only thinking of themselves, and the children paid the price.

James said, "Bessie was a good girl at first; George made Bessie do the things she did. George created that monster."

Bessie quickly learned the streets and had become better than George at the game. He could dish it out, but he couldn't swallow the bitter pill when it was his time to take it. Most of the time, George made it home before Bessie did. By the time she finally made it home, his anger had come to a boil and the battle was on. George would beat Bessie and she, in return, would run out of the house to avoid the blows. She would then stay gone for days at a time. She had gotten a taste of what he was doing all the time. George and the children were no longer her top priority, Bessie was now taking care of her own needs, wants, and everything else in her life was second and third. She was living the nightlife, drinking, gambling, and having sexual relationships with men and women. George had lost Bessie and when he realized this, he thought beating her would change this. But it didn't and never would. It only made Bessie get the strength to start fighting back instead of running.

There were times that Mattie (Bessie's sister) came to stay a few days with them. This still didn't slow Bessie down. Mattie recalls George coming home from work and Bessie not being there. George was hungry and tired; he'd ask Mattie to cook him some bread. Mattie didn't mince words with him; she just went to the kitchen and shot her best shot. Mattie was just a child and really didn't know what she was doing. George always ate the bread and never complained.

Betty was the oldest of Bessie's children and she was just a child, not even a teenager yet. But she had to take on the responsibility of taking care of the other children in her parents' absence. Betty was a little girl, but she became Mama to her siblings, and the smaller children even called her Mama. She made sure the children took a bath and got dressed, cleaned the house, and fed them when there was food at the house. When Bessie left the house, she would tell Betty to lock the door and not let anyone in. When there was no food in the house and the children got hungry, Betty and her siblings went out of the back door to the neighbor's house. All of the children would be right behind her in a straight line wherever she went. They would follow her like ducklings following their Mama duck. When Betty knocked on the door, Mrs. Mean would come to the door and look down at the children. Betty would look up at her and say, "Mrs. Mean, we hungry," and Mrs. Mean would reply, "Come on in and fix you something." Betty would go into the kitchen and fix herself and her siblings some peanut butter and jelly sandwiches. Mr. and Mrs. Mean didn't have any children together, but Mr. Mean had children. They were always so nice to the children and there were many days that they fed Betty and her siblings.

When they didn't get food from the neighbors, Mom Fannie and her husband would drop food off at the house. Bessie hated Mom Fannie and her husband, perhaps because of their constant attempt to advise her that she needs to change her lifestyle. However, if it hadn't been for her in-laws, there would have been many hungrier days for the children. On school days, Betty had to make sure all the children were dressed and ready to go to school. They would all line up behind Betty and follow her to school.

There was this gentleman named Benny who knew Bessie's situation, so he started leaving money in the mailbox for her to feed the children. This gentleman really liked Bessie, but she didn't care much for him. He knew her circumstances and knew just what to do to get her attention. Every week, he left money, and then he started leaving his whole check in the mailbox. Some of the women who knew him would tell Bessie, "All right, you keep taking Benny's money, he's gonna want something in return and he's going to pull a gun on you and make you do what he wants you to do." Bessie said, "I don't care; I'm taking this money so I can feed my children."

Benny wasn't easy on the eyes; he was a big, black, ugly man. Soon Benny started telling Bessie that he would get her a house for her and her children. When he got the house, Bessie left George and moved in the house. Benny soon moved in with her, but Bessie wasn't expecting that. Bessie left the children with George and his Mama, promising she would come back to get them to move in with her later. The children didn't move with her, but they came to visit.

Benny and Bessie's relationship went sour quickly. They started arguing and fighting frequently. This was because she realized she didn't care anything for him. She didn't want to be with him sexually, but Benny wasn't having it. He would pull a gun on Bessie to make her sleep with him. She grew tired of this quickly and decided that all money ain't good money. Benny was holding a gun on Bessie one day while they were riding in the car, headed for Stuttgart. Bessie decided enough was enough and made up her mind to jump out of the moving car to kill herself. She would rather be dead than stay in this situation. She opened the door, put her feet out to jump, and he grabbed her by her belt and held on to her while he stopped the car. Before he could get the car stopped, Bessie's feet dragged on the ground and were now hurt.

Bessie decided to move out of Benny's house while he was at work, but he found her. He had someone watching her, and at three o'clock in the morning he showed up at the door. Bessie was horrified. She moved seven times that week, but he found her each time. This was the price she was paying for taking Benny's money. He felt as if Bessie belonged to him, and he wasn't going to let her go that easily.

Finally, Bessie moved back in with George. Benny would knock on the door in the wee hours of the morning. She would tell George, "That's that old man." He would get his gun but wouldn't open the door. She would tell him to shoot, but George wouldn't. Bessie told George, "Give me the gun, I'll shoot." Benny would knock for a while, but eventually he left. Bessie finally had to go to the police for help. When she told the police her story, they told her they would be watching for him. When Benny finally showed up, the police were watching, and they arrested him. The police ordered Benny to stay away from Bessie.

This was when Bessie made up her mind that her children would not go hungry or without clothes again. She knew she couldn't depend on anyone but herself to take care of her children's basic needs. Bessie might not have had much of an education, but she knew how to count her money. She was better at gambling and playing cards than George was at rolling dice. Bessie had learned to sew and made most of her children's clothes -- that is, before she started stealing. Bessie had heard some people talking in the club one night about boosting clothes (designing clothes with hidden compartments for stealing). She paid attention to every word that they said and thought, "I can do that." Thus began Bessie's boosting career.

The fighting between George and Bessie only grew worse as the years passed and both continued their infidelity. Both had conceived children by other people while they were married to one another, and they both knew it. There was too much misfortune between them to repair and now when they were fighting, Bessie was standing toe to toe with George. The last fight they had, Bessie almost killed George.

They were separated, but ended up in the same place, drinking together. George got Bessie drunk with some Five Brother's Whiskey. Then he told her she was going home with him. Bessie had no intention of going home with George; she had plans to go home with one of the men from the band and the night was still young.

She told him, "No I'm not going home with you."

George said, "Come on now and come spend the night with me."

Bessie looked at him, eyeball to eyeball, and said, "I'm not going."

This made George mad, so he reverted to what he knew best. George beat Bessie until she was dusty, and her clothes torn halfway off. Instead of bystanders helping her, some of the men began to yell, "That's right, whoop her, she needs it."

Bessie picked up a knife that was nearby and began chasing him and swinging the knife, trying to cut George. As they ran around the cars that were parked, Bessie impelled the knife through the roof of someone's car. One of the bystanders tried to pull the knife out, but it broke.

Bessie looked down at the broken knife and said, "This enough for me."

George kept running around the cars, but he wasn't quick enough for Bigfoot Bessie. Every time he cut a corner; Bessie would cut him. She kept doing this until George fell. The same men who had encouraged George to beat Bessie were now saying, "You done killed the man."

Bessie still drunk and dazed said, "What man?" When she looked down and saw all the blood around George, she took off running. She ran to her house and got in the bed and went to sleep.

Early that morning, the police came to her room, knocking at the door. One was at the door and the other policeman was crawling through the window. When they got in, they told Bessie that she was under arrest. Bessie yelled, "For what?"

The police replied, "You done killed your husband."

Bessie quickly said, "I didn't kill anybody." She had to get dressed and go with the police. George was not dead and did not press charges against Bessie, so the police had to let her go. She went to the hospital, and when she got to George's room, Jun (George's brother) was standing in the door. He looked up at Bessie and said, "You can't come in, Miss." Bessie then threatened to cut him like she had cut his brother. Jun stepped to the side and said, "Come on in, Miss."

The police told Bessie, "You are lucky that you didn't kill him."

George wasn't so lucky; he was paralyzed for three months. The worst cut was in the bend of his arm. He almost bled to death before his friends could get him to the hospital. George looked up at Bessie and told her that she was going to have to get a job and take care of him since he was paralyzed. He knew before he let those words come out of his mouth, that wasn't going to happen.

George's Mama and father were outraged at Bessie for doing this to their son. Mom Fannie told George to stay away from that woman – she was crazy. But Bessie wasn't messed up about what they thought about her. There had never been any lost love between Mom Fannie and Bessie. She didn't like Mom Fannie at the beginning of her and George's marriage. Mom Fannie didn't mean any harm; she was just trying to tell Bessie the right thing to do. She would say to Bessie, "Baby, why don't you stay at home and take care of your children?" Bessie would simply just give her a good cussing out and tell her to mind her own [expletive] business. George eventually recovered, and he and Bessie never got together again after this.

This was one of the best things that could have happened for the children, because they got to live with George's Mama and father for five years. George and Bessie got to live their lives like they wanted to, carefree and in the streets. The children were safe and didn't have to worry about the necessities of life. Betty did, however, still have to take care of the children while Mom Fannie was at work.

Mom Fannie would come home from work and fix supper for everyone. Sometimes her husband, James, was not at home, so she would put his plate up until he did come home. Mr. James would sometimes be around the corner at his girlfriend's house and Mom Fannie knew it, but she never said a word. That was the way George wanted Bessie to be, but he had picked the wrong woman for that role.

For five years, the children had the best of both worlds. The best thing that happened to the children was both of their parents letting them go. George rarely brought them money or anything. Betty recalls asking their dad for some money and he gave her $25. And that was $5 apiece for each one of them. Betty got mad at him and threw the money back at him and said to him, "What is $25 going to do for us? That ain't any kind of money." George pleaded with Betty and asked her to please take the money. She finally took it.

George never really spent quality time with the children when they were small. Betty asked her father one day, "Daddy, why don't you take us anywhere? Take us somewhere." George loaded up the children and took them around the block to his girlfriend's house. He would sit in the chair and go to sleep when they got there. The children sat there quietly for about an hour before they got up and walked back home. This was what George wanted; he knew sooner or later they would get tired and go home. He would then wake up and go gambling. George even took the children to the gambling house once or twice and left them in the car for hours.

The children sat in the car for practically a whole day. It got dark, and the children were hungry and cold. Whenever someone passed by the car, the children would tell them to tell George to come out and take them home. The children did this with several of the people who passed by. Their father had forgotten about them. The children knew their father had finally gotten their messages when someone came to the car and started the car so they could turn the heat on to keep warm. The children sat in the car a few more hours before their father emerged from the gambling house broke, with his head hung low, to take them home.

Bessie may not have had the money or means to take good care of the children while she had them, but she had pepped up her game since they were with Mom Fannie. She brought them all kinds of clothes, shoes, bicycles, toys, and a TV for their birthdays and Christmas. She even brought food by so Mom Fannie wouldn't have a hard time feeding them. Mind you, Bessie stole just about everything she brought to them, but she did what she did best to make ends meet. Bessie had gotten pretty good at boosting stolen goods. She not only stole for her children, but for others in the family also. Bessie said that Mack would report that she brought them a lot of underwear throughout the years. Momole never had to buy them any underwear if Bessie was in business. She could go in a store and not just shoplift, but lift the shop. When she went to steal, she hurt the store profits. It was rare that she ever got caught. She was the original OG (Original Gangster) Booster.

Bessie was so tough at boosting that she went to bed one night and dreamed how to make some boosting underwear. They wore petticoats back then, so the dresses were wide, and you couldn't tell when they had stolen goods. They had pockets in the front, back, and side. Bessie only made two pair, one for herself and one pair for her boosting partner. Lots of her friends wanted her to make them a pair, but she wouldn't. After Bessie and her fellow boosters got to the store and filled up the boosting drawers they were wearing, they had to make sure they were even all the way around. So, Bessie would bust out with a song and say, "Hey am I even all around." One of fellow boosters would look and then sing back to her. "Oh yes you're even, you look just fine." Although there was one time, she got caught that she will never forget.

Bessie decided to come to Lonoke and visit Momole. She brought one of her friend girls along with her. Well, while visiting, Momole decided to go to McCray's Clothing Store. Darnell was Momole's baby at this time, so she brought him along. While Momole was shopping and paying for her things, Bessie and her friends were stealing, and they got caught. The store owner called the police and they went to jail. They locked them all up, including the baby. Well if you know Momole, you got to know she didn't take this standing still. Momole lay on that jail cell floor and screamed and yelled at the top of her lungs. When her sons, Finnie and John, found out they were in jail, John brought his boss down to the jail to see what he could do for them.

When John's boss went to the back where they were locked up, he told the police, "If you all don't want to get sued, you better get that baby out of there."

Momole yelled out, "I got a receipt for everything I got, I didn't steal anything."

John's boss then said, "Better yet, let them all go. I'll pay."

When Momole got outside, she looked at Bessie and cursed her out and told her, "Don't you ever come back to my house."

Bessie knew her Mama meant what she was saying at the time and that she would come around in time.

She was so good at boosting, different people in the neighborhood would literally go shopping at her house. Bessie stole and boosted things until her children got grown. She tried to continue boosting but got caught three times. The last time, the judge told her if she came back in his courtroom, he was going to lock her up. This ended Bessie's career of boosting. They took her boosting underwear, and they became famous after they showed them on the news.

Bessie hadn't even named the underwear; the news people named them boosting drawers.

During the five to six years the children were with Mom Fannie, Bessie went from house to house, staying with different girlfriends and men. Bessie's bisexual relationship angered George, and sometimes he would refer to Bessie as "that ____ dyke" in front of the children. Bessie was free at last to do as she chose to do. Sometimes she managed to get a place of her own for a while and the children would go stay overnight with her. Whenever they stayed at her house, Bessie still went out and left them by themselves. When her date came to the house and saw the children there, he didn't want to stay and take care of business with the children in the house. So, they would leave the house. Before Bessie left, she would give the children instructions to clean house, lock the doors, and not to let anyone in.

After staying at their mom's house for a few days, Betty would finally call Mom Fannie to come get them because she was gone most of the time and they didn't get to spend much time with her, which was the main reason they wanted to go with her. Some of the children felt like the only reason she even wanted them to come over to her house was because she wanted them to clean the house and hang her clothes up.

Bessie did what she had to do to provide for the children. Granted, most was illegal and immoral, but she did what she thought she had to do. The children had clothes on their backs, shoes on their feet, and toys to play with. But the thing they wanted the most, they did not have. All they really wanted was to spend time with their Mama and father. But this would never be, because their Mama and father were both lost in their own selfish worlds.

It was 1966, and Bessie was now living with her boyfriend, Grady. They had been in a relationship on and off even when she was still married to George. Bessie was in love and now pregnant with Grady's child. They named the baby Janice, and all was going well for three months. Janice was a good baby and didn't cry much, but God had only given her three months on this earth. This was a hurtful situation for them both, but three years later, in 1969, Bessie got pregnant again and Grady decided that they would get married, so they got married after the baby was born.

Bessie & Grady

After Janice was born, Bessie decided she wanted all her other children back and went to court to get them. When the judge asked the children who they wanted to stay with, all the children said they wanted to stay with their Mama. The children figured that their mom would be the better choice because they were looking at all the things that she had bought for them. The courts ruled in Bessie's favor and the children went to stay with their mom and Grady. It didn't take long before the children realized that they had made the wrong choice. With this realization came the knowledge of why their mom really wanted them there. Bessie was having children and she needed the older children to care for the younger children and to keep the house clean.

It only took a few days for them to get the big picture of how big a mistake they had really made. Bessie went out and told the children to clean the house while she was gone. The children thought they had done a good job, but when she got home, their good job was not up to her satisfaction. She beat the children from the oldest to the youngest. James was the youngest and he was only two years old. The children were terrified and in shock. They were not used to getting whippings like that. They made up their minds that they were not going to get another one. So, they all ran away and went back to the place where they felt loved and safe, Mom Fannie's house. The children didn't know that it was not going to be that simple to leave their mom's house. When Bessie realized they were gone and they had run off, she went to the police station to tell them her plight. The police went with Bessie to Mom Fannie's house to get her children back. When they arrived, the children were horrified to see their Mama and didn't want to go with her. Bessie repeatedly apologized to the children for whipping them and told them it was not going to happen again. The police asked the two oldest children if they wanted to go back with their Mama. They were scared to say no, because they were afraid if their Mama got them alone, she would beat them senseless. They had to go back because Bessie had legal custody of them now. They really didn't have a choice in the matter.

Hearts heavy, filled with fear, and tears rolling down their cheeks, they reluctantly loaded into the car and went home with their Mama. Bessie didn't keep her word and had no intention of keeping her word. The first time the children did something wrong that she didn't like, she beat them. The children lived in constant fear. When Bessie went out, she expected the children to have the house spotless when she returned home. The children did their very best to make sure the house was clean before they went to bed. But there were times that their stepfather, Grady, would get up and cook something and mess up the kitchen while they were in the bed, and leave the dishes in the sink. Bessie would come home the next morning and see the dishes in the sink and go ballistic. The children were awakened by the sting of an extension cord sinking into their flesh. The children tried to tell their Mama they had cleaned the kitchen before they went to bed, but she wouldn't listen. Grady sat in the other room or lay in the bed as Bessie beat the children and didn't mumble a word that he was the one responsible for the dishes in the sink. The children realized he really didn't like them and didn't want them there. The children even heard him talking on the phone one day saying what he really felt about them.

He said, "I married her not all these children. I don't want them here."

Betty had gotten tired of being beaten for something someone else was doing. They were getting enough beatings otherwise. She got wise to Grady's tricks and would wake up when he came home in the middle of the night. When he got through eating, Betty eased out of her bed and cleaned the kitchen. This deterred some of the beatings, but not all of them. For fear of waking to an extension cord tearing at their flesh, the children put on extra clothes when they went to bed. But when Bessie realized what they were doing, she made all of them strip naked and then she would beat them, and sometimes she drew blood.

When Bessie came home after a night of fun the next day, the children would be listening for her car to pull in the driveway. When they heard her car finally pull in the driveway, fear gripped their hearts and they began running around the house, almost stumbling over one another, trying to check and see if everything was done. Just before she walked in the house, they all hurried and sat down almost on top of one another. Breathing hard and holding their breaths at the same time, if it were possible, holding on to each other, they trembled as their Mama walked through the door. They were all hoping this was going to be a good day. They never knew what kind of day it was going to be until she walked in and said something. It all depended on how their Mama greeted them when she came through the door as to what kind of day it would be. Sometimes she would enter the house and say, "Hey, how are my babies doing today?" When she did this, they all exhaled a big sigh of relief. It was a good day. The children knew everything had gone in their mom's favor the night before. They knew she had won some money gambling and her boyfriend had treated her right.

But then there were those days Bessie would step through the door after a long night of partying and complain about everything in sight. On these occasions, nothing the children did was right in her eyesight. Even though they had tried with everything in them to make sure everything was in place, it didn't matter if their mom had had a bad night. The children sat there holding on to one another, hearts racing because they knew they were in for the beating of their lives.

The days they went to school before their mom came home were just as bad as the weekends. If she had a bad night, when they came home from school, clothes from all the dresser drawers and closets would all be on the floor. She would do this when she saw anything hanging out of the drawer or the clothes were not hung right in the closet. They preferred this over those days that she would show up at the school. If Betty was at school and looked up and saw Bessie coming, she would almost hyperventilate, wondering who she was coming to get, while praying and hoping it wasn't her. Whichever one of them she was coming to get, she would whip them on the spot. The embarrassment of this was almost too much to live through.

Even when the children were out playing with their friends near the house, they couldn't get comfortable and enjoy themselves. It might have appeared to the other children that they had no worries. But while the children laughed and played ball, the fear of their mom coming home was still in the back of their minds, and so they never truly could relax, because they knew she could show up anytime. No matter how engrossed in the ballgame or intense the ballgame became, the children could hear and recognize the sound of their mom's car a block away from the house. When they heard their Mama's car, it didn't matter if they were up to bat, on first, second, or third base, their fight or flight response kicked in and they took off running toward the house, trying to beat their mom home. Bessie had such a fear in her children, the neighborhood children even feared her. The children would make it to the house before their mom would pull up in the yard. Panicking and running over one another, they all ran in the house to give it one more looking over to see if they had missed something. Once they had checked out the house, they would all sit down with their hearts pounding, waiting to see what the verdict was going to be, beating or no beating.

Annie, Bessie's third child, will never forget the beating of her life for losing one of her Mama's forty-five cent records. Annie was in the fifth grade and they were having a Christmas party the next day at school. Annie's teacher had told the class they could bring records to the school to play at the Christmas party. She was excited about this because she knew her Mama had plenty of records. When she asked her Mama if she could take some of the records to her Christmas party at school, she said no. Annie was so disappointed by her Mama's reply, but her desire to take the records to school altered her judgment. She decided to disobey her mom and took five of her Mama's records to school anyway. All was well until Annie realized that one of the records was missing at the end of the day. She knew this was not going to be a good outcome for her, and fear gripped her heart as she made the journey home. After she got home and her Mama found out about the record, it was on and popping. Bessie beat Annie from one end of the house to the other.

It was wintertime and they lived in a shotgun house, and it was hard to keep the house warm. There was water in the tub and the children had filled the tub with soiled cloth diapers that they were supposed to wash. It was so cold in the bathroom until a thin layer of ice had formed over the water in the tub. Bessie was still beating Annie when she ran in the bathroom and jumped in the tub. Annie sat her hurting behind down in ice water and feces, trying to soothe the sting and pain she was feeling. As she sat down in the water, she said, "Awe!" For years, her sibling teased her about that and told her when she sat down, steam was coming from the water as she said awe. Annie quickly told me the reason she said "Awe," was because the water was cold.

Bessie stayed at home sometimes, but these were the times when the card game was scheduled to be played at her house. The children felt as though she treated her friends better than she treated them. The children would clean the house all day to prepare for the company that night. Bessie even fixed her friends a full course meal. She was the perfect hostess and she did everything to make her friends comfortable. The more comfortable they were, the longer they stayed gambling and partying. There were a couple of Bessie's customers that were more than friends. Bessie had gotten pregnant twice by one of her friends who hung out at her house. One other problem with this situation, other than the obvious, was that another lady friend of hers who hung out with them was also pregnant by the same man. This caused some friction, but it didn't stop the card games. Bessie got pregnant by this same man twice.

In between the partying, Bessie was still having children. While Grady and Bessie were together, she had six children and only two of them were Grady's. Bessie even told Grady that James was his child when she was pregnant with him. But when James was born, he looked like George's twin. Bessie was no angel and Grady was no saint; he hung out and did his thing also, but he had enough sense to come home before Bessie. He would take a bath and be in bed by the time Bessie made it home. Then he would fuss at Bessie for staying out all night, like he had been at home all night long. When Grady and Bessie got together, she was married to another man. They were a man and woman of like passions. Grady and Bessie had their fights and when they did, Bessie would threaten to leave but never did. She would go through the motions, but always ended up staying.

In the heat of the argument, she would tell the children to pack all their clothes and get in the car. The children were happy to do this because they felt as if Grady didn't care for them anyway, so they were glad to be leaving. They quickly loaded all their belongings in the car, sat, and waited for their mom to come out of the house. She would be in the house talking to Grady trying to settle their differences. The door finally opened, and the children's hearts were glad, but that soon changed after Bessie told them to bring everything back in the house because they were staying. Bessie and Grady went through this a few more times. The only difference was Betty didn't move when her Mama told her to pack their things and put them in the car. After Grady and Bessie calmed down and settled their differences, everything went back to normal. The closest Bessie ever came to leaving was sitting in the car with one leg in and one leg out of the car.

Bessie's oldest son, Barry, was about thirteen years old. He played football during the week and worked on the weekends with his father. He came home after a long day of school and football, unaware that his siblings had just got a whipping. When he walked in the house, his Mama informed him that the other children had already had their whipping and now she was going to give him his. When Bessie drew back the belt to hit him, he caught it in midair. Breathing hard, teeth gnashed together, he looked at his Mama eyeball to eyeball and told her that he was not going to take another whipping. This made Bessie furious, but by the time she could think of what to do, he had gotten his clothes and left the house. He moved to Lonoke to stay with his Aunt Lena Mae. He stayed with them over a year and then moved back to Pine Bluff with his father. He had it made; it was just him and his father, and life was a lot better.

Meanwhile, back at Bessie's house, the other children who were left were still going through difficult times with their Mama. Terry and James got a beating one day, and they decided that enough was enough. Bruised and battered, they packed a few things and ran away to their father's house. George wasn't perfect, but he didn't beat the children like Bessie did and this was what the children were running from. Terry and James showed up on their father's doorstep, pleading for him to let them come and stay with him. They showed their father their battered bodies. George didn't know what he was going to do, but he knew he had to do something. He loaded the children in his vehicle and took them to the police station. He informed the police of the circumstances and showed them the scars and bruises on the children's bodies. They were very sympathetic to the situation and advised George to take the children home with him and keep them. The police knew Bessie wasn't going to do much to cause trouble because she was in the wrong. George and the children were pleased with the solutions that the police had given them, so they happily went home.

Terry and James were safe now and it was no longer George and Barry, it was George and all his boys hanging out together. Betty had gotten married by this time and Bessie would call Betty, crying because Terry and James had left. Betty would console her by telling her, "Don't worry about them, Mama, they will come on back home after they realize what they're missing." Betty knew this wasn't true and she had to ask the Lord to forgive her. She knew where Terry and James were and that they were happy and content.

There would be days Bessie would go by George's house looking for the children. When Terry and James saw her car pull up at their father's house, they would panic and go up to the attic and hide most of the day. Bessie would knock at the door, but the boys would be quiet as a church mouse until she got in her car and left the house. They came out of the attic, knowing they had dodged the bullet one more time.

After a few years, Terry and James overcame the fear that had been instilled in them by their Mama. I listened to James as he told me the story about when he was standing at the bus stop, waiting for the bus to take them to his father's house after he had gotten out of school. While waiting, he thought he heard his Mama's car coming and fear gripped every fiber of his being. He just took off running. His father lived about four to five miles from the school. But James was so panicky about his Mama catching up with him, he didn't think about that, he just ran. The bus driver saw James running and tried to pick him up down the street, but James never stopped running until he reached his father's house safely. I believe James was feeling the fear that he felt back then in that moment as he said, "No man should have to fear a woman like that." Not long after Terry and James moved in with their father, their sister, Annie, followed. Annie was the last of George's children to leave Bessie's home.

James Ray (Bessie's brother) often said Bessie was a good girl in the beginning, "It was George's fault that Bessie did the things she did. She didn't have too much of a choice, he didn't bring any money home and she had to do what she had to do to survive. George created that monster."

Even when Bessie married Grady, she never stopped her hustle. Some nights Bessie and Grady went out and danced the night away. Grady had grown tired of Bessie hosting the card games at the house. He complained about the bills increasing because her friends were hanging out at the house. So, Bessie told him she would pay the bills and he could save his money. Grady was a butcher and was well capable of paying all the bills, but he agreed to Bessie's suggestion. Bessie did as she said she would do. She hustled and paid the bills with some of the money she made for years. After several years passed, Grady got tired of Bessie hosting the card games at the house and asked her to stop. It wasn't until then that he started paying the bills. After Bessie stopped hosting games at her house, she didn't have money in her pocket like she was used to having. So, she would go to Grady and ask him for money and his reply would be, "Where is your money?" He had saved his money for years and had started paying the bills but wouldn't give Bessie money when she needed some. She didn't know how she was going to make it.

She fell on her knees and talked to God. She said, "God, I need a job, I don't care if it's a job shoveling [explicit], I need a job." Bessie went to bed that night and about three o'clock in the morning, she got a call from a friend who needed some help at a club, and she went to work for him. After working for him a while, he gave her a club of her own to manage. Bessie ran the club for a few years, and then she finally let it go after Grady ran her customers away. This time when Bessie prayed to God, she prayed a different prayer. She prayed to the Lord and asked Him to take her appetite for the clubs, drinking, men and women, and God did that for her.

Grady and Bessie slowed down tremendously in their golden years. As this book in being written, she has a clothing store selling secondhand clothing. But she still enjoys playing cards and the slot machine on occasions. Her children are all grown up and have their own families. They all get together on some holidays and enjoy one another's company. I'm sure they all have their struggles, but not enough to keep them from moving forward in their lives. Bessie and Grady still would argue and fight about the years gone past. But they chose to stay together. Many may not understand their relationship, but it doesn't matter, because despite all their struggles they loved one another in their own way. There were times that Bessie refused to argue with Grady, and during those times he would say, "Mrs. Bessie, you don't love me anymore." Then they would argue about that and he was satisfied.

Grady passed away in 2016 of a heart attack. He loved Bessie and wanted to make sure she was taken care of after he was gone. They were married over forty years and chose to stay together despite the changes they had gone through. He trusted the children to do the right thing. At Grady's funeral, Mattie talked about the times when they needed shoes or any type of clothing. Momole would load them up in the truck and head to Pine Bluff. They would go to Bessie's house and literally shop like it was a store. They would get everything they needed. Not only did they shop for clothes, they would look in the refrigerator and cook whatever they needed. Grady would pass through the kitchen while they were cooking and smile. He never stopped them from eating whatever they wanted. Mattie said, "He might have had a mean streak, but we never saw it, he was always nice to us."

Will (aka Gabby)

Gabby was Momole's eighth child and I tell his story because his life was cut short at such an early age. It was 1968 and Gabby was a lot like his brother, Louis. Gabby was twenty-one years old and full of life. Besides fighting, he loved dancing and the ladies. There weren't too many people his age or even older who could beat him in a fight. His brother, Louis, was the only one who could truly give him a run for his money. There were many people who feared him and tried to stay out of his way. This fear that had been instilled in different ones cost him his life at a time that seemed to be too soon. Gloria Scarborough was the main lady in his life even though there were others. She was pregnant with Gabby's daughter and had already given birth to his son. Gabby and Gloria's brother, Arthur, were best of friends. Whenever Gabby hung out and was not hanging solo with one of his lady friends, Arthur was with him.

When Gabby went out on the weekends, he would borrow his brother, Shaffer's 1966 Chevy. After getting his brother's car, he would pick up his friends and they would hit up the popular juke joints. One weekend, Gabby decided to go to Little Rock to visit one of his lady friends instead of hanging out with the fellows. His brother, James, decided to go to Kool Kat Inn Juke Joint in England, where they all hung out from time to time. James was one of those people who talked a lot of jive talk whether he was drinking or not. If you spent any time around him, he would make you laugh, if you weren't the one he was talking about. Well, James got into an altercation with Tommy, a young man who sang in the band that night. The altercation was serious enough that Tommy tried to kill James. He stabbed James in both of his legs. The only reason he stabbed him in the legs and not in his upper body was because while James was on the ground, he was backing up and kicking him at the same time. This stopped Tommy from being able to reach James's upper body with the knife. Once James got Tommy off him, he ran for his life. James went home and took care of his wounds and went to bed.

When Gabby came home that night, he had already heard the news about James before he made it to the house. He walked to the bedroom, turned the light on and pulled the covers off James to see how badly he was hurt. Gabby asked if James was all right and he replied, "I'm all right." After James explained what happened to Gabby, they called it a night, and both went to bed.

Tommy knew Gabby was James's brother. He was not afraid of James, but he was terrified of Gabby. He figured Gabby was going to come after him for what he had done to his brother. The owner of the juke joint knew he was scared, and they all knew of Gabby's reputation. Everyone was expecting Gabby to retaliate. The owner gave Tommy a .25 automatic pistol just in case there was trouble and he had to defend himself. Having the pistol gave him confidence that he wouldn't have otherwise had.

The next night, Gabby decided to go to the Kool Kat Inn. That evening, Robert (Louis's son) was standing in the yard when Gabby stopped and talked with him. Gabby told Robert he was going to England to kick some [expletive]. Then Gabby handed a glass pebble to Robert and said, "This is my good luck charm, hold onto it until I get back." Robert was just a child and was excited about the good luck charm his uncle had given him. They picked up a few of their friends and headed to the juke joint, and Arthur was among those friends. The thought of what had happened to James the night before was in the forefront of all their minds as they conversed with one another about it.

Gabby had come to terms with the anger he might have felt about James getting stabbed, and decided to just let it go as they drove to England. He interrupted their conversation and said, "Listen, ain't going to be any trouble tonight, so, don't start any trouble. We just want to have a good time." When they arrived, the place was hopping, the music could be heard with the car windows rolled up, and cars were everywhere. Yes, there was a good time to be had. They got out of the car and headed for the door. The incident from the night before was firmly etched in the back of their minds, even though they didn't want any trouble.

The place was packed; the people were shoulder to shoulder and smoke filled the air as they made their way in. The music was loud and this, coupled with the chatter of different conversations, made it hard to hear anything being said. Gabby, being the lady's man that he was, grabbed a young lady's hand and headed for the dance floor. After dancing, they just stood around and looked, taking in the things happening around them. Gabby was unaware that Tommy was scared and had murder in his heart. He wanted trouble even if Gabby didn't. He had no idea that Gabby had come in peace and only wanted to let bygones be bygones and have a good time. Gabby had grown tired of standing around and decided to leave. Before he could reach the door, Tommy approached him. Gabby stopped and turned to hear what he had to say. After hearing what Tommy said, he turned to continue his journey toward the door, while simultaneously saying, "Man I don't want any trouble tonight. I didn't come to fight."

Tommy was unable to hear what Gabby was saying because of the loud music. He reacted to Gabby's comment by reaching for his gun while asking, "What did you say?" Before Gabby could turn completely away, Tommy pulled the trigger and shot him in the side of his head.

Gabby never saw it coming, and for about five seconds, he was still on his feet and then he fell. It wasn't until after he fell that chaos broke loose and everyone began running and screaming. Arthur was standing right beside Gabby when he fell to the floor. He may have wanted to run like everyone else, but his feet wouldn't move, he was in shock. His mind was trying to sort through what had just happened when Tommy turned the gun on him and pulled the trigger. The gun jammed and would not fire. Before Tommy had a chance to pull the trigger again, the security guards snatched the gun from his hand and said, "Give me that gun."

Gabby's friends picked him up off the floor and rushed him to the little clinic in England, and they said there was nothing they could do. They rushed Gabby to UAMS Hospital in Little Rock, and that's where he was pronounced dead. Gabby tried to avoid trouble that night, but the only way he could have avoided that trouble was to have stayed at home.

This was one of the longest nights of James's and Arthur's lives. Their brother and friend was gone, and it was so surreal and hard for them to wrap their minds around it. It all happened so fast, if they could only go back to yesterday. Robert, being a child, still had Gabby's good luck charm and thought he should have taken it with him. It has been over fifty years since Gabby's senseless death, and his absence affected so many he had left behind. When Gabby died, six ladies were either pregnant with his child or had his child already. The children who were already born were all under seven years of age. Arthur and James were never the same after what they witnessed.

Not long after Gabby died, Tommy came to talk with Momole. He cried as he apologized for killing her son. A few years after Gabby died, Arthur, Fat Albert (a friend) and Gloria ran into Tommy singing in a juke joint in Pine Bluff. Seeing Tommy again only made Arthur think of his friend Gabby, and oh how he longed to see him again.

Arthur is now active in the church and sometimes he lets his mind rest on the night that Gabby died and how God spared his life. Arthur testifies in church from time to time about how God spared his life by jamming Tommy's gun that night. The last thought that crosses Arthur's mind after reminiscing about days gone by is how young and foolish they were. "If only we knew then what we know now, we wouldn't have done half the things we did."

I don't remember much about Gabby because he died when I was a small child. The memory is a funny thing, because all I remember about Gabby was him getting dressed up and leaving the house with one of Momole's small towels hanging out of his back pocket. Momole would yell at him while he was walking across the yard, "I told y'all about carrying my towel off time and time again." But Gabby wouldn't listen; he just kept on walking.

I will never forget the day he got shot or the day we went to the funeral home to see his body. I didn't understand what was going on, but I remember Momole lying in the bed, crying. There was such a sadness that filled the atmosphere. When they took me to the funeral home to see Gabby, I still didn't understand what was going on. Mama tried to pick me up so I could see Gabby in his coffin. Fear gripped my heart as I backed away from my Mama to keep her from picking me up. As I backed away from her, I bumped into another coffin that had someone else's body in it. This coffin was low enough for me to see inside. I stared at the corpse, and for several moments I couldn't move. My legs got weak and I had nowhere to run. So, I squatted in the middle of the floor and began to cry. My Mama came and picked me up to comfort me. While comforting me, she walked back over to Gabby's body.

The image of Gabby lying in the coffin caused me to have nightmares for a long time. There were nights that my Mama had to sleep with me. As time passed, I got better until my brother decided to play a prank on me. It was about three years later. My Mama had a picture of Gabby in his coffin; it was face down, so when we looked at the pictures in the album, we wouldn't see the picture. My brother knew I was scared to look at that picture. So, he thought it would be a good joke to put the picture inside the clothes I was folding up. There wasn't too much that scared me, but dead people did.

Mama use to tell me, "Baby, a dead person can't do anything to you, it's the people that's living you have to worry about." It wasn't long before the picture fell out of the clothes onto the floor. My heart began racing as I yelled. When my Mama ran to the room, I was crying hysterically when I showed her why I was crying. She asked, "Who did this?" When I told her that Clyde had done this, the joke was no longer on me but on him." Clyde got a whooping that night, but that was of little comfort. Mama had to sleep with me for a couple of nights before I was able to get over the fear.

I've had to face many situations in my life since I've been an adult when fear and many other emotions overwhelmed me. It is no longer my Mama's comfort that I depend on, but Jesus is the one who wraps His loving arms around me and reassures me that everything will be all right. "For God hath not given us the spirit of fear; but of power, and of love, and of a sound mind." (2 Tim 1:7) One of the fears that I have had to overcome with the help of God was writing this book. I was writing about things that a lot of people didn't know about me and wondering how they were going to take it. I had to let that worry go and obey God and let God have the rest.

Mattie

Mattie was Momole's eleventh child and I'm only telling her story because of the strange circumstances surrounding her death in 2016. Our family in Arkansas had gotten the news about Uncle Jack's death. Finnie knew that a lot of the family would want to go to California to give our last respects. But he also knew that money was an issue with most of us. So, he got the church van, and gave me gas to drive my car there and back. Two other people drove their cars. Seventeen of us were able to make the trip to California. Jack's death weighed heavily on our hearts and minds as we returned to Arkansas.

Little did we know that our hearts were about to get heavier. Four days after we got back to Arkansas, Mattie died while she was at work. That within itself was a bit much to bear, but the unbearable thing about the situation was she had been dead for five days before any of the family found out she was dead. She worked at a facility that cared for mentally challenged adults in Jacksonville, Arkansas. Mattie was already sick when she arrived at work. As the night progressed, she became even sicker and began running into walls. The staff called their boss in the middle of the night to tell her about Mattie being sick and they also asked her if they should call 911. Their boss, for whatever reason, didn't deem it necessary to call 911 even though Mattie was foaming at the mouth and disorientated. She worked the evening shift. By eleven o'clock, Mattie was so disoriented that she didn't know how to clock out. Instead of calling 911, they told her to lie down on the sofa, and that's where they found her dead at 2:30 in the morning. Then they deemed it necessary to call 911. When the ambulance came to get her, no paperwork was given to them to properly ID who Mattie's family was. When she arrived at the hospital, she was dead upon arrival. The hospital then called the coroner to come get her body and she was sent to the Little Rock coroners with a toe tag that said no family. There Mattie lay for four, almost five days like she had no family. Mattie is one of sixteen brothers and sisters. Some had preceded her in death, but there was plenty of family left who loved her.

Finnie called me the night before we found out she was dead, to ask if I had heard from her. I told him no and gave him her new cell phone number. Right after I hung up, Fatina (her niece) called me and asked if I had heard from Mattie. I explained that I had talked to her Tuesday and she was supposed to be coming by the house to pick up some DVDs, but she never showed. Someone called and told Fatina they heard that Mattie was dead. I responded without any hesitation and said, "They are lying. I am going to her job to see if she's at work."

Mattie's job was right around the corner from where I lived. When I walk in the facility, I asked a young lady if I could speak to Mattie Woodard. She was unable to help me, but two ladies walked out of their office by that time. I knew something was wrong as one of the ladies began to talk. She said, "Ma'am, Mrs. Mattie died on the job Thursday morning and we have been trying to get in touch with some of the family." I began to scream; I couldn't believe what I was hearing. I didn't understand then or now how they couldn't get in touch with any of the family, because her contact information was in her file. They didn't even know where her body was. Finnie made calls and found Mattie's body and the family was able to do what it took to put her to rest.

I didn't finish the book before Mattie passed away, but I was able to read Uncle Jack his story from the book before he passed away. Mattie and Finnie are responsible for giving me Momole's story, and I will be forever grateful to both.

Stine, Annie Momole, Mattie & Mary

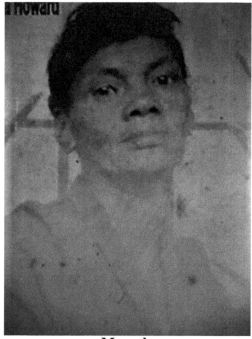

Momole

James

James was Momole's twelfth child. After James and Stine got old enough, Bessie would get them to babysit her children. The times Bessie didn't come get them, they would catch a ride to Pine Bluff, running away from home. Momole always showed up in Pine Bluff to bring them back home. They would tell her they wanted to stay with their Mama. She would reply, "Fool, I'm your Mama. Y'all can't stay with Bessie. Bessie barely can take care of her family."

Stine finally gave up and decided to stay at home with Momole. But James kept running away, and as soon as he could find a ride to Pine Bluff, he was gone again. The last time Momole came to get James, he had run away to Pine Bluff twice in one day. When she showed up the last time, she told him, "I'm not coming down here to get you anymore." He was happy about this and said, "Good." Momole didn't bother James anymore about coming home; she let him live his life.

James was working and living with Bessie and Grady. He would hang out and party with his big sister lots of the times. Drinking and partying the night away, James let the alcohol get the best of him. When this happened, he would get into a fight with someone sooner or later. Most of the time, James started the fights and most of the time Bessie had to end the fight. While she was finishing the fight that James had started, he would disappear and be nowhere to be found after the smoke cleared.

All the children loved James, but Annie was his favorite. There were times when Bessie was whooping the children and Annie would beg James to save her. He would do his very best and step between Annie and Bessie and try to convince Bessie not to whoop her. But it was to no avail, Bessie would start hitting James with the belt and he soon moved and let her finish what she had started.

James had gotten comfortable living in Pine Bluff and had no intention of moving back to Lonoke. He was a smooth talker, loved the ladies, and loved the fast life just like his big sister. But hard times were brewing for him around the corner when James lost his job. To make things worse, Bessie told James he had to move out. He knew it was more Grady's idea than his sister's. He was upset at first, but later in life James understood that Bessie did what she had to do to keep peace in her home. James refused to go back to Lonoke even if he had to sleep on the street. He would go by Bessie's house and Annie would bring him a plate of food so he could have something to eat. She would give him half the food off her plate and get some food off her brother, Terry's plate to make him have a full plate.

Since James had moved out of his sister's home, he would hang out in the streets most of the day. But at nightfall he would stay with his girlfriend, Willora. She still stayed in the house with her parents. Young and innocent, she was in love with James and willing to take a chance on getting in trouble with her Mama. Willora knew he didn't have a place to stay, so she told him he could stay with her at night. She told James, "I will have to sneak you in because Mama ain't going to let you stay here if we're not married." When nightfall came, Willora would sneak James in the house to her bedroom. Her Mama and father were unaware of what was going on right under their noses. She did this on the condition that James understood that he could not have her most prized possession. James said he understood, but this didn't keep him from shooting his best shot. Willora was true to her word; she did not give in to James's smooth talking, and she would sneak him in the house every night.

The times they spent together only made her fall even more for him, and James for her. They got comfortable with the situation and grew too relaxed. James got a job with the railroad and was tired because they had worked hard that day. He fell asleep holding Willora in his arms when her Mama walked in the room and caught them. She was upset, but the next words out of her mouth may have surprised them. Willora's mom looked down at James and said to him, "All I want to know is one thing-- are you going to marry my daughter? She is helping you out and giving you a place to stay." James answered her without any hesitation. "Yes, I'll marry your daughter; I love your daughter." Her mom then told James, "She yours and you going to marry her too." Willora and James thought her Mama didn't know about him being in her house, but somehow she had gotten wind of the situation.

James was grateful for Willora; she took care of him until he was back on his feet. He didn't have a car, so he would go down to the end of the road and catch a ride with someone going his way. Willora worked for the school and she drove a red Ford that wouldn't back up. She had to always park where she didn't have to back up. But one day, she got off from work and someone had her blocked in. James and some of his friends went out to her job and pushed her back so she could have enough room to pull out and go forward.

James and Willora were soon married, but they didn't have much of anything but one another. They moved into a shotgun house near Willora's family, and not too long after their marriage, they started having children. The house they lived in was just a roof over their heads. It didn't have any plumbing, so they didn't have a bathroom and had to use the bathroom in a bucket. The house didn't have a door. There was a blanket hung over the door frame in place of a door and they lived like this for years. Even though they were both working, James didn't always do what he was supposed to do with the money. Regardless of James's actions, Willora stuck by his side.

Momole went to Pine Bluff every weekend to the flea market. When she left the flea market, Momole would go visit James and Willora. When she got to their house, she had to use the bathroom. When she asked James and Willora to use the bathroom, they had to inform her that they didn't have a bathroom. Momole looked at James and told him, "James Ray, get them children and your wife out this house. Y'all can live better than this. Y'all working, so you all need to go buy a house."

James and Willora heard what Momole was saying loud and clear. They started saving their money. When they got enough, they went to Jacksonville to the trailer dealer to buy a trailer. They found a double wide trailer that they wanted. They had enough money but needed someone to cosign for them. They called Momole and she went to the bank and talked to Pete Bennett and he called to Jacksonville and told them to give James and Willora whatever they wanted. James moved his family in the trailer. Every Sunday, like clockwork, Momole came to town. This time when she went to James's house, she was able to use the bathroom.

James and Willora stayed together for years, but James loved the streets and was still blowing a lot of his money. They had gone through a lot together, but they survived it all. They eventually separated but never divorced. They survived losing two of their sons. James lived around the corner from Willora and they saw one another daily. They became the best of friends and would look out for one another. James would go to her house daily and they would talk on the phone every night. Sometimes Willora would say, "James, why don't you come out of those streets and stop all that drinking? Those niggas out there don't care anything about you." Whenever there were any family functions on James's side of the family, Willora was the one to drive James there. They were together but not together. Someone on the outside looking in may not have understood their relationship, but they loved one another until the day she died.

After Willora died, James wished he would have done a lot of things differently. It was hard for him to believe she had died before him, but he had come to terms with the fact that God knows best. Every since Willora died, I called James every day during the day. We prayed together and read a scripture or two. We discussed the scriptures, and there were times that James took over the conversation and explained the scripture himself. When he did that, I told him, "Preach preacher!" We both laughed and said our goodbyes until the next day. James still hung under the tree with his friends, and if he was under the tree with his friends when I called, I prayed for them also.

James was diagnosed with throat cancer in 2018 and he passed away in December of 2018. Out of seventeen children, only four of Momole's children are left: Finnie, Bessie, Sam and Darnell.

THE END

CPSIA information can be obtained
at www.ICGtesting.com
Printed in the USA
LVHW010225180620
658261LV00005B/118